Stopping the Presses

Published with assistance from the Margaret S. Harding Memorial Endowment honoring the first director of the University of Minnesota Press

Stopping the Presses
The Murder of Walter W. Liggett

Marda Liggett Woodbury

University of Minnesota Press
Minneapolis • London

The author thanks the following resources and libraries for permission to reprint material from their collections: Minnesota Historical Society; Alfred Bingham Papers, Herman Haupt Chapman Papers, Manuscripts and Archives, Yale University Library; Thomas J. Mooney Papers, The Bancroft Library, University of California, Berkeley; The Lilly Library, Indiana University; Seeley G. Mudd Manuscript Library, Department of Rare Books and Special Collections, Princeton University Libraries; Walter William Liggett Papers and Victor Francis Calverton Papers, Rare Books and Manuscripts Division, The New York Public Library, Astor, Lenox and Tilden Foundations; Minneapolis Public Library, Minneapolis Collection.

Published by the University of Minnesota Press
111 Third Avenue South, Suite 290
Minneapolis, MN 55401-2520
http://www.upress.umn.edu

Library of Congress Cataloging-in-Publication Data
Woodbury, Marda.
    Stopping the presses : the murder of Walter W. Liggett / Marda
Liggett Woodbury.
        p.   cm.
    Includes index.
    ISBN 0-8166-2929-3 (pb : alk. paper)
    1. Murder — Minnesota — Minneapolis — Case studies.   2. Liggett,
Walter W. (Walter William), 1886–1935.   3. Murder victims —
Minnesota — Minneapolis — Biography.   4. Journalists — Minnesota —
Minneapolis — Biography.   I. Title.
HV6534.M66W66   1998
364.15'23'09776579 — dc21   97-51443

To my parents,

Walter W. Liggett and Edith Fleischer Liggett

For my children,

Mark Walter Evans, Brian Woodbury, and Heather Woodbury

There is no truth, because history is written by assassins.

—from the film *The Official Story*

What I want more than all in this last hour of agony is that our case and our fate may be understood in their real being and serve as a tremendous lesson to the forces of freedom — so that our suffering and death will not have been in vain.

—Bartolomeo Vanzetti, August 22, 1927

Contents

Preface. A Daughter's Journey

The research and writing of this biography was a ten-year odyssey as I followed my parents through time and space. I concentrated my energies and research skills on exploring newspapers, histories, letters, and documents, rather than my own psyche. Although a personal story would be briefer, I felt I needed to document our life in Minnesota and to date and quote the ugly, if imprecise, accusations against my father.

I knew I wanted to show my parents' lives and beliefs in the context of their times. Thus, I tried to provide an overview of my father's early life and times, and a substantially fuller account of our lives in Minnesota before and after his assassination. Although I cannot claim to be truly objective, I also cannot, seemingly, write a purely personal account of a family tragedy. Although I know where I stand, I have provided other perspectives and independent documentation. I've tried to let readers in on the process of research, so they can draw their own conclusions.

From 1986 on, I spent most vacations tracing and visiting my parents' old haunts from Minnesota to North Dakota and Alaska to Cape Cod to Washington, D.C., tracking their lives and sometimes catching glimpses of myself as a child. This endeavor has put me in touch with family and family connections across the United States. I now feel much more a part of a family continuity, and closer to relatives, near and distant, dead or alive.

Family, near and extended, helped in many ways. My brother, Wallace, wrote his own memoirs to supplement my memories; he faithfully helped with the drudge work, busing to the University of California library in Berkeley to pick up and return books for me — a much-appreciated delivery service. He also scanned newspaper microfilm and copied hundreds, maybe thousands, of pages at our local copy centers. He devoted New York vacations to research. Above all, as a history buff, he encouraged me to include substantial historical background.

My older son, Mark Evans, another history buff who insists on arguing with me about the politics of the period, has sharpened my political insight, and sometimes called my attention to materials I might not have seen. He made a few major runs for me to Stanford and the Oakland Public Library, where he managed to amass a huge amount of material in a day or an afternoon. He has suggested, correctly, that my parents' story would make a good movie.

I drafted my second son, Brian Woodbury, to look for details in the Liggett files in the New York Public Library and to interview Morris Forkosch, my mother's lawyer when she sued the *Daily Worker.* Brian critiqued the whole book, while his wife, Elma Mayer, read chapters and provided helpful comments, as did my daughter, Heather Woodbury. I'm not sure that I always heeded her advice to "make it more personal, Mom," but I appreciate her encouragement.

My niece Susie Williams put me up on my visits to New York City and plied me with delicious food. My uncle Walter Fletcher, a wonderful raconteur, searched his memories for details on my parents and sent me photos, clippings, and other mementos. Other New York relatives, especially my cousin Hilda Pearlman, examined their memories and their scrapbooks for tidbits on my parents and grandparents. In Minnesota, my cousin Mary Vidovic met me at the airport, put me up and drove me around, and provided a sense of family away from home. In Brooklyn, Peter Kondrat, then my niece Jenny's husband, researched my parents in the *Brooklyn Eagle* file at the Brooklyn Public Library.

From 1986 until I retired in September 1995, the administrators at Life Chiropractic College West encouraged me to organize my time for research and writing; library staff members also were unwaveringly supportive. Thus, almost every May I managed to tack a few days' or a week's personal vacation time onto a medical librarians' meeting, frequently returning to document collections and county and city records in Minneapolis and St. Paul. There, I found myself simultaneously screening documents and writing down memories.

These memories lingered on in Berkeley, California, where I started my research with basic reference tools like the *Readers' Guide,* the *New York Times Index,* union lists of newspapers, and biographical dictionaries. Evenings, I immersed myself in the sweep of American radical history, scanning histories of Minnesota and the Farmer-Labor Party, and writing as many query letters as I could fit in.

I'm grateful to colleagues in libraries, archives, and records collections all over the country for arranging their materials so well. Many went far beyond the call of duty in providing access to their collections. I would like to extend special thanks to Ruby Shields and Steve Nielsen at the Minnesota Historical Society for ingenious and tireless help, and to Steve for putting me in touch with Thomas L. Baker and Douglas H. Holden; the former supplied student papers on my father's murder, the latter, occasional documents. Many thanks to Beverly Johnson, records supervisor at the Minneapolis Police Department, who made pleasant what could have been a grim experience. I also greatly appreciate the Special Collections staff at the Minneapolis Public Library.

For historical overview, specific source information, and reading sections of my manuscript, I'm greatly indebted to historian John Earl Haynes, now at the Library of Congress. Crime historian Paul Maccabee was extremely generous in providing names and addresses that greatly expedited my research in Twin Cities and state files. I have also learned from exchanging letters with historians Peter Rachleff, Stephen Fox, David Riehle, and Harvey Klehr, among others.

I am most grateful to Professors Tom Leonard and Tom Goldstein of the University of California, Berkeley, journalism faculty for accepting a bulkier version of the manuscript as a belated master's thesis in journalism in 1995.

I am particularly appreciative of the nonagenarians and octogenarians (both historians and participants in history) who offered details, insights, opinions, contacts, and documents. These remarkable human sources include Joe Murphy, Svend A. Godfredsen, Hertha Schwisow, Robert Wilson, Irma W. Ask, Al Rothman, John Winkles, Al Rathert, John B. Thayer, Morris D. Forkosch, Warren H. Guilford, Judge George E. MacKinnon, Irving Dilliard, Seldon Rodman, and Alfred Bingham.

An article on my work-in-progress by Peg Meier of the Minneapolis *Star Tribune* and a story done by Tom Gasparoli, formerly of WCCO-TV in the Twin Cities, brought new leads and contacts. I'm also grateful to Steve Weinberg of Investigative Reporters and Editors.

Over the years, I've read chapters to friends and to my writers' group, Thursday's Child. I particularly appreciate the moral support and editorial suggestions of Rephah Berg, Carol Talpers, and Karla Huebner. When I came to a frenzied period of shortening the book in the summer of 1996, Jane Lewis, Joan Rankin, Lewis DeSimone, and Brian Woodbury were all kind enough to read the whole manuscript and make thoughtful suggestions. My brother, Wallace, also helped in this chore, while Joan and Karla acted as sympathetic computer consultants. I appreciate the thoughtfulness and sensitivity of Lynn Marasco, my copyeditor at University of Minnesota Press.

Many others have helped through research or by reading chapters, holding my hand, or offering general encouragement.

With this book, I feel I've finally paid a debt to my parents. I have tried to use their skills — and sometimes their words — to tell their stories.

Introduction. Starting Point

I always associated my father's murder with hard times and the bitter Minnesota winter of 1935–36. His death in December of the waning year forever cast a shadow on our family's Christmas celebrations. Perhaps it was appropriate. If Jesus Christ had died for our sins, as I had learned in Sunday school, I figured — in my ten-year-old way — that my father had died for the sins of Minneapolis.

On the blustery evening of December 9, 1935, my mother and I, seated beside the groceries in the back seat of our Ford V-8, saw my father gunned down in the alley behind our apartment. I had seen a dark car purposefully and somehow ominously round the corner as soon as my father stepped out of our car. He was reaching for the groceries when he noticed the vehicle. Always courteous, he motioned my mother and me to remain inside while he moved close to give it room to pass. Suddenly a gun appeared in a window of the moving car. I ducked down and almost simultaneously heard five shots. When I looked up, my father lay stretched out in the alley.

My father, Walter W. Liggett, was forty-nine years old when he was killed — a veteran of thirty years of radical journalism. At the time of his death, he was the editor and publisher of the weekly *Midwest American.* In a bitter print battle with Minnesota governor Floyd B. Olson, he had accused Olson of betraying the ideals of the Farmer-Labor Party. My mother, Edith Fleischer Liggett, who would be thirty-five in January, was a reporter and the associate editor of the *Midwest American.* My brother, Wallace, almost twelve, was upstairs in our apartment.

My father had left his Lake Street office earlier than usual. He had worked at home that day, and had gone to the newspaper office only to deliver copy. He had been working on a speech that he intended to deliver to the Minnesota Legislature that week, demanding the impeachment of Governor Olson. It was a course my father had been pursuing in print for the past six months.

My father, I would later learn, was not the only Minneapolis newsman to be shot down while investigating government corruption. Fifteen months earlier, in a residential district only a few blocks away, local muckraker Howard Guilford had been killed by a shotgun blast fired from a moving car. Guilford had just announced a radio series that would "tell the whole story of Governor Floyd Olson's connection with the underworld."[1]

Nine years later another nosy newspaperman, Arthur Kasherman, would be gunned down while running and begging for his life. The latest issue of Kasherman's tabloid, *The Public Press,* had denounced the corruption of Minneapolis mayor Marvin Kline and the police.[2]

This is a unique record for an American city. Although journalists have occasionally been threatened, jailed, or beaten, they have rarely been murdered. That usually draws too much heat. During the thirties, unwanted newsmen were usually gotten rid of with phony indictments or charges of blackmail. Indeed, exactly one month before his death, my father had been acquitted of a sex charge designed to put him in prison for twenty years.

After their deaths, all three murdered newspapermen were accused of blackmail or ties with the underworld, yet little evidence supported these charges. Police investigations were cursory; none of the murders was officially solved. Guilford's and Kasherman's murders were one-day stories in the local newspapers, but my father's murder received national and international coverage. It dominated the Minnesota press from the day the bullets were fired until the acquittal of the mobster identified as his assassin.

It took me more than fifty years to get back to Minneapolis. My last vivid impressions were of my father's body lying on the pavement and the tumultuous sadness that followed his death. When I returned in 1986 to attend a library convention, it seemed natural for me, an inveterate researcher, to do some digging.

To start my busman's holiday, I visited the Minnesota Historical Society. As I settled in an oak chair in the decorous Reference Room, I anticipated a comfortably reminiscent afternoon. Instead, I found my father characterized as a brawler and a drunkard, a blackmailer, a publisher of scandal sheets, a radical who sold out to the Republicans, and a man who had shady dealings with the criminals he denounced. These sources looked authoritative, I realized with dismay, although there was little documentation to back the charges. And on closer examination, I saw that terms like "obscure," "it was said," and "generally believed" modified the allegations.[3]

As I studied the documents, I was astounded at the picture that was emerging: Walter Liggett had been omitted from or disparaged in nearly all of the histories and analyses of the Farmer-Labor Party.

There seemed to be two vastly different views of Walter Liggett. Our family and friends, along with the bulk of the American press, had considered him a crusader who lost his life fighting an alliance of crime and crooked politics. I remembered him as a man of honor who brought me up to tell the truth. The books and articles I was now finding, on the other hand, implied that his death was an "underworld vendetta," that he was somehow involved in blackmail or extortion.

Perhaps naively, I had thought such allegations had been discredited fifty years earlier, when my mother successfully sued the Communist Party's newspaper, the *Daily Worker,* charging civil and criminal libel for comparable statements. In six years of painful and protracted litigation, the *Daily Worker* had completely failed to document its accusations that my father was a "blackmailer" and a "scavenger" with ties to reactionaries.

Yet here these defamations were stated as facts.

It was hard for me to credit statements that my father had been a blackmailer, a friend of mobsters, or an editor of scandal sheets. Still, such statements appeared frequently enough that I determined to learn the truth.

Restless and in turmoil, I found it hard to sit still. I felt an urge to do something concrete. Out in the lobby, I leafed through Twin Cities telephone directories looking for the authors of the books and articles I had just read. Finally, I reached Arthur Naftalin, who had cited the *Midwest American* in a much-quoted thesis on the Farmer-Labor Party.

Naftalin seemed surprised at my call. "Your father," he stated baldly, "had a bad reputation."

"That's why I called you," I answered.

Naftalin was affable enough on the telephone but said he was too busy to talk to me in person. He suggested that I write, but he never answered my letters. Unfortunately, this lack of response was typical of many Minnesota historians.

During the Depression, a time of political legends, left-wing proletarian literature presented images of heroic workers and leaders. The words *myth* and *golden legend* are still used to promote the portrait of Floyd Olson as a larger-than-life Titan. I wondered whether my father and other opponents had been demonized to preserve a heroic portrait of Olson.

I felt I owed my parents something. My father, though careless with his life, was proud of his reputation as a political investigator. And my mother, who maintained her idealism throughout a difficult life, had revered my father's memory and fought for his good name.

As a reference librarian and the author of seven reference books, I knew the methods and difficulties of research, and I knew just how long it could take to nail down a fact or a precise date. Shortly before my Minnesota visit, I had finished proofreading the galleys for my book *Childhood Information Resources.* I had also signed a contract for a similar work on youth.

After the new book, I thought, I would investigate my father's murder and try to account for the vastly different interpretations of his life and death. Newspapermen, I knew, leave paper trails. And I was willing, if not eager, to learn the worst.

Part I. Walter's Story

1. Prairie Activist

[The editor] is the town confessor, the town boomer, and the town goat, doormat, rock of refuge, errand boy and the vicarious sacrifice.

— *Pasco Express*, **June 21, 1912**

Growing Up in Minnesota

My father, Walter W. Liggett, was born on St. Valentine's Day in 1886 on his father's stock farm near Benson on the gently rolling prairies of western Minnesota.

I saw this family homestead once when I was seven or eight, on a summer day when my dad took us down to Benson to show us where he was born. I remember a square white farmhouse, two or three stories high with a porch on two sides, set in a huge yard with leafy, nurturing trees. I was impressed that my father had lived in such a big house on such a big lot.

The Liggett family had moved to Minnesota with their two young children, Madeleine and Robert, after my grandfather (then in the Ohio state militia) was wounded while he was helping end the bloody Cincinnati Riot of 1884 (one of many in that troubled decade).[1] Walter and his younger sister, Gladys, were born in Minnesota.

Before coming to Minnesota, William Madison Liggett had had a full and adventurous life. He left college at seventeen to join the Ninety-sixth Ohio Regiment and was immediately thrown into a series of bloody battles. A sergeant when the Civil War ended, he turned down a commission and returned to Ohio after a brief stint in Texas. In 1876 he married my grandmother, the strong-minded Mathilda Root Brown.[2]

At Benson, my grandfather managed a two-thousand-acre scientific stock farm. A strong advocate of diversified farming, he specialized in stock adapted to Minnesota's climate and soils. His model farm drew so much attention that he was appointed a regent of the University of Minnesota in 1888 and assigned responsibility for the School of Agriculture; two years later, his farmer peers elected him to direct the Minnesota State Fair. Then, in 1896, he became director of state agricultural experiment stations and the first dean of agriculture at the university. As dean, he opened the college to women in 1897 and converted a struggling school with seventy students and three buildings into the nation's best agricultural college.[3]

Mathilda threw most of her considerable energy into women's causes: the Minnesota Federation of Women's Clubs, the Daughters of the American Revolution, the Women's Welfare League, the Women's City Club of St. Paul, and the (Progressive) Republican Women's Club of St. Paul.[4] In 1905, she urged the "daughters of our time" to use the "weapons of knowledge" to combat "ignorance and darkness and the . . . deadly limitations of an artificial social standard."[5] In an era when women were known by their husbands' names, she always signed her letters Mathilda Root Brown (or R. B.) Liggett.[6]

Although the first white child was not born in St. Paul until 1839, St. Paul had 216,000 residents — mostly immigrants and first-generation Americans — when the Liggetts settled there around 1890.[7] The period when Walter was born was neither as idyllic nor as innocent as we like to imagine. In the cities, rapid growth brought factories, industrialism, and labor unrest; in the country, farmers were restive. Walter's birth year of 1886 was a year of strikes and a rapidly growing Knights of Labor. Grassroots members became more and more militant, striving to attain a universal eight-hour day.[8] Militant farmers considered themselves the most radical group in America. The Populist or People's Party began in the 1880s as the Farmers' Alliance and developed rapidly during the next decade. During the 1880s, the Alliance elected many state legislators as well as a few governors and congressmen.[9]

Midwestern farmers' groups focused not on ownership of the means of production (these farmers, after all, mostly owned their own farms), but on access to capital and credit through free silver, banking reform, and cooperatives. They demanded regulation of monopolies and railroads, and creation of warehouses for grain and farm commodities. While William Liggett urged farmers to escape boom-or-bust economics through diversity, the "Pops" contended that railroads, millers, and grain exchanges controlled the price of wheat.[10]

Walter grew up in St. Paul but spent most summers in the country — at farms, experiment stations, and logging camps. I have a picture of him with some dour-looking farmers displaying a long string of fish, and I recall another in which he, barefooted and bare-legged, red-haired and freckled, could have won a Tom Sawyer look-alike contest. The Liggetts were all readers and collectors of books, and the children devoured the enchanting children's magazines of the period.

Walter spent several youthful summers at the Grand Rapids Experiment Station, then managed by Herman H. Chapman, who was later professor of forestry at Yale. Chapman described Walter as "sensitive and impressionable . . . warm-hearted, fearless, and impetuous." Walter's outstanding trait, according to Chapman, was "an indomitable courage and a burning desire to right wrongs regardless of personal risk."[11]

In the city, Walter played sandlot baseball with Lyle Pettijohn and Joseph Granbeck (later his lawyers), who remembered him as an idealist from childhood. Dr. Ernest Powell, another childhood friend, similarly recalled that "many of his youthful and formative years were spent on the frontier. He was always hoping to find an opportunity to apply his ideals, for he was an idealist."[12]

Newspaper Days

In January 1903, just before Walter's seventeenth birthday, *McClure's Magazine* launched the muckraking era by publishing three articles dealing with what publisher Samuel S. McClure called "American contempt for law." The lead article, Lincoln Steffens's "The Shame of Minneapolis," was accompanied by a chapter of Ida Tarbell's *History of Standard Oil* and Ray Stannard Baker's exposé titled "The Right to Work."[13] Soon one popular magazine after another entered the investigative field.[14]

The muckrakers exposed what newspaper critic Marlen Pew called the "crass materialism" of post–Civil War America, where "machine politics joined hands with privileged business. . . . The muckraker's science was to do a real investigating and reporting job, dramatize the situation in print, fearlessly call things and men by their true names and get action."[15]

The muckrakers' ascendance coincided with Progressive Republicanism and with the peak years — 1897 to 1917 — of the Socialist Party in America. The muckrakers tended to ally with progressive politicians like Robert "Fighting Bob" La Follette, Al Smith, and Theodore Roosevelt (in his trust-busting, Square Deal phase).[16] With their aid, the muckraking movement achieved a long list of reforms, including child labor laws, a federal pure food law, a tariff commission, and workers' compensation.[17] The muckrakers also raised readers' awareness with explanations of such tricky phenomena as special interests, vertical trusts, interlocking directorates, and "boodle."[18] Muckraking books and magazines established a national journalism that demonstrated the universal nature of American misgovernment, nationalizing news in a way that local dailies and press services could not.[19]

Indeed, local crusading could be hazardous. Shortly after the San Francisco earthquake of 1906, editor Fremont Older was kidnapped at gunpoint when the *San Francisco Bulletin* pursued his campaign against grafters.[20] Crusader Marlen

Pew lost his job on the *Boston Traveller* after an irate advertiser purchased the paper and Pew's contract as editor.[21]

Sam McClure always demanded legwork, interviews, and documentation from his authors. Consequently, each of Lincoln Steffens's articles on cities required about six months of research, as well as sworn statements, interviews, photographs, and documents.[22] His detailed study of Minneapolis's turn-of-the-century corruption portrays detectives who managed the police force "to protect, share with, and direct the criminals," while a former gambler recruited out-of-town thieves, pickpockets, and gamblers into Minneapolis. One police captain's job was to sell places on the police force, while decent cops were marked for dismissal. And the county prosecutor was too corrupt or too frightened to act.

Although Walter was excited by the idea of fearless journalism, he entered his father's agricultural college in 1904, following in the footsteps of his brother, Bob. Like his brother, Walter was active in college football and boxing. And, like Bob, he became a journalist. He had a scholarly side and maintained a life-long interest in agriculture, but he was too restless, and perhaps too competitive, to stay in college.

Walter left school in 1905 to conquer and reform the world as a full-time newspaperman. He was only nineteen years old, six feet, four inches tall, slender but hardy, and strikingly handsome, with blue eyes and curly auburn hair.

The early twentieth century, when Walter started his career, was a boom period for American newspapers: the number of papers grew twice as fast as the expanding population. This rapid growth was partly a response to lowered prices and partly a manifestation of the era's passion for progress and knowledge. Certainly the new technologies of the time — improved graphics, cartoons, and half-tones — made for a more interesting product, while press services and syndicates extended national reporting.[23] A skilled newsman like Walter could find work almost anywhere.

Walter started out close to home, as police and general reporter for the *St. Paul Pioneer Press,* the *Minneapolis Journal,* and the *Minneapolis Daily News.*[24] He moved on to Duluth, a rambunctious mining port on Lake Superior, and then to the *Fargo Forum,* just over the border in North Dakota.

Before long, Walter headed for Seattle, and then was offered the position of managing editor of the Skagway *Alaskan,* an eight-page tabloid — America's smallest daily newspaper.[25] Walter always had fond memories of Skagway, a beautiful tiny seaport on the northern tip of the Lynn Canal, surrounded by magnificent mountains. By the time he arrived in 1909, Skagway was a resort town trading on its gold rush reputation.[26] Walter — always an admirer of honest cops —

was struck by the stark difference between law enforcement in Skagway and a few miles away in Canada's Yukon Territory.[27]

While Canada had the Mounties and stringent law enforcement, Skagway had Soapy Smith, a confidence man whose gang had moved to Alaska after losing control of Colorado mining towns. At its peak during the gold rush, Smith's gang included two or three hundred confidence men, gamblers, pimps, whores, and gangsters. Smith himself played the role of a public-spirited citizen—and at times conned himself into believing he was a town benefactor. In this lawless town, few except Jim Dunbar, the elderly editor of the *Alaskan,* had the courage to defy Soapy Smith. Even when Soapy's gangsters threatened to shoot him on sight, Dunbar continued his vivid denunciations.[28]

During Walter's stint on the *Alaskan,* he focused on issues of good government and conservation of public lands, with a balance of local and outside reporting. He also served as correspondent to several Eastern newspapers and liked to provide political tidbits from all over. Many items came from the new Alaskan News Bureau, which provided telegraph connections with the outside world; others came from muckraking magazines. In May 1910, for example, he outlined a *Hampton's* magazine article on the Morgan-Guggenheim syndicate's takeover of Alaskan resources.

Walter resigned shortly after he was appointed town clerk, but continued to be a close friend of the *Alaskan*'s publisher. The *Alaskan* recounted Walter's romance with and marriage to Norma J. Ask. Norma, tall, stately, and adventurous, was the only daughter of the Ask merchant family, who had moved their store from Seattle to Skagway when gold fever struck. Norma grew up in Skagway with her younger brothers, who enjoyed teasing her about her year in an Eastern finishing school.[29]

Walter's last job in the north was as express messenger for the White Pass & Yukon Railroad. This post heightened his admiration for the Royal Canadian Mounted Police and provided him with material for two books and innumerable articles on the Mounties. Walter noted that the Canadian police cooperated across jurisdictions, while in the United States the police often failed to cooperate across state lines and even ignored pleas to look for known lawbreakers.[30]

In October 1910, Walter and Norma, with Norma's teenage brother Harry, traveled to Tacoma, Washington, where Walter worked at the *Tacoma Ledger.*[31] From there they moved east to Pasco, where Walter and another young reporter bought the weekly *Pasco Progress.* Pasco newspapers were Progressive and Populist, and in general backed reform legislation. Even though Walter considered the rival *Express* rather conservative, it supported William Jennings Bryan and

Robert La Follette. Prohibition was an ongoing issue, nationally and locally, and Walter made himself unpopular with the saloon set by advocating liquor controls in the *Progress*.[32]

World War I began while Walter and Norma were in Pasco. In 1915, when Walter's young sister Gladys died of appendicitis, he and Norma sold the *Progress* and moved back to Minnesota to comfort his mother.

Insurgent Farmers

Shortly before Norma and Walter left Pasco for St. Paul, a handful of North Dakota farmers launched the Nonpartisan League. Although few today have heard of the League — Walter's favorite radical cause — it was perhaps the most successful democratic mass movement in American history.[33]

In late February and early March of 1915, Arthur Townley and two other farmers trudged and bobsledded from farm to farm on the windswept prairies of North Dakota to muster support for a simple five-point program: state ownership of grain terminals and milling facilities, state inspection of grain and grading, state hail insurance, rural credit banks, and tax exemption for farm improvements. With these dollars-and-cents reforms, it was surprisingly easy to persuade farmers to gamble on the Nonpartisan League.[34] Within a week, the group had pledges from seventy-nine farmers. Within a few weeks, dozens of Fords loaded with organizers — idealists, farmers, and Socialists — covered the entire state. The organizing proceeded rapidly but quietly. Few except farmers learned of the League.

From the beginning, organizers distrusted the existing press and wanted to develop their own publications. By the time the first issue of the weekly *Nonpartisan Leader* appeared in September 1915, proclaiming that "this journal belongs to the farmers of the Northwest," twenty-two thousand farmers had joined the League. Before long, the circulation of anti-League newspapers began to decline.[35]

Through the next winter, the League continued organizing. On Washington's birthday, forty thousand Leaguers met to select Nonpartisan candidates — mostly farmers — for the North Dakota primaries. (The League was not registered as a separate political party, but chose candidates to run in party primaries.)

Despite one of the worst thunderstorms ever recorded in North Dakota, farmers voted in record numbers on primary day 1916. Though rivers were flooded and roads were wet trails of gumbo mud, farmers managed to get to the polls. The candidates backed by the League, mostly Republicans, won the election handily, capturing the governorship, three supreme court judgeships, and all state offices except treasurer, as well as a strong majority in the state House of Representatives. But only half of the Senate seats were contested and the League did not win the Senate, although it captured the Republican Party machinery.[36]

With the aid of study, nightly caucuses, and a committee of attorneys, the new legislators were able to enact a few mild League reforms and some leftover Progressive reforms. They gained women the right to vote for presidential electors and for state and local officers; tripled aid to rural schools; and established adult evening schools and a public welfare commission with a woman commissioner. On the farm front, they installed a state inspector of grains and weights, and gained partial tax exemption for farm improvements. But the holdover senators proved to be roadblocks to the rest of the League's program. Soon, the remaining Republicans and Democrats banded together to oppose the Leaguers in a truce that held until 1921. Undeterred, the League redoubled its efforts to build membership. It raised dues to establish a financial base. At the same time, it organized out of state, concentrating on Minnesota, home of the monied interests that controlled the price of North Dakota wheat.

Joining Up

On September 20, 1917, Walter, then working for the *St. Paul Dispatch,* was assigned to cover a speech by Wisconsin's Senator Robert La Follette. It was an evening destined to change both their lives. "Fighting Bob," a Progressive Republican, was addressing the Producers' and Consumers' Conference (read farmer and labor) in St. Paul. As a result of incorrect Associated Press reporting of his speech, La Follette would be accused of treason and nearly hounded from the U.S. Senate.

Because of the Nonpartisan League's perceived antiwar stance, it was probably foolhardy to schedule the conference in St. Paul in September 1917. In April, five short months earlier, four out of ten Minnesota congressmen had voted against declaring war. Yet as soon as the United States entered World War I, the state legislature hastily created a Minnesota Commission of Public Safety and gave it sweeping authority to "defend the state and nation, and prosecute the war." The commission could force anyone to appear before its agents and furnish any records the commission wished to see; it could review the performance of all public officials, and had "all necessary power not specifically enumerated."[37]

Although Governor J. A. A. Burnquist theoretically headed the commission, it was dominated by Judge John F. McGee, who saw traitors everywhere. In a state where 70 percent of the people were immigrants or children of immigrants, McGee required all "aliens" to register. He developed card indexes dividing citizens into patriots and traitors. In McGee's opinion, most immigrants, most of labor, and all the leaders of the Nonpartisan League were traitors. So far, however, the commission had failed to impugn the League's loyalty. Even McGee's informants reported that League speeches were patriotic. Still, Twin Cities newspapers had denounced the League as pro-German before the Producers' and Consumers' Conference began.[38]

The strategy for the conference was to emphasize the League's loyalty while attacking monopolistic aspects of the war program and the failure to tax war profits. Behind the scenes, the organizers warned speakers to avoid the explosive issue of American involvement in the war.[39] The conference began auspiciously in Fargo, in a gala atmosphere of flags, bunting, and patriotic airs. Still festive, it moved on to St. Paul. La Follette, who spoke on the last day, was undoubtedly the star of the conference. More than eight thousand people packed the auditorium to hear him, and as many as seven thousand were outside to welcome him.

Beginning with a hearty endorsement of the Nonpartisan League, La Follette went on to discuss taxation and war finance. Then, responding to a heckler, he threw aside his notes and told the crowd that he had not favored entering the war. He went on, "I don't mean to say that we had not suffered grievances: we had, at the hands of Germany... they had interfered with the rights of American citizens to travel on the high seas on ships loaded with munitions for Great Britain."[40]

At the close of the speech, Walter forgot journalistic objectivity and leaped to his feet to join in a standing ovation. While La Follette thought his speech had gone over well, Twin Cities newspapers accused him of disloyalty and the Associated Press misquoted him. Five days later, the Minnesota Commission of Public Safety passed a resolution demanding that La Follette be expelled from the Senate "as a teacher of disloyalty and sedition." Then Senator Frank Kellogg of Minnesota introduced this resolution to the U.S. Senate.[41]

La Follette's speech turned out to be a dramatic focal point for Nonpartisan League opponents, and it triggered a campaign of violence against the League and its members. It was in this climate that Walter left the *St. Paul Dispatch* to work as head of publicity for the League. He was more than ready for the move. During his stint at the *Dispatch,* he had persuaded a janitor to bring him the managing editor's wastebasket, and he concluded that most of the discarded stories were more important than most of the articles that were published. The behavior of Twin Cities newspapers following La Follette's speech convinced him that he was right to move on.

By December, Walter was writing publicity and a weekly Washington newsletter at the League's national headquarters in St. Paul — an informal office where farmers dropped in at all hours and organizers brought political gossip from the thirteen Midwestern and Western states where the League was beginning to campaign.[42] He kept up a barrage of letters to newspapers, arguing the League's case and reiterating its right to speak out.[43]

The Lindbergh Campaign

Charles A. Lindbergh Sr., one of the few politicians Walter ever admired unequivocally, was chosen by the Nonpartisan League to run for governor in the 1918 Republican primary, opposing Governor Burnquist. A former congressman and leader of the Republican Progressive League, Lindbergh was famous for opposing what he called the Money Trust, and for his die-hard battle against establishment of the Federal Reserve Bank in 1913.[44] From 1915 on, Lindbergh had focused on opposing American entrance into the European war, and later he wrote a book entitled *Why Is Your Country at War?*

Although Walter wrote some of Lindbergh's speeches and was slated to become his private secretary if Lindbergh was elected governor, Walter recalled that it was "no picnic" to be assigned to campaign with him. Because of the ever-present danger of violence, Walter carried a revolver to protect himself. Still, League members never actually returned violence with violence.[45]

In May, Walter campaigned with Lindbergh near Cloquet. They and three others had just come from Duluth, where the mayor and the police had forcibly prevented their meeting.[46] When the group arrived in Cloquet by auto around 9:00 P.M., they found that agents of the Public Safety Commission had gotten there first and had spent the early evening hours buying drinks and inciting the town to violence. A dozen delegations of "pool hall patriots" had driven in from nearby towns, drinking and looking for action. These troublemakers vastly outnumbered the farmers.

"One could fairly smell trouble," Walter wrote, but Lindbergh decided to go ahead. When their entourage reached the movie theater they had rented for the meeting, the owner met them at the door and handed back their deposit, declaring, "There ain't going to be no pro-German meeting here." Someone turned out the lights in the theater lobby, and Lindbergh and his group were jammed up against the wall, surrounded by a crowd of belligerent drunken patriots. Walter heard later that a dozen men in the crowd had ropes. "Their hostility," he wrote, "beat against us like a hot wind."

Lindbergh, tall and slender, towered above the mob. He stood there silently, Walter wrote, like a lion trainer outfacing a row of crouching beasts. They couldn't look him in the eye. Finally Lindbergh asked the crowd to step aside, and as he started through, it parted like water before a swimmer. The mob grumbled and cursed, but didn't attack. But as soon as Lindbergh stepped into the car, a dozen rocks rattled off its side. Walter always believed that he was close to death that evening.

While opponents painted the houses of Lindbergh's supporters yellow, or tarred and feathered his backers, the League stepped up its campaign meetings to sixty a week. League advocates arranged for meetings in every precinct, and for mammoth automobile parades: long lines of cars traveled through counties carrying "We'll Stick" pennants and the American flag. Opponents cut car tires and poured shot and gravel into the crankcases of League automobiles, strewed nails across roads, and sometimes hung Lindbergh in effigy.[47]

Governor Burnquist, taking a stance of being above politics, avoided domestic issues as much as possible. As titular head of the Public Safety Commission, he scheduled loyalty meetings all over the state to campaign against Lindbergh at state expense. Another campaign tactic was to indict League members for unlawful assembly; a week before the primary election, Lindbergh himself was arrested in Martin County and charged with attempting to hold a disloyal meeting.[48]

Ultimately, Lindbergh received 150,626 votes to 199,325 for Burnquist—not a bad showing considering the circumstances.[49] It was the League's first defeat. Walter believed that Lindbergh might actually have won the election; he claimed that Lindbergh ballots were changed in St. Paul and on the Iron Range.[50] In fact, the voting total of nearly 350,000 was at least 150,000 more than in any previous Republican primary in Minnesota history. While perhaps 60,000 of the votes might have been Democratic crossovers, the difference is still huge.[51]

Undeterred by Lindbergh's defeat, the Nonpartisan League decided to join with labor to run a third-party ticket in the fall, although the League was philosophically opposed to separate parties. To this end, the League and the State Federation of Labor set up a cumbersome joint committee for endorsing candidates. Walter was present when for the first time, in simultaneous August meetings, the farmers' Nonpartisan League, the Working People's Nonpartisan Political League, and their joint committee agreed to endorse a partial ticket for the fall election. It was a historic occasion, the first awkward farmer-labor alliance, tagged with the obvious name, the Farmer-Labor Party.

North Dakota Whirlwind

In the summer of 1918, Walter was still in Minnesota actively promoting farmer-owned papers as a counterforce to the establishment press. In September, League founder Arthur Townley transferred him to North Dakota, where the League was engaged in a heated campaign for the state Senate. The Independent Voters' Association—a conglomerate of Republicans, Democrats, and disaffected Leaguers—was trying to recapture the state. Walter played a vital role in this North Dakota campaign as editor of Bismarck's *Capital Daily Press* and managing editor of the daily *Fargo Courier-News.*[52]

In the spring of 1919, Walter took command of the Northwest Service Bureau (soon named the Publishers National Service Bureau), where he organized and supervised an expanding chain of weekly farmer-owned newspapers.[53] By July, he had set up Nonpartisan League newspapers in fifty of North Dakota's fifty-three counties. It was not easy work. Between May and October 1919, for example, Walter mailed eleven letters to one editor, H. A. Knappen, requesting regular financial statements, urging Knappen to provide more local news and telling him how to find it, and counseling him to report an assault objectively: "I think you will have a stronger case if you...do not allow any abuse or editorializing to creep into your accounts."[54]

In September 1919, Walter wrote reformer Upton Sinclair, who was then collecting information on newspapers for *The Brass Check,* that the bureau had "some hundred weekly newspapers under its supervision." In October, he wrote Sinclair: "The farmers of North Dakota now have a cooperatively owned newspaper in every single county in the state and we are starting them in Minnesota at the rate of two or three a month. When we have Minnesota covered, we will then step into Wisconsin and South Dakota and other adjoining states....I believe that with this humble beginning, we are destined to change the entire American press."[55]

It was not to be. In October, Walter lost his post because of differences with a former bureau head whom Walter considered self-serving.

North Dakota law called for a Commission of Immigration to recruit European farmers to its empty farms, and although Walter had written in mid-1919 that he wasn't interested in the job of deputy commissioner of immigration for North Dakota, he agreed to take the position in December 1919. In part, I believe, he wanted to be a team player.[56] And since this position was based in Washington, I suspect that he chose to leave North Dakota's frozen fields to help fight the national anti-Red sentiment that was sweeping the country in late 1919 and early 1920. One year after the Armistice, the nation was suffering from coal strikes, race riots, and anticommunist hysteria.

2. The Roaring Twenties

Walter . . . believed it was the sacred duty of the press to expose corruption, to guard . . . the public welfare, to lead the fight against special interests. . . . He seemed to feel that he, personally, had been singled out by providence to protect the unfortunate. . . . He was just one of those people who could never be an innocent bystander.

— **Edith Liggett, unpublished manuscript**

Home Base Washington, D.C.

When Walter and Norma Liggett moved to Washington, D.C., in January 1920, the government was still caught up in a wartime mentality, with a void at the center of power. The presidency was run from behind the scenes by President Wilson's wife and doctor after Wilson suffered a series of strokes. Those who managed the country in his name tried to conceal his illness from reporters, from the cabinet and the vice president, and certainly from the American public.

Prohibition took effect just two weeks after Walter and Norma arrived in Washington. The ban on the sale and consumption of alcoholic beverages, which was to last fourteen years, spawned thousands of shady endeavors and corrupted government at all levels.

Norma and Walter lived in a handsome, spacious building on a sunny street in northwest Washington. The apartment they shared with two other radical couples was the unofficial Washington headquarters of the American Civil Liberties Union's letter-writing campaign to get Eugene Victor Debs out of prison.[1] Debs had been tried for a supposedly subversive speech in Canton, Ohio, in June 1918 and sentenced to ten years for "tending to" persuade. In the federal penitentiary at Atlanta, Debs charmed the warden and won one and a half million votes when he campaigned for president from prison.

Although Washington was Walter's home base during 1920 and 1921, he worked in New York and Chicago during the summer of 1920, publicizing the Chicago National Convention of the Committee of 48, a party of "men and women of the forty-eight states" founded in January 1919 by a broad spectrum of radicals, reformers, and progressives.[2] His publicity went well, but the convention failed to be the great political event the 48ers hoped for.[3]

In October 1920 Walter proposed that the Committee of 48 publish a magazine to be called *Searchlight*. My mother, then Edith Fleischer, was working for McAlister Coleman, a Socialist writer and labor historian, who suggested an alternative news service.[4] My parents probably met at a discussion of these alternatives.

Working off and on as North Dakota's deputy commissioner of immigration, Walter tried to set up a Washington conference of immigration, labor, and agricultural officials, but he found U.S. immigration commissioner Anthony Caminetti more interested in deporting radicals than in encouraging immigration. On January 3, 1921, Walter testified before the U.S. Senate Committee on Immigration: "Everytime I went down to [Caminetti's] office to discuss plans for getting new citizens into this country, I found his desk stacked high with deportation matters, and his mind seemed to be so firmly fixed on the question of getting people out of the country that he never had time to consider how we ought to get citizens into the country."[5]

The very next week, the *New York Times* identified Walter as the secretary of North Dakota's newly elected senator, Edwin Fremont Ladd, a distinguished chemist and president of the University of North Dakota who had been elected against the conservative tide. Ladd and the other insurgent senators elected with Nonpartisan League support — Robert La Follette of Wisconsin, Burton K. Wheeler and Thomas J. Walsh of Montana, Smith W. Brookhart of Iowa, Henrik Shipstead of Minnesota, Robert Howell of Nebraska, and Gerald Nye and Lynn Frazier of North Dakota — were among the few honorable politicians in Washington during the Republican regimes of the next twelve years.[6]

Warren Harding assumed the presidency in March 1921, accompanied by Attorney General Harry Daugherty's "Ohio Gang," colloquially known as "the Forty Thieves." As Walter put it: "Other choice cronies and a few score of itching fingered retainers descended upon the national capital with the apparent purpose of stealing everything that was not nailed down."[7] And although Walter did not consider Secretary of Commerce Herbert Hoover one of the light-fingered crew, he would clash with Hoover soon enough.

In the last quarter of 1921, Walter worked with and for Minnesota congressman Oscar Keller, who recommended him to Senator Joseph France of Maryland to head the new American Committee for Russian Famine Relief. (At that time 25 million Russians were on the verge of starvation while typhus was spreading.) But just as the organization was getting off the ground, Herbert Hoover came out against it. He believed that the committee was set up by a foreign government to circulate propaganda, and he asked the Bureau of Investigation to provide a report on Walter and asked the post office to trace his mail.

"So far as I am able to determine," the assigned agent wrote, "the movement in securing the services of subject comes from Senator France and . . . Congressman Keller." I was amused by the agent's undoubtedly accurate assessment that "nothing is known as to his [Walter's] financial situation; in fact he is not known to financial circles at all in this city."[8] Despite the report, Hoover continued to consider Walter a Communist.

Newspaper Romance

In the midst of this tumult, Walter took time off to go to New York City to attend my mother's twenty-first birthday party on January 21, 1922. He opened the door to discover sixteen celebrants—Edith included—writhing in pain on the floor. They had shared one bottle of champagne to toast Edith's coming of age, and like so many bottles of bootleg booze, it had been poisoned with wood alcohol. Walter was kept busy that evening administering first aid to the Prohibition casualties.[9]

In the late spring of 1922, Walter moved to New York City to take the position of city editor of the *New York Call,* a Socialist daily famous both for staying afloat during wartime repression and for underpaying its scholarly reporters and editors. My mother also worked on the paper, holding down at least two positions, crime reporter and feature editor, at a salary of twenty-five dollars a week.[10]

Walter's wife, Norma, more socialite than socialist, remained in Washington, supporting herself handily as a bookkeeper and manager of the Penguin Club. The Ask family told me that Norma enjoyed the cultural life of Washington and the knowledge that she could make it on her own. And while she admired Walter's radical ideals, she had never shared them. Whatever their differences, she and Walter seem to have had a lifelong respect for each other.[11] The Ask family suspect that Edith was "the other woman." Although it is hard for me to envision my idealistic little mother as a femme fatale, they may be right.

While my father's roots were in Minnesota, my mother's were in New York City. Although her mother had grown up on the northern Minnesota frontier, Edith was born in Manhattan in 1901 and grew up in Brooklyn when there were still farms, estates, racetracks, and unpaved roads with original Dutch milestones within walking distance of her home in Flatbush.[12]

Edith was a middle child, the second daughter in a family of three daughters and one son, the rebel in a cultured, conservative family that ran to teachers, writers, and lawyers. Tiny and precocious, she had a tendency to run off, even as a toddler. In an era when little girls traditionally wore white and pastels, my grandmother dressed Edith in red to increase her visibility.

All of Edith's grandparents, assimilated Jews with some Christian admixture, came from Europe. Her father's parents came from Bohemia, her mother's from Sweden and Germany. It seemed that the women in both families always married the handsome stranger from out of town. Her own parents had met when her father's train was snowbound in Minnesota and her mother, Ida, was clerking at the nearby Indian trading post. Usually Ida taught Indian school, but the blizzard had made the long horseback ride impossible.

Edith's father, Charles Fleischer, was something of a maverick in his family. As the oldest son in an immigrant family, Charles did not receive the college education that his younger brothers and sisters took for granted. Instead, he traveled across the country as a photographer, and later became a traveling salesman. Married in Aitkin, Minnesota, at the Congregational church, Ida Rosenblatt Fleischer arrived in New York in 1897 with a good working knowledge of Swedish and Ojibwe and a complete deerskin outfit, but little knowledge of her own Jewish heritage.

When the Fleischer family moved toward Christian Science, Edith joined the Young Peoples' Socialist League (the Yipsels) at fourteen. An early feminist, she was a reporter in her high school days, getting assignments from the *New York World,* the *Brooklyn Eagle,* and the Socialist *New York Call.* Despite her diminutive size, she was a formidable basketball player. Although she was an outstanding student, she was nearly refused graduation from Girls' High in Brooklyn for not signing a wartime loyalty pledge. My uncle recalls that Edith also got into trouble at school for leading a women's suffrage demonstration. Ida belonged to a more decorous suffrage group; Edith belonged to the radical group that marched on Washington. Indeed, Edith and her sisters were part of the first generation of young women who assumed they would work after high school.

A slender brunette, five foot two, with a heart-shaped face, large green eyes, and black hair, Edith always looked younger than her years. She cut her heavy black hair short sometime in the flapper period, revealing a shapely head and the only pretty ears I've ever seen.

Like Walter, Edith attended college for only one year. She took the train to Los Angeles to attend UCLA, chatting en route with the young Marion Davies.

But when Edith developed appendicitis, the Los Angeles doctors packed her appendix with ice and sent her home by train.

After Edith's return from California, she worked for a time for McAlister Coleman, then went on to work more than full time for the *New York Call.* Although there were many daily newspapers in New York City, and the *Call* was not known for its pay, it offered great perks for young reporters. Since the *Call* assigned its most seasoned reporters to Wall Street, Albany, and union politics, its copy boys and student space writers covered local crime and the World Series. Edith as a young cub reporter was literally green with nausea when she covered her first murder. She worked from ten in the morning until two the next morning as police reporter, women's page editor, and occasional secretary to Walter, who was then managing editor. She and Walter shared long work hours, ideals, and a common goal. She considered him the handsomest man she had ever met.

Walter obtained a Mexican divorce from Norma, and, after a courtship followed by most of the working press in New York City, he and Edith signed a contract marriage—legal then with the signatures of husband and wife and two witnesses—in July 1922. Walter considered this more decent than taking vows that might later be broken. Edith called it "a life partnership of two free people who loved each other."[13]

Walter and Edith worked for the *Call* until it succumbed to Socialist infighting in 1923. The left, no longer the broad-based movement it had been before the war, had splintered into language and interest groups after the Bolshevik revolution. Walter was attacked for printing a report condemning the lack of free speech in the new Soviet society and finally resigned after the editorial board ordered him to fire a reporter because of a board member's personal grudge.[14] After the paper folded, Charles Ervin, its longtime editor, wrote: "The battle between those who stood for the social democratic principles and those who stood for the dictatorship in Russia . . . finally resulted in doing what all the forces of reaction in the United States could not do—put an end to the *Call* and the magnificent fight for human rights it had waged for over fifteen years."[15]

After the collapse of the *Call,* Walter, believing he could get a job on any paper he chose, put the names of ten New York City dailies into a hat and drew out the name of the *New York Sun.*[16] He might well have saved the names. Between 1923 and 1926, Walter worked for the *Sun,* the *New York Times,* the *New York Post,* and the *New York News.*

Edith, pregnant with my brother Wallace, did not look for another newspaper position. Wallace was born in January 1924, and like me after him, was delivered by Dr. Mary Halton, a friend of Edith's who had studied at the Sorbonne. Though Edith's liberated friends thought her foolish to give up paid employment and have two children on a freelance writer's uncertain income, it never occurred to Edith to be sensible. She was young and in love and ready to face whatever life might offer.

3. Freelance Writer, Freelance Radical

Mr. Liggett . . . does not mince words: he has little charity towards political parasites; but he is far too astute a newspaperman to be caught making statements that are not thoroughly well-documented. . . . He does not inform us vaguely and urbanely that graft exists. He tells us exactly what is done, who the thieves are, how they operate, and how much they get away with.

—**William H. Cunningham, in** *Understanding America*, **1934**

Writers' Paradise

Walter launched his career as a magazine and book author the week Edith learned she was pregnant with me, a month after Wally's first birthday. On February 14, 1925, Walter's thirty-ninth birthday, my parents took five dollars from their savings to see a show and drink to the luck I would bring them.

Edith listened to Walter's tall tales of the Mounties and his days as an express messenger. Next morning, she went to the library and came back to tell him that no American magazines had recent stories on the Mounties. That afternoon, Walter phoned a friend at *Collier's*. After an interview with the editor-in-chief, Walter got an advance for a trip to Ottawa to gather material and pictures for a series of "dramatic stories on the Royal Canadian Mounted Police," which *Collier's* bought for three hundred dollars apiece. They came out just about when I was born, in September 1925. My dad always told me that I brought him luck.[1]

Although being a freelance writer has never been easy, Walter could not have done better than to start out in New York during the mid-1920s. If Washington represented corruption at all levels, New York represented cultural vitality. In this period of postwar expansion, prosperity spilled over into everything from construction and electrification to music and theater. Even with the inroads of Hollywood and the radio, the twenties were a golden era for publishing. Writers had a profusion of outlets in newspapers, magazines, and books.[2]

The magazine world ranged from the high-quality publications known as "slicks" to mass "pulp" publications. Walter wrote for many of the slicks, including the old *Scribner's;* the brash, irreverent *Plain Talk;* and H. L. Mencken's *American Mercury.* He also wrote for more middle-of-the-road magazines like *Collier's* and *Everybody's,* and for left-wing publications like *Modern Quarterly* and *New Leader,* as well as writing boxing and adventure stories for the pulps.

Many high-quality magazines were launched in the twenties, out of both careful thought and casual impulse. The debonair *New Yorker* started out in 1925, the caustic and opinionated *American Mercury* in 1924.[3] To my mind, neither embodies the refreshing irreverence of the twenties quite as well as *Plain Talk,* a monthly journal of opinion launched in 1927. G. D. Eaton, *Plain Talk's* founding editor, asserted in his first editorial that *Plain Talk* would be "dedicated to Tolerance, and naturally to locking horns with Intolerance." But since Eaton was highly intolerant of cant, the magazine was less tolerant than engaging and literate, with a good balance of articles on literature and public affairs. Walter, with his series on Prohibition enforcement, was one of the mainstays and circulation builders, and was the magazine's final editor after Eaton's death in 1930.[4]

By the time of my birth, our family had moved from Greenwich Village to the family-centered borough of Brooklyn.[5] In the summer of 1926, we headed north to Cape Cod, where we lived first near Manomet in a pretty farmhouse on a lake, then moved to Provincetown, an artists' haven packed with writers, some surprisingly poor: Edith was always giving "something for your dog" to poet Harry Kemp. It was a happy time for her.

On Cape Cod, Walter, with Edith's help—she typed and critiqued his work and helped out with dialogue—wrote three books for the Macauley Company. *Frozen Frontier* (1927) was straight adventure fiction glorifying the Mounties, while *The River Riders* (1928), under the guise of adventure fiction, dealt with the abuses of Minnesota's logging industry and the dramatic wartime Minnesota forest fires. *Pioneers of Justice* (1930) was a history of the Mounties that reflected Walter's concern for justice.[6]

Walter was incapable of staying away from radical activities for long. And, as usual, there were plenty to choose from. In 1925, Minnesotan Frank B. Kellogg, who had been promoted to U.S. secretary of state after losing his U.S. Senate race, launched his diplomatic career by protesting Mexico's laws regulating oil lands owned by foreign interests. By November 1926, Kellogg had sent the Mexican government fifteen escalating protests. Then Kellogg insisted to the Senate Foreign Relations Committee that Mexico was trying to establish a Bolshevik hegemony through Central America.[7] Progressive senators suspected that the United States might back into war by sending armed forces to Mexico while Congress was not in session. North Dakota senator Lynn Frazier submitted a Senate resolution opposing sending armed forces to Mexico, while Minnesota senator Henrik Shipstead headed a subcommittee on this resolution.

Meanwhile, Walter researched the financial background of Kellogg's complaints, following the money trail. On February 27, 1927, Walter spoke to Shipstead's subcommittee, testifying that only twenty companies in Mexico had refused to submit to the Mexican government's oil regulations. It turned out that 87 percent of these companies' total acreage was owned by three individuals: U.S. Secretary of the Treasury Andrew Mellon, and Harry Sinclair and Edward Doheny. The latter two had just figured prominently in the recent Teapot Dome oil scandals.[8] After Walter's testimony, Kellogg dropped his attempt to force a quarrel on Mexico. Edith always believed that Walter's investigations were a major factor in keeping the United States from going to war with Mexico in 1927.

Although Walter certainly felt strongly about unwarranted interventions in Latin America, he had a more personal interest in the case of two immigrant Italian anarchists sentenced to death in Massachusetts for their supposed involvement in a payroll robbery that resulted in the murder of two guards. Our Manomet house was less than eight miles from Plymouth, where the two men, Nicola Sacco, a shoemaker, and Bartolomeo Vanzetti, a fish peddler, had lived. Walter, a gregarious man, had met their friends and neighbors and heard the story firsthand. He learned that when the two men were first arrested in May 1920, they believed that they were being arrested for their anarchist beliefs.[9] To their surprise, they were charged with murdering a paymaster in a holdup in South Braintree.

Neither Sacco nor Vanzetti had a criminal record. Both had convincing alibis, but long histories as anarchists. The evidence was tenuous, the witnesses dubious, the atmosphere tense, the judge prejudiced, and the defense political and erratic. Although the Morelli gang, an organized crime family from Providence, were far more likely suspects, Sacco and Vanzetti were sentenced to death for murder.[10]

Since Walter had, for once, money in the bank, thanks to advances for his books, he took a month off from writing to work without pay for the men. Other Provincetown writers, including Frank Shay, John Dos Passos, and Mary Heaton Vorse, were also active in the defense of Sacco and Vanzetti. In the final month before they were executed, Walter with four other men founded the Citizens National Committee for Sacco and Vanzetti. While the primary defense committee and the defendants' lawyers worked for a commutation of their sentence, the Citizens National Committee also demanded that the Department of Justice open its files and make public its evidence on Sacco and Vanzetti.[11]

Walter managed to get wide attention with a letter signed by prominent authors. He spoke at eight mass meetings in Wisconsin and Minnesota. He got the support of governors and senators, but to no avail.[12] Sacco and Vanzetti were executed at midnight on August 23, 1927; Walter was with a group trying to reach the governor, while Edith, waiting at home with friends in Provincetown, listened to the news on the radio.[13]

In the summer of 1928, we pulled up our Cape Cod roots and hit the road. My clearest memories of our family are of us traveling together by car, my parents joshing in the front seat and pointing out scenic and historic highlights, while Wally and I played road games or squabbled quietly in the back.

I have faint memories of Montana, where Walter investigated the administration of the Bureau of Indian Affairs for the Senate Indian Affairs Committee in the fall of 1928. I remember the sun-baked prairies, the fields of wheat, and the towns with shacks and teepees as well as houses, and I have a nightmare recollection of hissing and of dead snakes wound through the spoke wheels of an old Ford truck. Most of all, I remember the Indians: the old men, tall, straight, and handsome despite their wrinkles; the children with puffed faces and scabs and running sores on their eyes.[14]

Walter spent some time aiding Montana senator Burton K. Wheeler in his 1928 reelection campaign,[15] then, always a supporter of the underdog, moved over to North Dakota to campaign for Alfred E. Smith, Herbert Hoover's opponent in the presidential race.[16] Hoover, whom Walter believed to be a master of propaganda, handily won the election as custodian of what soon proved to be the false prosperity of the twenties.

Washington, D.C., and the Mooney Case

Our family moved to the Washington, D.C., area in the winter of 1928–29, perhaps to be nearer the action. We lived in Chevy Chase in a nice two-story house that was our major essay at gracious living and the only house we ever owned. Wally started school there, crossing a woodland field with houses under construction, leaving me home with my mother. Walter sat writing in his study, but kept popping out to read good paragraphs to Edith, while I used to throw my shoes out of the window to get his attention. He had to interrupt his work to rummage around in the bushes to find them. "Make Daddy nervous," I told my mother smugly.

Walter had been writing about the imprisoned Thomas Mooney off and on ever since Mooney was jailed in July 1916 on charges of bombing a Preparedness Day Parade, but his involvement with Mooney really began in January 1929.[17] At the height of war fever, Mooney, a longtime San Francisco labor leader, had been prosecuted by a hostile district attorney with perjured testimony even though a photo with a clock showed him miles away from the scene. The two witnesses before the grand jury were an unemployed waiter and a prostitute once accused of murder. (Prostitutes, of course, have always been easy prey for crooked district attorneys.) Frank Oxman, a traveling businessman, made a more convincing witness, but it turned out later that he was actually transacting business elsewhere at the time that he testified he saw Mooney planting the bomb in San Francisco. While Mooney, his wife, and several friends and acquaintances were originally indicted, only Mooney and a young labor activist named Warren Billings were convicted.[18]

Fortunately, Mooney had friends abroad. One was Emma Goldman, who got an anarchist faction in Russia to demonstrate in front of the American embassy in Petrograd. This was the first of a series of foreign demonstrations that circuitously brought the case to American attention. It quickly became an international cause célèbre. Largely because of "effects on international affairs which his execution would greatly complicate," President Wilson persuaded the governor of California to commute Mooney's sentence to life imprisonment in 1918.[19]

By January 1929, however, the Mooney case was out of the public eye, except in California. As a result of the dedication of a few Mooney advocates and tireless marshaling of evidence by newspaper editor Fremont Older, all of the witnesses had recanted. By that time, the presiding judge, three assistant prosecutors, two of the police officials who had helped prepare the evidence, the next district attorney, and ten of the twelve jurors in the case had all come to believe in Mooney's innocence. But the governor and the Supreme Court of California still refused to free him.

On January 15, 1929, Walter mailed a letter to Tom Mooney at the state penitentiary in San Quentin, California: "You, of course, don't know me from Adam's off ox, but if you desire you can get my record from . . . anyone connected with the radical movement. . . . I have persuaded a certain U.S. Senator to go to bat in your behalf and also have lined up a magazine of national circulation which has agreed to make an issue of the case."[20]

The senator was Thomas D. Schall, Republican maverick from Minnesota and a longtime acquaintance of Walter's. Schall, who had grown up in extreme poverty and had been blinded in an accident as a young man, tended to identify with outcasts and underdogs. The magazine was *Plain Talk,* then hitting its stride with lively fiction and crackling exposés of everything from birth control to national politics.

Whatever they thought, Mooney and Mary Gallagher, who organized the work of his defense committee, responded with documents and hope. Walter researched and wrote an article titled "Why Is Mooney in Prison?" that appeared in the May 1929 issue of *Plain Talk* (ascribed to Schall) and brought Mooney's case once again to the forefront of public attention.

By dint of "an enormous amount of polite pressure," Walter convinced Senators Gerald P. Nye, Burton K. Wheeler, and Schall to bring Mooney's case to the floor of the Senate. On June 19, 1929, Nye spoke for nearly an hour, claiming that President Hoover's call for law enforcement was being undermined by the Mooney case. After Nye finished, the blind Senator Schall declared that he had listened to the transcripts and was sure that "Tom Mooney is as innocent of the crime of which he was convicted as any man in the Senate." Wheeler called the case "one of the foulest conspiracies ever perpetrated in this country."

"Getting those speeches made has almost driven me to the verge of nervous prostration," Walter wrote Mooney the next day. "Day after day, Nye and Wheeler have been held up by legislative jams and as the closing hour drew near I actually commenced to fear that they would not get in. . . . I certainly was the most relieved man in America when Nye actually started to speak."[21]

Walter continued to press for Mooney's release between articles for *Plain Talk,* writing potboilers for rent, and investigative journalism. By the time he died, Walter had spent nearly twenty years on the case.

Prohibition: "Noble Experiment" or the Shame of the Cities?

Immediately after Walter's burst of activity for Mooney, *Plain Talk* hired him to undertake a series of investigative articles on Prohibition. This spirited but scholarly series, which appeared between September 1929 and August 1930, recounted specific violations in city after city and state after state and left a trail of grand jury investigations and legislative probes in its wake.

The first article, "Why Dry Killers Go Free," was a detailed inquiry into 136 "accidental" deaths caused by Prohibition agents' careless shooting. In "How Wet Is Washington?" Walter used arrest records, mash liquor confiscation records, and interviews to estimate the number and location of Washington bootleggers and commercial stills, as well as the quantities of moonshine, medicinal whiskey, and home-brewed beer they produced. He charged that many "dry" senators, cabinet members, and congressmen flagrantly violated the laws they advocated.[22]

The article corroborated the stories of three *Washington Times* reporters who had been jailed for refusing to name their sources, and Walter was asked to appear before the grand jury that had sentenced the *Times* reporters. I remember him eating bread and graham crackers soaked in milk, which I later learned was then the recommended treatment for ulcers.

Walter proved a cooperative witness, if not exactly what the district attorney had in mind. The *New York Herald Tribune* quoted Walter as saying, "I believe these conditions are public property, but where I got the information is my own property."[23]

"I do not intend to be a snooper or a stool pigeon for the police or District Attorney," Walter told reporters beforehand, "but I don't see why I should protect hypocrites in high places—Senators, Representatives, and Cabinet officers who are personally wet, but who go back to their districts and tell their constituents how dry they are."[24] Evidently he made the same statement to the grand jury: in no time at all, he was handed his hat and excused. His testimony had taken less than ten minutes.[25]

After serving forty days in jail, the three *Washington Times* reporters were released to a festive reception in Washington's Belasco Theatre. The publisher of the *Times,* who had doubled the reporters' salaries while they were in jail, now awarded them extra vacations. Colonel Frank Knox of the Hearst newspaper chain presented each with a check for a thousand dollars and a gold watch inscribed "for loyalty to newspaper ethics."[26]

Walter's "Bawdy Boston" appeared in *Plain Talk* in January 1930 and "Holy Hypocritical Kansas" in February, while news of the upcoming article on Michigan was rocking that state. Walter always checked historical records and official documents like shipping invoices and arrest records, and cast a wide net for possible sources. In Kansas, for example, he first spent several days at the state capitol and the historical library, then visited sixteen counties and investigated conditions in the three largest cities.[27]

Soon after the Kansas article appeared, Walter was called to testify before the House Judiciary Committee as the major witness at the first open hearing on the merits of Prohibition. He spoke for almost three hours, frequently interrupted by applause. A Universal Service correspondent reported that Walter provided "a startling portrayal of a prohibition machine, broken down and greased with graft and corruption."[28]

He began with background on his research, explaining how he had surveyed Boston, Kansas, Minnesota, North Dakota, Michigan, and the District of Columbia for his *Plain Talk* articles. "Liquor is the basis today for all underworld crime," he told the committee:

> Every racketeer, every gangster, every rat of the underworld, regardless of whether he is holding up dry-cleaning shops or kidnapping brewers or murdering for a consideration, regardless of what his specialized activity is, he gets his main income and his certain, steady source of income from some connection with the liquor racket, with a rum runner or a bootlegger. It affords criminals a sure steady means of support and causes large sums of money to be at their disposal, and furthermore, when you go to your sheriff or your Federal enforcement officer or your county constable, and you slip him some money to let you ride in with a load of rum, you have him in your power the moment you corrupt him, the minute you give but $10, for that moment he has surrendered his integrity and his manhood to your keeping. It is a matter of progressive corruption.[29]

Walter asserted that the huge profits from illegal liquor were invested in other criminal enterprises — prostitution, gambling, extortion, loan-sharking, and rackets of every kind — often converting them into criminal syndicates and spreading crime and corruption from the cities to state governments and the boondocks. Prohibition had produced corruption at every level and caused a permanent change in the scale and sophistication of American crime. To the question of whether the law was worth enforcing, Walter replied, "If we have ten more years of Prohibition, the nation will be ruled by gangsters, underworld rats, and crooked politicians." The crowd responded with thunderous applause.

The hearing was reported across the nation, and the *Plain Talk* articles that followed were in hot demand. The *Plain Talk* series encouraged the newspapers that had tried to report honestly on enforcement of Prohibition and inspired or shamed others to greater efforts.[30]

Savvy reporters were only too aware of the dangers of crusading journalism. Throughout the twenties and thirties, *Editor & Publisher* recorded incident after incident of intimidation and harassment, from Atlantic City to Indiana to California.[31] The most celebrated case of the twenties was the assassination of Don Mellett, editor and publisher of the Canton, Ohio, *Daily News,* who was shot in the back by a man lurking in the bushes outside his home less than a year after he had started a campaign to investigate ties between crime, city authorities, and the police. The murder conspiracy involved two businessmen (bootleggers branching out into brothels), a former police detective, and the Canton police chief.

Mellett's widow had to sue the men accused of murdering her husband in order to obtain indictments.[32]

As Walter's series continued, government officials attempted to suppress particular issues of *Plain Talk;* the more corrupt the area, the more serious their attempts were. Boston banned the "Bawdy Boston" issue, but it sold out in less than a day. After "Holy Hypocritical Kansas," the Kansas Legislature officially defeated a motion that Walter be called a liar and another motion to pay his expenses to come to Kansas to prove his statements to a legislative body. As one representative put it, "We all know liquor can be bought. Liggett will prove it if he comes, and I think it will be bad advertising."[33]

When "Michigan, Soused and Serene" was on its way to the newsstands in March, the head of the Michigan State Police tried to induce a circuit court judge in Detroit to suppress the issue. After state officials frightened off an independent distributor, *Plain Talk* had to hire its own trucks to circulate the issue. Despite the threats, fifty thousand copies were sold in Michigan. People borrowed issues, resold them, and rented them out for fifty cents a day. One Michigan editor estimated that some three hundred thousand Michiganders had read the article.

While one letter writer declared Walter's articles "an intoxicating mixture of fact and fiction," *Plain Talk* editor G. D. Eaton declared, "After each article by Walter W. Liggett comes a host of letters corroborating the picture he has drawn of Prohibition conditions within a given community."[34]

"Minneapolis and Vice in Volsteadland," Walter's report on his home state, portrayed Minnesota as a state where farmers—who often voted dry—made liquor from corn developed by the state's agricultural college, while better liquor was transported from Canada past federal, state, county, and city police. Walter reported that the Minneapolis police force was "utterly demoralized" and that rackets were started with police connivance. Even though Walter accurately reported the extent of vice in Minnesota and its cities, the article was less hard-hitting than others in the series. He did not mention Floyd B. Olson, who, as Hennepin County attorney from 1920 through 1929, had been responsible for prosecuting Minneapolis violations. Friends had told him that Olson had turned over a new leaf and was working responsibly.[35]

"Georgia—Godly but Guzzling" followed in May 1930, "Whoopee in Oklahoma" in June, "Ohio—Lawless and Unashamed" in July, and "Pittsburgh—Metropolis of Corruption" in August.[36] By this time, Walter had taken over as editor of *Plain Talk* after Eaton's death in June. "All his life," Walter wrote, Eaton "had waged a slashing fight for principle, for the utmost in human liberty, against sham and oppression."[37] *Plain Talk* did not survive Eaton long. Walter wanted to keep it going as a forum for Tom Mooney, and was planning a ten-part series on President Hoover, but he was to be editor for only two more issues.[38]

Chicago, Chicago

By my fifth birthday, on September 20, 1930, our family had left Washington for a comfortable hotel in Chicago, far removed from the increasing penury of the Depression. Frank Knox of the *Chicago News* had hired Walter to investigate the ties between crime and government in Chicago. My mother and uncle told me that Knox had made Walter an unrefusable offer—a hundred dollars a day plus expenses, an incredible sum for a newspaperman in the Depression. Apparently, Knox was willing to pay extravagantly for an honest and thorough investigator.[39]

Knox's largesse probably stemmed from the June 1930 murder of Alfred "Jake" Lingle, a leg man and street crime reporter for the *Chicago Tribune*. Although the press initially thought he was a martyr, it turned out that Lingle was a streetwise gambler who had led a double life for nearly a decade, working for and protected by Al Capone. To complicate the matter further, the Chicago commissioner of police was a boyhood chum of Lingle's, and they shared a joint $100,000 stock account.[40]

The family story is that Walter pursued his investigation with gusto and sometimes with a bodyguard. In December, he brought Knox a thick sheaf of papers—apparently too hot to print and too hot to act on. The corruption in Chicago went clear to the top: judges, high state officials, U.S. senators and representatives, bankers and wealthy merchants, prominent socialites, and members of the bar association and the Association of Commerce. Walter's research was not completely wasted. In March 1932, the *American Mercury* published his article "The Plunder of Chicago," which was later incorporated into a social studies anthology, *Understanding America.*

"Criminals," Walter stated, "are delighted when the newspapers make a clatter about melodramatic events in the Chicago underworld. So long as they feature the colorful gang feuds of the town, or savagely attack the labor racketeers, no attention is paid to inquiries into the municipal finances. There is drama when some squealer is taken for a ride, or groups of mobsmen are chopped down with machine-guns, but digging into dusty records is drab business at the best."

"The Cities Reap the Whirlwind," which appeared in *Scribner's Magazine* in August 1932, represents Walter's appraisal of the hazards and possibilities of honest city government in a Depression environment. Although the neglected science of city government could improve the odds, he wrote, "no government can rise above the character of the men who conduct it."

I don't know what happened to Walter's fabulous salary. I vaguely recall hearing that he lost it in a venture in gold dust on the Chicago Exchange. But then, he was never comfortable with money.

The American Dreyfus: San Quentin Prisoner 31921

In December 1930, Walter, having just completed his investigation for Colonel Knox, received an urgent telegram from Aline Barnsdall, one of Tom Mooney's supporters, and agreed to go to San Francisco to head the Tom Mooney Molders Defense Committee.[41] We arrived in San Francisco on a damp Friday evening in January and found an apartment on Geary Street. On Monday, Walter had a three-hour conference with Mooney.[42]

Our Geary Street apartment, though less posh than our Chicago digs, had a fascinating fold-down Murphy bed in the living room. But our stay in San Francisco was a strenuous period for the family. Everyone in the family got sick. Wallace and I had to have our tonsils out, while Edith had an emergency mastoid operation. Then my dad and I got pneumonia. Even the private school Wallace and I went to burned down one weekend.

Sometime after my recovery from pneumonia, my dad took me to visit Tom Mooney at San Quentin. Tom had a round, worn, very Irish face and wore a clean short-sleeved white shirt open at the neck. Somehow, I knew that meeting him was important, but I didn't know what to say. We smiled at each other, full of goodwill if not many words. Eventually, we chatted about my health and my school.[43]

Early in February, Walter began a campaign to get California newspapers to take up the Mooney cause again, writing to friends and acquaintances in the labor press. As a consequence of a letter to activist Clara Lee, most unions in Colorado passed resolutions demanding that Mooney be freed.[44] Walter also appealed to old allies to draft new articles, editorials, and special issues on the case.[45] Heywood Broun promised to do a column for the *New York Evening Telegraph,* while the *American Guardian* put out a special issue of 156,000 copies.[46]

In Minnesota, Henry Teigan arranged for articles in the *Farmer-Labor Leader* and the *Union-Advocate.* Walter then prodded Teigan to use his influence to get the state legislature to pass a resolution urging release of Mooney.[47] "Can't you get Floyd Olson and the other members of the Labor Party to do their damnedest?" Walter queried, informing Teigan that the state of Wisconsin had already passed such a resolution. Floyd B. Olson had just been elected governor on a Farmer-Labor ticket, and it seemed to Walter that a Farmer-Labor administration in Minnesota should do as well by Tom Mooney as had the Wisconsin Progressives.[48]

Working with writer Travers Clements, Walter helped the national Mooney committee set up a California chapter.[49] Walter also worked with lawyers to prepare and distribute a succinct legal critique of the California Supreme Court decision on Mooney.[50] In May, thirty-one noted authors signed a protest against Mooney's continued imprisonment.

Amidst his hard work, Walter found himself in conflict with both Tom's sister, Anna Mooney, and Aline Barnsdall. Anna may have resented his coming to the office as savior. Aline questioned his travel expenses.[51] All were proud and ungiving. Walter kept on working through March, but the committee did not come up with funds for his April salary. Still, his presence had given a jump start to the floundering effort. Much of his work came to fruition in May, when California's Governor James Rolph was deluged with resolutions from workers' organizations and "Our American Dreyfus" by Lillian Symes appeared in *Harper's*.[52]

Herbert Hoover: The Man and the Book

Walter had long been collecting tidbits about Herbert Hoover and had actively begun researching a biography. In February 1931, he began contacting book and magazine publishers.[53] The prospective book was a hot property — and Walter knew it. Albert Boni of Boni and Liveright offered royalties of 17.5 percent after 15,000 copies, pointing out that this was higher than royalties paid to best-selling authors Thornton Wilder and Will Rogers.[54]

During our last month in California, Walter spent time investigating Hoover's early life and California connections. On our return auto trip to New York City, we stopped in Iowa so Walter could check on Hoover's background. By June, we were living at the Kew Bolmer apartment house in Kew Gardens, Queens, where we lived until we left for Minnesota in the summer of 1933. Although Walter always had an office where we lived, he usually worked on his book at Boni's Fifth Avenue offices in Manhattan, where he had a marvelous research assistant. In between bouts of writing, Walter filled in the book's gaps by persuading a host of people to ferret out odd facts. Edith, too, was put to work; I recognized her handwriting on abstracts of articles from the *Nation*.[55]

When Boni and Liveright sent out notices about the forthcoming book, one evidently got into the hands of the Treasury Department and was later mentioned in a report to the head of the Secret Service. Walter either did not realize, or did not care, that government and private detectives were investigating and reporting on him while he worked on the biography.[56] But the government investigations may have hurt his rapport with his publisher. Walter wrote journalist Harry Elmer Barnes that "after reading much of the manuscript and personally urging me 'to make it hotter,' [Boni] suddenly changed front, developed a very bad case of cold feet."[57] Boni abruptly asked him to eliminate certain sections. Then he found another publisher—which later unexpectedly dropped the book.[58]

Peggy Walton wrote in April 1932 in the new *Plain Talk* that "government dicks reminded the publisher that his penchant for taking ladies on weekend parties to his villa" was a violation of the Mann Act. The next publisher's printer was warned that his father's estate taxes might balloon if he finished printing the book—and Walter was trailed by government agents when he accompanied the type that was removed from the shop.

(Sam Roth, who had published John M. Hammill's *Strange Career of Mr. Hoover under Two Flags,* had a similar story. After Hammill's book appeared, three income tax detectives ransacked his office. A few days later he heard that a postal inspector was warning booksellers not to buy his other books.)[59]

The Rise of Herbert Hoover: The True Story of His Progress from Promoter to President was finally published by H. K. Fly Company, publishers of the old *Plain Talk,* in February 1932. In it, Walter examined what he called "the Hoover myth" and found that myth at variance with the record of Hoover's actions, with Hoover's statements, and with the recollections of Hoover's friends and professional acquaintances. Walter believed that all through his career, Hoover had consistently used what we would now call disinformation or spin control. From 1914 through 1922, Walter wrote, Hoover always had at least a dozen publicists on his payroll.

Walter had not been the only writer preparing a critical biography of Herbert Hoover. While he was arguing with his publishers, several hasty efforts had been issued. Walter's book surfaced amidst a disinformation campaign directed against these biographies.[60] After discarding the idea of libel suits, Hoover's supporters tried discrediting the authors.[61] They retained Arthur Train, whose article titled "The Strange Attacks on Mr. Hoover" appeared in *Collier's* in February 1932. Then they commissioned political reporter Herbert Corey to write *The Truth about Hoover* and indemnified both Corey and the publisher against libel suits. The group sent agents to bookstores to gather sales statistics, initiated a nationwide campaign of letters to newspapers, and distributed Corey's book gratis to libraries and high schools across the United States. Long after Hoover lost the 1932 election to Franklin Roosevelt, they continued to buy up copies of unfavorable biographies.[62]

Soon after Walter's book appeared, laudatory, if somewhat hasty, biographies of Hoover came pouring off the presses. As more and more books on Hoover came out, reviewers tended to group them. The *Nation* lumped four books together, with the demurrer that "it would be manifestly unfair... to condemn Mr. Liggett's biography for the sins of the others. . . . Mr. Liggett gives the impression of seeking to be scrupulously fair, although occasional cases of malice creep in."[63] Journalist Arthur Robb wrote that Walter had "approached the subject with the technique of the investigating reporter," and he found Walter's book "probably more accurate than the run of 'official biographies' since every statement is carefully documented."[64]

Looking for a Magazine

We lived in our comfortable middle-class apartment in Kew Gardens until July 1933. Although the Depression cut deeply into the income of many freelance writers and newspapermen, Walter still sold adventure, boxing, and detective fiction to the pulps and, increasingly, articles to the slicks, where he was considered a crackerjack investigator and an authority on both Hoover and municipal government.

His articles on cities came out in *American Mercury, Scribner's,* and the new *Common Sense.* Both the *New Leader* and *Modern Monthly* published his materials on Hoover. In March and April 1932, *Popular Aviation* sent him to Washington as a special investigator for a three-article series on airline monopolies, airmail subsidies, and wasteful government procurement practices.

During our time in Kew Gardens, Walter kept trying to establish a national journal of opinion, a successor to *Plain Talk.* He worked with Dell Publishing on *Spotlight,* a satirical monthly journal whose first issue came out in June 1932.[65] It was not a good year to launch a magazine, and Dell cut its losses after a couple of issues. Walter then briefly produced his own *National Spotlight,* partly to print more on Hoover.

After Hoover's 1932 defeat, Walter wrote Upton Sinclair on behalf of *Common Sense,* seeking "trenchant, factual articles dealing with politics, finance, industry, and economics in general."[66] *Common Sense,* which propounded a non-Marxist American radicalism, was launched by Alfred M. Bingham and Selden Rodman, two recent Yale honors graduates who decided to run the magazine with volunteer labor. Walter, with a family but no family inheritance, did not volunteer to serve on the staff, but he contributed the first issue's lead story, "Mr. Mellon's Pittsburgh," which tracked corruption from gangsters to the Supreme Court and the Cabinet. *Common Sense* ultimately devoted itself largely to promoting a third party. Walter would remain on the masthead with the other original contributors until he broke with Floyd B. Olson.[67]

The first (probably the only) issue of *Liggett's Searchlight* came out in June 1933, turning the searchlight on Boston. Walter wrote Upton Sinclair that his magazine had "been kept off the newsstands in Boston and the police have been chasing my news boys all over the historic Common."[68]

I don't know exactly why Walter suddenly decided to return to Minnesota to run a country newspaper, the *Northland Times,* in Bemidji. Among other considerations, the move seemed financially imprudent. Bemidji was a very small town, and two newspapers besides the *Northland Times* were publishing there.

Further, on July 9, 1933, Walter wrote Upton Sinclair that he had just signed a contract to prepare a history of the American press. Judging from that letter, he was eager to get started.[69] Probably V. F. Calverton (George to his friends) had acted as Walter's agent, since Walter, over the next hard-pressed years, kept apologizing to Calverton for being so slow to complete this work. Sadly, he was too busy living a chapter of that history to write the book.

I suspect that Walter was nostalgic for small-town journalism and the shirt-sleeve friendliness of small Minnesota towns. Unlike most newspapermen who hankered to run a weekly paper, he had considerable experience with country journalism, and he felt he would have ample time to work on a new book in a leisurely setting.

And, although Walter was best known for his expertise on municipal corruption, he was increasingly concerned with the plight of farmers and wrote three articles on farm issues for major magazines: "The Farmers See Red" appeared in the *American Mercury* in June 1932; "Our Machine-Tilled Acres" came out in *New Outlook* in November 1932; and *Scribner's Magazine* published "What Future Has Farming?" in March 1933. In the *Scribner's* article, Walter noted that in the capitalistic United States, "the farmers, as the result of wholesale foreclosures and tax evictions, are making really radical demands and today offer the only substantial nucleus for an independent third party."

I'm sure that Walter, a longtime believer in a third party, was in part drawn back to Minnesota by the seeming resurgence of the Farmer-Labor Party under Governor Olson; many old friends from Nonpartisan League days were now working for the Farmer-Labor regime; others were applying. Although Walter had doubts about Floyd Olson's record as Hennepin County attorney, mutual friends assured him that Olson had changed after being elected governor and was taking his job very seriously.

But although the Farmer-Labor Party had captured the governorship and held on to the rhetoric of the left, it had changed radically during Walter's long absence.

4. Meanwhile, in Minnesota

You can't have an underworld without an overworld, if you know what I mean. You can't have rackets unless you have the mayor, the chief of police, and the county attorney in your corner.

—**Nate Bomberg, reporter for the** *St. Paul Pioneer Press*, **quoted in Fred Friendly's** *Minnesota Rag*

Floyd B. Olson, County Attorney (1920–1930)

While Walter was exploring the connection between crime and Prohibition, Minneapolis had become the headquarters and distribution center of the Northwest's illicit liquor traffic, led by gangs from Minneapolis's north side. Many were boyhood friends of county attorney Floyd B. Olson, who had grown up in poverty on the wrong side of the tracks.[1] The only son of unhappily married immigrants, Olson grew up in a neighborhood of tumbledown shacks where the only brick buildings were houses of prostitution. This area, a melting pot for immigrant labor, provided most of the city's criminals and crooked policemen.

The growth of vice and crime in Minneapolis in the 1920s coincides with the first ten years of Prohibition and with Floyd Olson's tenure as Hennepin County attorney.[2] A charming, persuasive, exceedingly smart politician, Olson had a good radio voice and a superb sense of public relations. Although he was nominally a Democrat until 1924, Olson was appointed by Republican bosses in 1919 to serve as assistant county attorney under Republican William "Bud" Nash.[3]

Nash himself was rather openly crooked; both a judge and a former bootlegger claim that he owned brothels while he was in office.[4] Shortly after the start of Prohibition, Governor J. A. A. Burnquist discharged Nash for corruption after Howard Guilford, an unpopular muckraker, publicly accused Nash of accepting bribes from criminals and gun runners. Guilford's evidence must have been convincing, since Burnquist removed Nash in the face of a determined letter-writing campaign.[5]

Although many applicants wanted the county attorney position, the Republican bosses unexpectedly offered it to Olson, only eighteen months after his appointment as assistant county attorney.[6] One of Olson's first acts as county attorney was to help draw up an indictment against Nash. When it was quashed, it left Nash free to pursue a lucrative career as a criminal attorney. My parents believed that during Olson's stint as county attorney, clients of Nash's firm received especially generous treatment; their cases slid through without trial.[7]

As county attorney, Olson set the tone for Minneapolis law enforcement and was its linchpin. In an avowedly crooked city, he had the power of indictment and nolle prosequi, the ability to bring cases before grand juries, and the power to recommend sentences.

Although he was a competent and charismatic lawyer, Olson made no efforts to be a crusader, and he was something of a pioneer in plea bargaining and suspended sentences. Hennepin County convicted significantly fewer accused criminals than neighboring St. Paul did. The *Owatonna Journal,* after examining Hennepin County records for the years 1925 to 1928, reported that 548 persons who pleaded guilty to major crimes had received suspended sentences and 402 others were dismissed without trial. Altogether, 950 felons received no punishment at all. Many were habitual criminals with prior records, charged with crimes ranging from forgery and receiving stolen goods to manslaughter and sexual crimes against children; 145 were later arrested for other offenses.[8]

During the twenties, both Minneapolis and St. Paul practiced an "open door" policy toward criminals, who were allowed in St. Paul as long as they didn't commit crimes in the city. In Minneapolis, the police demanded a cut in the take.[9] Notorious criminals like John Dillinger, Baby-Face Nelson, Machine Gun Kelly, and the Roger Touhy gang nested in the Twin Cities and built ties with local gangsters.

Walter considered Olson's ten years as county attorney to be a time when justice was bought and sold in Minneapolis, and when known criminals enjoyed immunity from prosecution.[10] A good example is Isadore Blumenfield, better known as Kid Cann, the man later accused of my father's murder. Born in Romania in 1900, Cann grew up in the street-fighting, crap-shooting alleys of north Minneapolis. Prohibition enabled him to progress from juvenile delinquency to a well-paid career in crime. Once a small-time pimp and bootlegger, Cann became godfather of a syndicate that controlled much of Minneapolis's liquor business. With a penchant for aliases, including variants of Blumenfield and Cann, he went by at least sixty-two false names over the course of his criminal career.

Cann was arrested at least eighteen times for a variety of offenses before being accused of murdering my father in 1935. He was charged with picking pockets and being in a disorderly house, with assault, with passing kidnapping money, and with the murder of cabdriver Charles Goldberg. He was also arrested several times for violating the federal Prohibition Act. The county dropped most charges against him. Charles Goldberg's murder, for example, was called accidental death even though Cann had argued with Goldberg before shooting him.[11]

Similarly, five federal charges against Cann were dropped. Despite the chain of charges and arrests, he spent little time in court or in jail. He paid a few fines and spent one year in the county workhouse after pleading guilty to operating a still, but essentially, Minneapolis police, politicians, and prosecutors protected him for life.[12]

Attempted Murder and the Minnesota Gag Law

Throughout the twenties and thirties, major scandals were kept under wraps by the Minneapolis daily newspapers, which belonged to the "see no evil" school of journalism.[13] Edith attributed their silence to implicit blackmail by Olson, although he also made a constant effort to charm reporters while denouncing their papers.

The resulting vacuum in Minneapolis political investigation and crime reporting was filled by controversial editors and publishers. The establishment press called their publications—the *Twin City Reporter,* the *Saturday Press,* the *Beacon*—scandal sheets. Some historians called them obscene. Their editors were a colorful lot whose lives were a constant battle with the police and the political establishment. In the end, two of them—Howard Guilford and Arthur Kasherman—were murdered because of their publications.

Guilford was a multitalented individual. A master builder, inventor, and published author of children's verse, he could have made his living in a dozen ways had he not been so strongly drawn toward combative journalism. From 1913, when he accused St. Paul detectives of beating him up, until his murder in 1934, he was continuously embroiled in controversy. While his writings ranged from sentimental to straightforward to sleazy, they were usually accurate.[14]

Indicting Guilford was practically a hobby with Nash and Olson; he ultimately accumulated nineteen indictments. Some of them—"publishing obscene article," "placing in the hand of minor newsboys papers chiefly devoted to news of crime"—were obviously intended to suppress publication. Counterfeiting charges were considerably more serious and even more spurious. Although Guilford lacked political clout and influential friends, he was never convicted of any of the charges.[15]

Jay M. Near was another opinionated individualist. Cynical and dyspeptic, he also had the tenacity to carry his fight for free speech to the Supreme Court in the famous Minnesota "gag law" case. This story began in the summer of 1927 when Near and Guilford announced their plans to start the weekly *Saturday Press* to show how the Twin Cities liquor, vice, and gambling ring was protected by crooked politicians. It was a dangerous venture. Near noted in the first issue that they had been warned "that if we persisted in our exposé of conditions . . . we would be bumped off."[16]

On the morning the first issue hit the street, Guilford drove to work with his sister-in-law. A touring car pulled up beside them and forced Guilford's car to the curb. Two men in the touring car had guns. Guilford and his sister-in-law tried to save each other: he opened the passenger door so she could jump out; she screamed and tried to cover his body with her own. Fortunately, she jarred him and the first bullet missed his head, but the gangsters shot him in the stomach, nearly fatally; one bullet left twenty-nine intestinal perforations.[17]

Because the shooting had occurred 100 feet outside city limits, neither Olson nor the Minneapolis police investigated. Indeed, on September 27, the day after the shooting, police chief Frank Brunskill ordered his officers to visit downtown newsstands and tell newsboys to keep the newspaper off the street because it was "inciting to riot."[18]

The *Saturday Press* responded by intensifying its attacks and naming names. The second issue noted that Brunskill had visited Floyd Olson to find some legal way to stop the *Saturday Press*. In fact, Brunskill used a city ordinance to officially ban the paper, but Near refused to be stopped. The following issues — all banned from the newsstands — asserted that the chief of police participated in graft; that the mayor was derelict and inefficient; and that the county attorney knew of the situation but failed to correct it. Near demanded a special grand jury to investigate the crime situation and the attempt to murder Guilford.[19]

In the meantime, the county sheriff went to Guilford's bedside with a stenographer to get descriptions of his assailants, whom the sheriff identified as Harry Jaffa and Paul "Irish" Gottlieb. Guilford withdrew his identification after he saw the two in person, and later described his assailants as "two of Chicago's cold-blooded gangsters."[20] Whoever they were, the gangsters do not seem to have been prosecuted.

But the editors were. After two months and nine issues, Olson closed the *Saturday Press* for "malicious, scandalous and defamatory" remarks about the mayor, the police chief, the county attorney, and the Jewish race (the last issue had contained Near's exasperated diatribe protesting being called anti-Jewish for naming Jewish gangsters).[21] Although Near had pleaded with Olson to indict him and Guilford under criminal libel statutes, Olson used the Minnesota "gag law"—a 1925 public nuisance law passed by the Minnesota Legislature that had never been invoked.[22]

By the time the Minnesota Supreme Court determined that "there is no constitutional right to publish a fact merely because it is true," the American Civil Liberties Union (ACLU) had commissioned attorney Carol Weiss King to begin work on the case.[23] King was struck by the fact that Olson, the complainant, was one of the persons attacked by the *Saturday Press*. "This law," she wrote, "then makes it possible for anyone subjected to newspaper attack to turn around and have the paper enjoined if a single county judge can be found to sign such an order." She concluded that "the case more directly involves essentially civil liberties than any other case that I have ever had anything to do with."[24]

The ACLU's Forrest Bailey wrote Near that the group was prepared to sponsor an appeal to the U.S. Supreme Court and asked if Near was willing to change his local attorney to George Leonard, the ACLU contact in Minneapolis. Near exploded in a telegram and a lengthy letter. He wrote:

> We have in this state a peculiar political situation as well as a damnably corrupt one. The corner stone of the vile political temple is the county attorney of Hennepin county. Around him the underworld dregs swarm like flies round the bung of a molasses barrel. He is their protector, their guardian, their god ... and George B. Leonard will consult with him, mind you, before he answers your letter (my main bet).[25]

Near predicted that Leonard would report back that the case was not a civil liberties case. And indeed, Leonard advised Bailey that the *Saturday Press* was scandalous and defamatory. Leonard also claimed that Floyd B. Olson was "a member of the Civil Liberties Union and not in sympathy with an attempt to bridge the liberties of the press," though Bailey could not find Olson's name on the ACLU's membership lists.[26] Although Bailey dropped his recommendation of Leonard, his ACLU colleague Roger Baldwin continued to consult George Leonard as his main source for Minnesota.

After a permanent court order shutting down the paper and the district court's final judgment enjoining Near and Guilford from publishing the *Saturday Press* or any similar paper, Near appealed again to the Minnesota Supreme Court. By that time, Near had abandoned the ACLU for lawyers supplied by Colonel Robert McCormick, publisher of the *Chicago Tribune* and head of the Freedom of the Press Committee of the American Newspaper Publishers Association.

In the second round before the Minnesota Supreme Court, Near's lawyer argued that Minnesota was amply protected by criminal libel law. Olson himself eloquently defended the gag law, insisting that the state should have the power to suppress publications: "Freedom of speech is not an absolute right and is subject to previous restraint. The press enjoys the freedom it now enjoys merely because of the generosity of the people."[27]

The law remained in force as the case, bankrolled by the *Chicago Tribune* and supported by the American Newspaper Publishers Association, slowly moved up the judicial ladder.[28] In January 1931, *Near vs. Minnesota ex rel. Olson* finally reached the U.S. Supreme Court. At the hearing, Justice Louis B. Brandeis praised the editors' "great courage" in exposing corrupt government officials and criminal leaders. "If that is not one of the things for which the press chiefly exists, then for what does it exist?" he asked.[29] In June 1931, Chief Justice Charles Evans Hughes signed a landmark decision declaring the law unconstitutional.

Although the decision drew national editorials and legal commentary, it had little effect in Minneapolis. At the very time that the Supreme Court was declaring the gag law unconstitutional, Minneapolis police seized two issues of Arthur Kasherman's four-page weekly *Public Press* and a judge refused to grant him an injunction restraining the police from interfering with its publication and distribution.[30]

From Nonpartisan League to Farmer-Labor Party

The Minnesota Farmer-Labor Party, which had started out as a legal label used by Nonpartisan League candidates running outside Republican primaries, joined two groups with somewhat different aims. Farmers and farm advocates wanted a separate league that would embody their ideals and political identity. Labor, more realistic and more radical, if more accepting of corruption, wanted to gain political power through a farmer-labor federation.

In the 1920s, the two leagues—the Nonpartisan League and the Working People's Nonpartisan Political League—needed each other. The farmers, hit hard by the farm depression, supplied votes and most of the candidates, while labor unions supplied money and political savvy. After the Minnesota Legislature adopted rules that kept the Nonpartisan League out of Republican primaries, the League reluctantly lurched toward becoming part of an independent Farmer-Labor Party.

In 1922 the League won national attention when Henrik Shipstead defeated the Republican incumbent, Frank Kellogg, to win a Senate seat. A few months later, the other incumbent Minnesota senator died in office, and dairy farmer Magnus Johnson handily won the seat in a special election. The election of a second Farmer-Laborite senator—a dirt farmer, at that—put the Farmer-Labor Party on the national political map and increased the pressure to merge the two leagues. It also made the leagues an appealing target for takeover by the American Communist Party, which was trying in 1923 to gain control of a united front.

To accomplish both ends, Clarence Hathaway, a union machinist who was simultaneously a member of the Labor Federation and the Communist Workers Party, called for a state conference to form a federation of farmer-labor clubs.[31] The coalition that supported the federation included William Mahoney, Henry Teigan, and Floyd Olson.[32] The federation would be open to all groups that had supported the Farmer-Labor ticket in 1922 and 1923, and all organizations affiliated with the Workers' League. These clubs, in turn, would become the basic units for allocating delegates. Opponents argued that this structure could give power to phantom delegates and organizations.

Still, in March 1924, the farmer delegates at the Nonpartisan League convention voted narrowly to join the farmer-labor federation, and, sentimentally, to continue the League. Then they moved on to another meeting and voted to join a national third-party convention to be held in St. Paul in June—a meeting that the Communists fully intended to control. Even before it convened, both Shipstead and Magnus Johnson repudiated the convention, which turned out to be a debacle that fulfilled the direst predictions of its opponents. Communist squads dominated the gallery and the floor, bitterly attacking La Follette. Eventually, most Minnesota delegates walked out of the hall.[33]

Although this failed convention drove a wedge between those who had supported it and those who had opposed it, the Farmer-Labor Party had eight candidates for governor—who ranged from Communist Workers Party candidates to Walter's hero, Charles Lindbergh Sr.—in the 1924 primary elections.

Backed by the Hennepin County Central Committee, Floyd Olson entered the gubernatorial primary campaign in April 1924, his first foray into Farmer-Labor politics. Four days later, Lindbergh, ill from a brain tumor, withdrew from the race; Lindbergh's supporters were delivered to Olson. Olson won the primary with a handful of votes, despite heated inquiries as to what he had been doing as a Democrat in 1918 and 1920. Although he lost the general election, his good showing indicated his talent for getting votes.[34]

A year later, the trade unions voted to expel the Communists and changed the name of the federation to the Farmer-Labor Association. Olson helped write the constitution of the new Farmer-Labor Association, which from then on would control the Farmer-Labor Party. Although the basic units still were Farmer-Labor clubs and affiliated unions, other groups—action groups or ethnic groups, real or imaginary—could also elect delegates. The structure remained wide open to fraud and the creation of paper entities.

Olson wavered about being the Farmer-Labor candidate for governor in 1928 and kept silent for most of the year. But in 1929, aided by newspaper publicity, he began a deliberate effort to create a positive public image. In the postcrash year of 1930, he ran for governor on a platform of generalities that defused charges of radicalism. One of his few unequivocal statements was that he would not make appointments "on the basis of political affiliation." He was helped by the All-Party Committee of Democrats and Republican supporters and a tactical alliance with the Republican senator Thomas Schall.[35] Herbert Lefkovitz astutely commented that "radicalism may be dead in Minnesota, but the Farmer-Labor Party still lives. The party has no program and no cry, but it has 'prospects.' "[36]

Henrik Shipstead, the honest if stuffy incumbent Farmer-Labor senator, at first refused to endorse Olson in 1930 because he believed that Olson had ties to the underworld. But George Leonard, Olson's close friend and drinking buddy, finally persuaded Shipstead to issue a rather tepid endorsement.[37] Olson won handily, and despite few tangible accomplishments in his first term as governor was reelected in 1932. Although patronage was an ongoing issue in the Depression year of 1931, Olson avoided either moving toward civil service or setting specific standards for office-seekers. Instead he used the All-Party volunteers and patronage to build a personal political machine.

Charming, empathetic, and politically adroit, Olson struck up an alliance with President Franklin Roosevelt across party lines, juggled competing constituencies, and kept a substantial retinue of press advocates on the state payroll.

5. Return to Minnesota

Without a vigilant press, no democratic government can succeed.

— *Midwest American*

Homecoming

Our family left New York with a sense of adventure in July 1933, looking forward to an exciting new life in Minnesota. My grandmother prepared a wonderful farewell Sunday dinner for us, with roast beef and glazed potatoes, my favorite spring salad, and Wally's favorite chocolate cake. We took pictures on the porch and promised to write.

On the train trip west, I sought out my father in the smoking car, where I found him talking expansively. I felt proud of my handsome father and equally proud of the pretty new dress with green and lavender rickrack that my grandmother had sewed for me as a parting gift.

When we reached the Twin Cities, we met Walter's brother, Bob, and his family. Although the two brothers were much alike — both newspapermen and former boxers and football players — they had been estranged because of political differences dating back to World War I. While Walter had opposed the nation's entry into war, Bob had taught boxing to recruits.

Uncle Bob was nearly as tall as my father. He had a stern craggy face, softened by a twinkle in his blue eyes, and he claimed that he had inherited the dour Scotch traits of the Scotch-Irish Liggetts, while Walter had inherited their Irish recklessness. The two big men approached each other awkwardly. My aunt Frida and my mother smiled encouragement, and my cousins and my brother and I smiled shyly at each other. When the men finally grasped hands, we felt like crying or applauding.

Bob and Frida took us to their home on White Bear Lake just north of St. Paul — the first of many lakes in my Minnesota life. In the book-lined living room, the titles in the bookcases seemed much the same as ours: sets of nineteenth-century classics and single copies of great and avant-garde works of the 1920s and 1930s. Despite his stern exterior, Uncle Bob had a soft spot for me and I for him. Aunt Frida was warm and motherly; our cousins, three wriggly little boys, were close in age to Wallace and me. Even though we did not see their family often, it felt good to have family in a strange place.

Before we went north to Bemidji, we bought a blue Ford V-8 and drove to Wood Lake, Wisconsin, to visit the Akermark family. They had been Walter's neighbors in St. Paul before they had homesteaded on Wood Lake; Wallace and I were to be frequent visitors at their Wisconsin farm while our family lived in Minnesota. I still recall the summer smells of Wood Lake—the fermented cereal smell of turkey mash, the light, clean smell of just-caught fish, and the fresh scent of the pines.

Bemidji was a small town in northwestern Minnesota, near the headwaters of the Mississippi River. The smells were of lake and pine—and printers' ink. I celebrated my eighth birthday with new schoolmates in a house surrounded by pine and oak overlooking Lake Bemidji. Around our house, we collected acorns to feed the bears and raccoons at the zoo, and, at Wally's insistence, played at being trappers and Indians.

But the Depression, too, had reached Bemidji. That autumn, for the first time, I saw tramps—often middle-aged men—lingering shamefacedly at our door, looking for work or meals. I had never experienced this in San Francisco, Queens, or Chicago. Two young men came by one day, more briskly than usual, asking for food to make Mulligan stew. When I asked my dad what Mulligan stew was, he took me by the hand and walked with me to the very edge of town. Near where the sidewalks ended, tramps had gathered and set up a huge kettle on a tripod over a fire. I was a little frightened and hung back, but my father stepped forth confidently, and, for a dime, bought me a tin cupful of stew from the gray-haired man who seemed to be in charge. It was delicious and tasted of the corn and tomatoes we had donated.

Bemidji newspapers provide details of drought and Depression in the Midwest summer of 1933: the grain harvest was the smallest in decades; 25 percent of our national population was still farming, although farm prices had dropped 63 percent since 1929; some desperate, angry farmers began organizing strike "holidays" for harvesttime.[1] And then, as now, 20 percent of American children were living in poverty.[2] Across the nation, people gritted their teeth and held on, looking toward President Roosevelt, who had brought hope to a discouraged nation when he assumed office in March.

For lovers of the sensational, the big story was the search for the body of Herbert H. Bigelow, a St. Paul millionaire who had disappeared on Basswood

Lake during a storm. Charles Ward, vice president of Bigelow's firm, directed a massive search.[3] The two had met in Leavenworth prison, Ward serving time on a narcotics charge, Bigelow for income tax evasion. Later, Bigelow gave Ward a job at Brown & Bigelow, one of the nation's largest printers of calendars and novelties. When Bigelow's will was read, Ward inherited almost a million dollars, including the firm of Brown & Bigelow.[4] This fortune would lead to behind-the-scenes political power.[5]

All across the country, newspapers counted down the states as they voted to end Prohibition. With Repeal looming, hoodlums and syndicates jockeyed for position in new rackets. Bank robbery and kidnapping were growth industries in the Midwest during the summer of 1933.[6] Even a kidnapping in Oklahoma turned out to have a Minneapolis angle: the supposed mastermind was a former Minneapolis nightclub owner who had left town suddenly after a local bank robbery.[7]

The Oklahoma grand jury implicated seven members of the Minneapolis liquor Syndicate in passing the ransom money. Cliff Skelly, Bernie Berman, and Isadore Blumenfeld (better known as Kid Cann) were indicted in September 1933, in the first trial held under the new Lindbergh kidnapping law.[8] Cann claimed that he got the money in a liquor deal from men he did not know and would not recognize if he saw them again. Skelly and Berman were found guilty, but Cann was acquitted—with the help of Minneapolis police chief Joseph Lehmeyer, who flew to Oklahoma City to testify for the Minneapolis defendants without notifying anyone of his departure.[9] This caper, a bit too much even for Minneapolis, cost Lehmeyer a demotion to captain.

Wally and I liked Bemidji, but Walter resigned from the *Northland Times* only a month after we had moved there. I have no idea what happened—perhaps a quarrel with his partner or the competition of two other newspapers.

He was considering editing a national magazine in Chicago when he was introduced to Governor Floyd Olson at the Minneapolis Athletic Club. It was their first meeting, and Walter was thoroughly charmed by Olson.[10] They reached an understanding that Walter would establish a Farmer-Labor newspaper in Rochester, to provide the party with a voice in southeastern Minnesota. Olson helped arrange a cash advance to purchase the plant and press of the *Red Wing Organized Farmer,* and soon we moved to Red Wing.

The *Organized Farmer* had at best nineteen hundred subscribers when my parents bought the creaky plant in the first week of October 1933. In the thirties, small-town publishers could still eke out a living from tiny weeklies. There were more than five hundred weeklies in Minnesota, many with even smaller readerships.[11] Unfortunately, the *Organized Farmer's* decrepit press dated back almost to the Civil War. Every roller was flat and the mechanism wheezed and clattered.

About all I can remember of Red Wing are Halloween and Thanksgiving. On Thanksgiving, employees and friends gathered in our print shop to eat two enormous turkeys, huge bowls of mashed potatoes, six or eight pies, and seemingly hundreds of dishes of fish, relishes, pickles, and creamed onions. After the plates were cleared, Barbara Ritchie, our fashion and shopping columnist ("Around Town with Babs") encouraged me to do a tap dance on the stone tables that had held the smorgasbord. Barbara, a slender young woman who hit it off well with my mother, shared our household in Red Wing and later in Rochester.

Walter was listed as editor and publisher and Edith as associate editor when the first issue of the *Midwest American* rolled off the press in Red Wing on October 27. The *American* pronounced itself "independent, but never neutral": "In state affairs," it proclaimed, "we strongly incline to the announced policies of the Farmer-Labor party . . . but even here we shall preserve our independence of party labels and always feel free to criticize any office holder who, in our opinion, is prostituting the party from its original ideals."

The *Midwest American* was then a weekly of twenty-four to thirty-two pages, with local, state, and national coverage; it included a church page, local and national sports, a Washington news page, a children's page by Aunt Edith, and the fearless feminist column "What Do You Think?" by Rena Gunderson (aka Edith Liggett). Like all Walter's papers, it had a "news behind the news" section. The masthead slogan changed over time, but always extolled the role of the press in a democratic society: "However it be, the truth must out." "Without a vigilant press, no democratic government can succeed."

The very first issue contained an editorial titled "The Menace of Hitlerism." The *Midwest American* was one of the few weekly newspapers in the country to provide continuous in-depth coverage of Germany under Hitler. Walter had reported on Hitler way back in 1923, as editor of the *New York Call*. Similarly, one of Edith's feminist columns contained a fascinating critique of the abuses of women under the totalitarian societies of Russia, Germany, and Italy.

Within its small compass, the *Midwest American* covered an immense variety of economic news in human terms: reports on sharecroppers, increasing desertification, evictions in Chicago, cooperatives in Denmark, homes in slum districts, Upton Sinclair's EPIC (End Poverty in California) plan, and always, always, stories on the well-being of children. The paper reported regularly on labor and farm strikes, and on farmers' movements in Minnesota and the Midwest, and also covered the nation's first sit-in strike — in Austin, Minnesota, in November 1933. The story told how striking workers, led by Frank Ellis of the Independent Union of All Workers, had taken over the Hormel plant there.

As part of national coverage, the *Midwest American* carefully reported on constitutional issues. Often, editorials supported individuals who worked to promote justice. For example, an editorial on December 1, 1933, applauded Sam Liebowitz, a conservative Democrat, who served without pay as lawyer for six Negro youths accused of rape in Alabama. Another editorial on the same page agreed with the Minnesota jury that had acquitted gangster Roger Touhy of kidnapping. "The government's case fairly reeked with signs of fixing and fraud," Walter wrote. "We have no sympathy with gangsters, but we have even less sympathy with the efforts of government prosecutors to 'frame-up' convictions." Walter, who had a good feel for frame-ups, was correct. Ironically, Thomas McMeekin, one of Touhy's lawyers, later defended Kid Cann when he was charged with murdering Walter.

Prohibition finally ended in December 1933 when Utah ratified the Twenty-First Amendment. It arrived with little fanfare in the *Midwest American,* although Walter had worked hard for its demise. Gus Wollan, our political columnist, announced that a special session of the state legislature would convene in December to legislate emergency relief and liquor control in Minnesota. He expected that liquor would flow freely during this special session, and he predicted heavy pressure from distillery and winery lobbies.[12]

Overall, the legislative session drew mixed reviews, but most of the Farmer-Labor press emphasized the positive. The *Union Advocate* recognized that the new liquor control act was "certainly not in accord with the principles of the Farmer-Labor party."[13] Still, the *Advocate* called the legislature's work good "as a whole," because Governor Olson's liquor tax bill — which funded the public relief program through taxes on liquor and beer — passed. Many conservatives and good-government advocates preferred not to tie relief to liquor consumption, but to fund relief through the general fund.

The editor of the *Milaca Times,* who had attended the special session as a legislator, was considerably less circumspect. "The bill passed by the legislature for 'regulating' hard liquor is a monstrosity," he wrote. "The disgusting feature of it all was the way that the liquor interests took control of the legislature. Distillery and brewery lobbyists were as thick as flies." He concluded somberly that "the liquor interests have already resumed control in Minnesota politics and they are going to be very hard to unseat."[14]

Governor Olson signed the liquor control bill on January 6, 1934, and appointed David Arundel, formerly secretary of the state boxing commission, the new liquor control commissioner.

Labor Hassles in Austin

In December 1933, my parents, carrying out Walter's agreement with Governor Olson, moved the *Midwest American* to Rochester. Since jobs were hard to find, Barbara Ritchie and several other employees moved to Rochester with their families. For the first few months of 1934, Walter attempted to juggle two Farmer-Labor papers, the *Midwest American* in Rochester and the *Austin American* in Austin. Rochester was a staid, pretty town of 21,000 set in dairy country and dominated by the Mayo Clinic. Austin, forty miles away and about half as large, was a tough packinghouse town dominated by conflict between the Hormel plant and the feisty IUAW — the Independent Union of All Workers.

In September 1933, the IUAW had set up a committee to investigate the possibility of starting a union paper to compete with the *Austin Herald*. A few months later, Walter met Frank Ellis, the union's business agent and chief organizer, and they hit it off at once.[15] Ellis, a folk hero in Austin, was a small, scrappy Irish-Indian who had led a strike at Hormel and succeeded in organizing just about everybody in Austin (clerks, bartenders, and waitresses — even some policemen) into the IUAW. A talented orator, Ellis somehow made the old slogans sound fresh.[16]

IUAW officials approached Walter in January, asking him to help them start a union newspaper. Walter was enthusiastic.[17] He threw himself into raising funds for the *Austin American* and setting up its plant, expecting to receive forty dollars a week and expenses from the IUAW, but this ill-starred undertaking trapped him in the crosscurrents of a bitter factional dispute over trade versus industrial organization between Frank Ellis and the other union representatives on the newspaper board of directors.[18]

John Goldie, a Minneapolis lawyer who was Governor Olson's personal representative on the board (Edith called him an "s.o.b."), persuaded the three other members — Emil Olson, Olaf J. Fosso, and Frank Prochaska — to support the American Federation of Labor rather than an industrial union, and to structure the newspaper to prevent Ellis's having a voice. Because Ellis was popular with the rank and file, the board had to act indirectly. Edith's notes identify Fosso as the "fat rival of Ellis in union." In fact, Fosso was then the IUAW president. Emil Olson was a state oil inspector at Austin, and Frank Prochaska an elderly printer who had worked with Walter in North Dakota.[19]

Other evidence of union infighting is preserved in the files of Vince Day, Governor Olson's secretary, who collected news, rumors, and tidbits from all over the state. Allegations against Ellis in Day's files date back at least to November 1933, when Emil Olson accused Ellis of trying to sabotage the governor's settlement of the Hormel strike and of hanging out at the Ritz Hotel in Minneapolis to stir up trouble in South St. Paul. Day's memos show that Fosso told him in January 1934 that Ellis was planning to bring machine guns into Austin—a most improbable story. Other Vince Day papers contain similar "confidential" reports of dubious accuracy.[20]

Vince Day's office was not the only state agency to collect background on Ellis in early 1934. The Bureau of Criminal Apprehension, then a twelve-person group supposedly devoted to law enforcement, wasted time interviewing women to find out if Ellis went out drinking or dancing while he was organizing out of town. Under Melvin Passolt, an investigator for Olson when Olson was county attorney, the bureau looked for damaging information on those who were out of favor with the power structure.[21]

Against the odds, Walter kept trying to persuade Governor Olson to back Ellis in the union dispute. Finally, on May 1, 1934, Walter resigned from the *Austin American,* claiming that the board would not allow him editorial discretion and was trying to keep Frank Ellis out of the newspaper.[22] In June, Walter mailed union leaders copies of a pamphlet titled "Why I Resigned as Editor of the Austin American." He claimed that he "worked day and night, for week after week," but that board members were working against the interests of the union. "I warned Governor Olson," he wrote, ". . . that the retention of Goldie on the directorate would wreck the entire enterprise and probably disrupt the Independent Union of All Workers."[23] Fosso forwarded the pamphlet to Governor Olson, urging him to "take what action as you may deem proper to eliminate further trouble with Mr. Liggett."[24]

About this time, my parents encountered the first of a series of dirty tricks designed to close down the *Midwest American.* Walter noted rumors that the paper was going out of business. Within a two-week period, he wrote, four employees were induced to leave without notice. One left without collecting his paycheck; another was offered a sixty-dollar bonus for leaving; another received a bus ticket by telegraph. Walter did not suspect either the governor or the directors of the *Austin American,* but believed the campaign to drive him out of business stemmed from business rivals or banks he had accused of laundering money. "The *Midwest American,*" he wrote, "has incurred powerful enemies . . . [but] we cannot be bought, bribed, or bluffed out of existence."[25]

Whoever his enemies were, Walter announced: "We don't know—and we don't give a damn. The *Midwest American* is here to stay—if you want it. After all, friends and readers, this is your paper and it is fighting your fight. . . . I am in this battle because I believe that America must be redeemed from the control of political crooks and financial pirates."[26]

Walter attempted more or less quietly to recoup $2,642 from the *Austin American* board for his services and expenses. He calculated that he had devoted seventy-six days to getting the paper established. He had traveled more than six thousand miles (including nineteen trips to the Twin Cities), spent $900 on car and hotel expenses, bought and installed the press, printed several issues, and raised $12,921 for the paper.[27] When the newspaper board refused to pay, Walter sued, and, on the advice of his attorney, named Governor Olson among other parties. When John Goldie learned that Walter was planning to sue, he wrote Vince Day a letter calling Walter "rampaging," "indiscreet," "a wild animal," and a "pirate" and suggesting that the "skipper"—the governor—take him in hand.[28]

Eventually, to avoid a scandal, Walter settled for a mere $490.[29] Despite Walter's decision to be a team player in the matter of the money, Olson was furious when Walter came to his office as part of a delegation a few days later.[30]

Because of a roller damaged in the move to Rochester and the time Walter devoted to the *Austin American,* the *Midwest American* missed some issues in early 1934. The paper that ultimately emerged was very much a part of the Rochester community, with strong local coverage as well as state and national reports. Its motto was "News the daily papers don't dare to print." Edith's intermittent feminist column was increasingly devoted to women's efforts to keep their families decently fed and clothed in the Depression. Outraged that children in dairy country were drinking coffee for breakfast, she initiated a successful campaign to establish a city milk depot.[31]

In our early days in Rochester, the *Midwest American,* though political, was relaxed and folksy. Walter liked to write graceful obituaries for national figures like editor Fremont Older and settlement worker Jane Addams, praising their unique contributions to the public welfare, and—sometimes—noting his own connections with the departed.

Edith found Rochester comfortable to live in, despite a middle-class stuffiness that persisted even though one-fourth of the city's families were on the relief rolls. I remember the mother of a friend telling me one day that, while I seemed to be a nice little girl, she didn't know who my father was. I duly reported that at home, and Walter, who took an innocent pleasure in his listing in *Who's Who in America,* told me to tell her that she could look him up in *Who's Who.* I repeated this to my friend's mother, who seemed unimpressed.

In Rochester, we had time for afternoon tea with friends and employees, and each week after the paper "went to bed," Edith enjoyed a luxurious free afternoon. A few workers left because of threats or bribes, but in general our employees had rather close relations with our family. Barbara Ritchie, the fashion and shopping columnist who shared our home, was something between an indulgent aunt and a big sister for me. She also brought out a girlish streak in my mother that I enjoyed—although I didn't completely approve. One afternoon they decided to try out some clay packs that had been recommended to Barbara. The dry clay on their faces looked like green mud, but was supposed to do wonders for the complexion. They drafted me to answer the door just in case anyone came by, and wouldn't you know it, the doorbell must have rung ten or twelve times that afternoon. I didn't mind answering the door and thought their plight was funny. Still, I felt embarrassed that every time the doorbell rang, Barbara and my mother giggled and whooped like a couple of schoolgirls. Mothers, I felt, should always be dignified.

Throughout the first half of 1934, the *Midwest American,* although it was still pro-Olson, became increasingly critical. Walter had returned to Minnesota recalling and probably idealizing the radical Farmer-Labor Party of his youth. Although he was aware of some shady deals Olson had made as county attorney, he initially believed that Olson was a man of great abilities who had put aside his early mistakes. But as a seasoned political reporter, Walter reluctantly came to realize that the Farmer-Labor record for progressive legislation was poor and that many All-Party appointees were reactionary or "hard-boiled political spoilsmen."

Walter strongly favored the idealistic platform adopted by the March 1934 convention of the Minnesota Farmer-Labor Association, supposedly inspired by one of Governor Olson's most stirring and fiery speeches. Before leaving the convention to lobby in Washington, Olson had declared: "I am not a liberal. I am what I want to be—I am a radical. I am a radical in the sense that I want a definite change in the system. I am not satisfied with tinkering." The platform, in turn, declared that "our capitalistic order, as at present constituted, is failing to function in the interest of the great Masses of people."[32] At the national level, it called for a cooperative commonwealth, nationalization of banking and credit, public ownership of railroads, munitions plants, steel, and utilities, and farm mortgage moratoriums. At the state level, it demanded state insurance, a state printing plant, and a state liquor dispensary. Despite these sweeping planks, platform advocates considered themselves more in the tradition of Jefferson, Jackson, and the Populists than that of Marx; the platform barred communists from the association "because of revolutionary tendencies." This was to change in late 1935, when the Communist party line changed to Popular Front and the party tried to use the Farmer-Labor Party as its major front in the Midwest.

Walter wrote that the Farmer-Labor platform was a "beautiful piece of thinking and plain talking," but he was annoyed that Olson sent out "interpretations" of it. He believed that pressure to undercut the platform came from the All-Party Democrats and Republicans who supplied Olson's private campaign funds. The spring primaries had indicated—to my parents at least—that the rank and file of the party were ready for constructive change.[33]

Despite the radical platform, the Farmer-Labor Party had changed vastly from its idealistic beginnings as a cooperative of farmers and workers. After 1930, the party had become an uneasy amalgam of machine-dominated county organizations, local Farmer-Labor clubs, old-time radicals and reformers, and an All-Party clique of Republicans and Democrats, who contributed to Olson's "personal campaign funds" and usually expected a quid pro quo. Racked with patronage problems, factional disputes, and the cult of personality, the party directed its efforts into pork-barrel enterprises and keeping up appearances rather than social reform.

Edith had her own criticism of the platform and of the Farmer-Labor Party. Her "What Do You Think?" column frequently dealt with the dearth of women as candidates and as influential persons within the party. She believed that the party needed women's voices and practical common sense: "Women on the platform committee . . . would not have neglected to mention maternity insurance and living mothers' and old age pensions." One of her columns described "most of the party locals" as job-hunting associations where men sat at club headquarters with their feet on the tables, spitting copiously, while women were not welcome.[34]

Still very much a part of the Farmer-Labor press, Walter was chosen to represent the First Congressional District when thirty-four Farmer-Labor newspapers organized the North Star Press Association in July 1934. He hoped this organization would help Farmer-Labor editors unite to reform the Farmer-Labor Party.[35] Walter's editorial titled "Take Highways out of Politics" was reprinted by several other Farmer-Labor papers.[36]

One reform the North Star Association hoped to effect was in the state printer's office; Jean Spielman, the state printer, was an Olson appointee accused by Farmer-Labor editors of "flagrant favoritism" and of limiting state printing bids to eight favored concerns.[37] Both Walter and the platform advocated a state printing plant, like the one still functioning today in California. Walter pushed this in print and in the governor's office, and he complained that the governor was sending printing out of state. His opponents claimed that he was hungry for state printing and broke with Olson when he couldn't get it. Walter apparently *did* want more business from the state, but Olson told him that he had given him all the business he could afford, saying, "Remember I'm ambitious and want to go places. I've got to take care of papers out of the state as well as in the state."[38]

A Free Press: Phonokus Bolognus?

For Governor Olson, the summer of 1934 was a political balancing act. Aside from concerns with the party platform and Walter Liggett, Olson was trying to keep the lid on a series of Teamster strikes in Minneapolis—strikes that kept the city in turmoil for months and kept him off the campaign trail longer than his advisers thought prudent.

Early in June, Olson had made both friends and enemies when he greeted the second convention of the newly formed American Newspaper Guild. It was a made-to-order photo and speech opportunity for Olson, who rarely missed a chance to ingratiate himself with reporters. In his welcoming address, he urged the delegates to be militant: "Do something for yourselves, don't muff your chance."[39] The speech went over well with most of the delegates. Guild head Heywood Broun was so beguiled that he pushed Olson as vice presidential or even presidential timber, while the local Twin Cities Guild made Olson an honorary member.[40] But Olson's flippantly calling concerns with free press "phonokus bolognus" infuriated *Editor & Publisher*'s Marlen Pew.

Nationwide, the summer of 1934 was notable for strikes by unions newly empowered by the National Recovery Act. Still, the violent Teamster strikes in Minneapolis were distinctive. In May, police chief Mike Johannes deputized the "respectable element," including members of the antiunion Citizens Alliance, as special officers and armed them with badges and guns. The truckers, armed with pipes and baseball bats, beat two special deputies to death.[41] When a new round of negotiations broke down and Teamsters Local 574 voted to strike, Olson mobilized the National Guard for "the preservation of law and order." *The Organizer*, the local's newspaper, blasted Olson and claimed that the only threat to public peace came from the bosses' use of scabs and deputized hoodlums.

On "Bloody Friday," July 20, 1934, the police sent an armed convoy to escort a strikebreaking truck. Despite police warnings, strikers sent out their own truck to block the convoy. The police opened fire, wounding sixty-seven strikers and bystanders; most were shot in the back. Within a few days, two died of their injuries. Troops were rushed to the scene of the shooting, only to be withdrawn. The governor ordered guardsmen to stand by for strike duty.

When federal mediators announced terms for a settlement on July 25, Olson gave Local 574 and the employers twenty-four hours to accept before he sent in the troops. The union, largely for tactical reasons, accepted the proposal by a vote of 1,866 to 147. The employers also "accepted with reservations," although they objected to the wage provisions.[42]

The next afternoon, Olson put the city under martial law, calling out the National Guard, forbidding picketing, and appointing a close friend, Adjutant General Ellard A. Walsh, military commander. Walsh prepared a lengthy document and ordered newspapers to publish the complete text for the next two days.[43] This Proclamation of Martial Law read, in part: "It shall be unlawful . . . to publish newspapers defaming the state of Minnesota or any member of the Minnesota national guard in the field." It banned not only obstruction of military forces, but also printing, publishing, distributing, or transmitting any notices, documents, or newspapers "defaming" the state or any member of the Minnesota National Guard. It also banned group meetings of more than 100 individuals except with permission of the commander. Nonresidents "having no legitimate business" in the city were ordered to leave.[44]

The front page of the *New York Times* announced on July 27 that "Governor Floyd B. Olson today established a military dictatorship over the press of Minneapolis." The *Times* was not alone in viewing the proclamation as an assault on freedom of the press. *Editor & Publisher* headed its August 4, 1934, special report "Press 'Gag' Threat in Minneapolis" An editorial in the same issue called Olson "an American Hitler," charged him with acting like a military dictator, and compared his assaults on civil rights with those of Huey Long: "His defense technique is to slander publishers and newspapers in general . . . but always to keep on friendly terms with reporters." Olson, the editorial continued, "is the type of politician who enjoys throwing stink bombs at the press. . . . It provides, in times of great public unrest, a convenient political smoke screen."

Jim Cannon and Max Schactman, editors of *The Organizer,* were the martial law's first casualties. Two Minneapolis detectives had arrested the pair in a Hennepin Avenue movie theater before the proclamation. After two days in jail, Schactman and Cannon were led into court surrounded by two squads of guardsmen led by an officer carrying a submachine gun.[45] "I never saw so many bayonets in one place in my life," Cannon recalled.[46]

By the time the union lawyer threatened legal action, the militia wanted to get rid of Cannon and Schactman. The provost marshal released the two journalists on condition that they leave town. They then wired Governor Olson, pointing out that they could not have violated military law since they were in jail when martial law was declared. They called the provision that they had to leave town an "outrageous violation of constitutional rights." They threatened to appeal to labor and liberal forces to "make the governor's direct and personal responsibility known, particularly to those who have hitherto regarded him as a progressive and liberal governor."[47] After all the rhetoric, they moved only as far as St. Paul, where they edited *The Organizer* under assumed names. Soon Schactman headed back to New York and Herbert Solow took over the *Organizer.*

In response to the outcry, Governor Olson announced that all classes of the press, "from the Tory *Chicago Tribune* to the radical militant," would be protected. Walsh told the press, "Forget this gag stuff. There's nothing in it. I will not interfere in any way with normal operation of the press."

Minneapolis newspapers denied being censored. *Minneapolis Star* editor George Adams wrote *Editor & Publisher* that out-of-town newspapers were creating a bogeyman: "Governor Olson, is much too clever a politician to . . . attempt to censor Minneapolis newspapers. . . . It is no secret that the Governor has his eye on the national political stage. A record of having tried to suppress free speech by military force would be a splotch on that picture, and he can be trusted to know it."[48]

Out in Rochester, Walter called for the end of martial law and its "harassing regulations" and deplored the actions of "kids in khaki . . . armed with a brief authority." Court-martials and press censorship and ordering Communist newspapermen to leave town could only damage the Farmer-Labor program, he wrote.[49]

Throughout the summer of 1934, Olson's secretary, Vince Day, fretted about the adverse effects of publicity on the governor's image. Day feared that the strike would interfere with Olson's campaign for governor.[50] Despite Day's worries, Olson had little cause for concern. Between martial law and Olson's honorary Newspaper Guild membership, Olson received either favorable or subdued coverage in most Twin Cities and out-of-town papers. And during the Depression, patronage was quite effective with certain newspapers. The *Duluth Plain Dealer,* for example, supported Olson in return for a job for a friend of the editor's.[51]

Several of Day's memos to the governor dealt with Howard Guilford's radio broadcasts. Indeed, Day had complained of Guilford's "inflammatory" broadcasts since January. Now Guilford, Olson's old nemesis, was broadcasting for the Employers' Association with documented charges. On August 10, Day pointed out that "the radio talks of the Employers' Association are turning sentiments against the strikers by using the charge of communism." Olson had already spoken on the radio during the strike, and Day urged him to take to the air again to "explain the situation to the public."[52]

Guilford, however, followed Olson on the air with a series contradicting Olson's assertions.[53]

6. Break with Olson

The All-Party machine . . . consists of professional politicians of all three parties, liquor and railroad lobbyists. It draws its support from the underworld, from brewers, distillers, bankers, and recipients of public contracts.

—**Editorial by Edith Liggett,** *Midwest American*, **February 7, 1936**

Walter's ultimate break with Olson started in Benson, Minnesota, at a Nonpartisan League voters conference held on Labor Day in 1934 to examine All-Party influence on the Farmer-Labor Party. Nearly five hundred old Leaguers attended. The stormy meeting began with League founder Arthur Townley's eloquent address tracing Minnesota's historic fight for better government.[1]

"When we formed the Nonpartisan League," Townley said, "we formed it to redeem control of the state government which was under the absolute domination of the Republican machine. . . . We chose as our candidate Charles Lindbergh, a man of the Lincoln type, a high-minded, honest statesman, a real patriot, and he fought our fight without ever flinching."[2] Now, Townley said, Governor Olson was entangled by reactionary interests that dictated his appointments. Townley declared that he would like to reelect Olson if Olson could keep his promises to free the state from reactionary control; otherwise, Townley would reluctantly run for governor as an independent.

Conference participants passed resolutions denouncing the policy of filling appointive posts with All-Party Republicans and Democrats and chose the Committee of 100 to meet with Governor Olson the next day. Walter was one of the delegates. The meeting started off badly. The governor stormed in an hour late, shouting, "This is my place of business." He demanded that those who would vote for Townley if he did not meet their demands raise their hands. When Walter objected, Olson snapped, "That will be all from you, Mr. Liggett." Again he asked for a show of hands, and added, "I'll see about you later."[3]

Although Olson refused to consider the committee's demands, he invited a smaller group to lunch the next day. Walter was one of seven or eight who attended. During lunch, Walter was surprised to hear Olson mention Howard Guilford three times. No one on the committee even knew Guilford, and there didn't seem to be any connection with the topics under discussion.

The following day, Guilford—who had recently announced a series of radio commentaries to "tell the truth about Governor Floyd Olson's connection with the underworld"—was killed.[4] The murder was obviously a professional job. Guilford was driving home from his office, listening to a Cubs game on his car radio, unaware that a maroon auto with an out-of-state license had drawn up next to him. Someone fired a shotgun through its window and killed him with a blast to the head. Apparently he had not taken seriously the death threats he had received over the previous ten days.[5]

Judging by the slender file, the Minneapolis police barely investigated the murder—even though the governor's chauffeur Maurice Rose was at the police station on the night of the murder.[6] (Walter initially assumed that this was to see that the police acted.) They did not look for fingerprints in a stolen maroon auto that was almost certainly the murder car.[7] Although one newspaper article stated that "veteran Minneapolis detectives" were convinced that the murder was "rooted deep in labor or political difficulties," this possibility does not seem to have been explored. It could have been difficult. In an anonymous letter to Mrs. Guilford, "a friend" wrote, "Floyd Olson was really his murderer (although he did not do the real act)."[8]

It took more than a year for the police to contact two St. Paul brothers who had heard the gunfire and followed the speeding murder car. One brother, H. B. Colestock, had told the *St. Paul Pioneer Press* that he was good at remembering faces and could identify the driver of the car. He tried to make a report to a Minneapolis policeman, who refused to take down the information.[9]

Almost by accident, the Minneapolis police questioned Colestock fifteen months later, five days after Walter's murder. Colestock supplied a detailed description of the murder car's driver—a man about forty or forty-five, more than six feet tall, with a close haircut and a sandy complexion, a heavy neck, a peaked nose, and a receding chin. Both the driver's face and his neck were very red, Colestock said. The two men in back had dark hair and dark complexions.[10]

Colestock saw the driver again in a downtown restaurant at Sixth and Nicollet on the very day Walter was killed. His description seems to fit Ed Morgan, a Minneapolis gangster who was headquartered near the restaurant shortly before Walter was murdered. Unfortunately, Colestock's interview was buried in the Liggett homicide files, where I found it in 1988; it was probably not followed up for either murder.[11]

Howard Guilford's son Warren, in his early twenties when his father was killed, told me that the Minneapolis police had opened his father's safe and shown him his father's address book with about a dozen pages missing.[12] Robert Wilson, an old bootlegger and a friend of Guilford's one-time partner Jay Near, suspected that the police were in on the murder; he told me that he learned about the impending murder the day Guilford was killed, but had not succeeded in warning him.[13] Near, on the other hand, thought that Guilford was murdered by professional gangsters hired by communists.[14]

Although the murder had some national coverage, it was only a one-day story in Minneapolis newspapers, with scanty coverage throughout the state. The *Farmer-Labor Leader*—which my parents called Governor Olson's house organ (its name was later changed to the *Minnesota Leader*)—accused Guilford of having been a blackmailer. This charge was spread, Walter wrote, through Henry Teigan's Farmer-Labor Press Service and was reprinted in half a dozen Farmer-Labor newspapers around the state. Ironically, Walter's distaste for Farmer-Labor editorials "that seek to justify a cowardly and cold-blooded murder" led him to investigate Guilford's death.[15]

Nationally, *News-Week* pointed out that there was no evidence that Guilford was a blackmailer.[16] In the *Nation,* "Eric Thane," a pseudonymous Minnesota writer, called Guilford a "mouthpiece for the Citizens Alliance." Since both Guilford and the Alliance were opposed to the striking drivers, this charge was more plausible than the *Leader*'s accusation of blackmail.

Although I have not been able to locate transcripts of Guilford's broadcasts, I have read his clip sheets carefully. At the time of his death, he was editing a clip sheet for four hundred rural Minnesota newspapers focusing on the radical leaders of the violent Minneapolis truck strike. The clip sheets reveal no opportunities for blackmail, although they certainly might have cut rural votes for Farmer-Labor candidates in the upcoming election. The October issue, presumably not distributed after Guilford's murder, had a summary of the truck strike with horrifying pictures of strikers using bats as weapons.[17]

My own belief is that Guilford was not bought or blackmailed by anyone, but was following his own convictions and fighting Olson in his own way. Guilford did not lack a social conscience. And if he was a blackmailer, he was a deplorably unsuccessful one. His parents in Massachusetts had to pay for his burial.[18]

After Olson rejected the demands of the Committee of 100, the group decided to meet at St. Cloud in mid-September. Before this meeting, state employees chased down committee members with promises of jobs and threats of dismissal, trying to get them to change their stand.[19] Despite these efforts, ninety-six members of the committee met again and, by a vote of ninety-five to one, adopted a report stating that the governor had been brusquely rude and that his reply was evasive and misleading. They also objected to Olson's naming Republican John J. Hougen his campaign manager. In another ninety-five-to-one vote, the committee demanded that the *Farmer-Labor Leader* print its original Labor Day resolutions and correct factual errors in the governor's reply.[20]

The *Farmer-Labor Leader* did not print a line. The editor, Herren G. Creel, told committee members that he had no authority to print anything without consulting others. This was true; the Farmer-Labor Association's Newspaper Committee, headed by Henry Teigan, had issued an order not to accept unsolicited communications.[21] As a consequence, an entire rebellion in the Farmer-Labor Party is largely undocumented outside the *Midwest American.*

Walter and the Committee of 100 saw themselves as Nonpartisan League stalwarts trying to stop a clique of politicians posing as radicals from controlling the Farmer-Labor Party for their own aggrandizement. When Olson filled patronage positions with All-Party Democrats and Republicans, it made bona fide Farmer-Labor voters responsible for administration failures and abuses, but without power to correct them.

On September 28, 1934, the *Midwest American*'s front-page editorial titled "Why I No Longer Support Gov. Floyd B. Olson" was followed by Walter's eloquent editorial "Why Do They Justify Murder?" Walter wrote that when he returned to Minnesota he had been charmed by Olson and impressed by Olson's knowledge of history, economics, and current affairs. He had hoped that Olson's association with the "sincere rank and file of the Farmer-Labor membership had made him an honest convert to the cause of good government." He denounced Olson for downplaying the party platform; he accused him of raising campaign funds in ways that committed the party to dubious compromises; and he charged him with handing the Farmer-Labor Party over to Democrats and Republicans who had no sympathy with its platforms and pledges. He believed that Olson was "using the Farmer-Labor Party as a ladder on which to climb to power" and would "kick that ladder aside" when he reached his ultimate goal, the U.S. Senate.

At first both Farmer-Laborites and third-party advocates welcomed a new voice airing doubts about Olson. Lieutenant Governor Hjalmar Petersen commented that it pepped up the campaign.[22] Alfred Bingham, editor of *Common Sense* and a tireless advocate of a third party, asked for "dope on the Townley-Liggett attack on Olson." Even though Olson deserved the attack for weaseling on the platform, Bingham wrote, he did not want to get involved, since he still considered Olson the "strongest man in the field" of potential third-party presidential candidates.[23]

While two Republicans, Senator Tom Schall and gubernatorial candidate Martin Nelson, called Guilford's murder a case of "shotgun censorship," Walter wrote that he did not believe "that Floyd B. Olson is the type of man who would hire gunmen to do away with an opponent. On the other hand, some of Olson's close associates have friends among the denizens of the Twin Cities underworld who ARE that type of men and who would not hesitate a moment at murder— especially to oblige an influential friend. Consequently, it is not only possible but highly probable that Howard Guilford was killed because of his political activities."[24]

"Why," he asked, "is the Farmer-Labor state-paid press bureau going to such pains to make it appear that the murder of Guilford wasn't such a serious matter after all?"

When Arthur Townley announced that he would run for governor as an independent, Walter supported him vigorously in the *Midwest American.* For the first time, he began to search for evidence of party corruption. He wrote about the efforts of Fred Ossanna and the Minnesota Liquor Dealers' Association to raise a war chest of $100,000 for Olson through assessing liquor dealers in the Twin Cities, with the guarantee—at least an implicit one—that liquor laws would be amended after the election. He also pointed out that the state was paying Charles Ward $12,240 a year in rent for a building formerly rented for $250 per month. Walter gave specific instances of hasty pardons and slow extraditions. He printed affidavits that indicated that the governor was selling court appointments. Other affidavits purported to show that the Highway Department, notorious for patronage, had been ordered to support certain Democratic candidates to whom Olson was indebted.

Walter also attacked Olson for handing over the Farmer-Labor Party to All-Party machine politicians; give Olson another term, he wrote, and little would be left of the Farmer-Labor organization or its principles.[25] Throughout Minnesota, remnants of the Nonpartisan League old guard, who had risked physical violence, imprisonment, and ostracism in 1917, flocked to Townley's forlorn candidacy, doomed to failure by lack of time and funds. Edith recalled one Townley collection bag containing perhaps one hundred dollars—more than sixty dollars of it in change and a number of large old-time dollar bills "dug out from family socks or under mattresses."[26]

Olson's resources, on the other hand, included the Farmer-Labor press, large sums from businessmen, a war chest from liquor lobbyists and the underworld, and an obligatory 3 percent donation from state employees—plus their unpaid labor.

Walter's attacks on Olson were not attacks on the Farmer-Labor Party; they were intended to aid in reforming the party. Nor was Walter motivated by personal hostility. He wrote V. F. Calverton that Olson, "with all his faults and crooked dealings, is a prince of a fine fellow, but absolutely the only way the party can be saved is to commence its reorganization along the old lines."[27]

The *Farmer-Labor Leader* claimed that Townley had sold out to Republicans and called Walter "a notorious scandal sheet editor" who "flooded the state with malicious fabrications," supposedly directed by an agent of the Republican National Committee.[28]

My parents prepared two special election issues of the *Midwest American*—filled with concrete examples of fraud, favoritism, and governmental inefficiency—for statewide distribution. Since our ancient, rattling press was not up to a run of 250,000 copies, Walter sent the larger issue off to Minneapolis, where the printers watched nervously for hijackers.[29] My parents never knew that one of Olson's coups was to suppress this issue almost completely. According to a columnist writing in 1936, the Hennepin County strategy board heard about the special edition a day before it was due for circulation. To counter it, they sent nearly a thousand telegrams from towns around the state, each requesting from five to ten thousand copies of the paper immediately. The copies were then "burnt or otherwise destroyed before they could reach the electorate."[30]

This story is probably true—at least in essence. Vince Day's daily memo for October 24 enclosed a copy of the *Midwest American* "grabbed in the course of printing," along with a copy of a pamphlet entitled "Twenty Reasons Why Thinking People Should Not Vote for Floyd B. Olson." Jean Spielman, state printing director, used his contacts with the typographers' union to get Olson's opponents' publications.

The *Midwest American* supported Farmer-Labor candidates my parents considered worthy: Hjalmar Petersen for lieutenant governor, Harry Peterson for attorney general. On November 2, before the election, Walter, who could never bring himself to support a Republican, wrote that "Olson at his worst is preferable to Nelson" (the Republican candidate for governor). After the election, he compared the Republicans to the Bourbons who had learned nothing and forgotten nothing.

Votes trickled in for more than a week. The results were probably a disappointment to both Walter and Olson. Despite the Depression and the plight of farmers, rural people voted against Olson and the Farmer-Labor Party, although they did not vote for Townley in any numbers. Most of Olson's votes in the state elections of 1930 and 1932 had come from rural districts;[31] in 1934 the Farmer-Labor Party was kept in office by votes from big-city machines in Duluth and the Twin Cities.

In Olmsted County, where my parents published the *Midwest American,* Walter wrote, "members of the Highway, State Banking, and Hotel Inspection departments all neglected their work for weeks so that they could campaign in and around Rochester" to discredit the *Midwest American.* But, Walter wrote, the county election results were a "smashing rebuke" for Governor Olson.

As several political commentators noted, Olson had made little effort to elect legislators. Consequently, only fifty-three newly elected legislators were Farmer-Labor supporters; seventy-seven were not, although they were not necessarily conservative. Lieutenant Governor Hjalmar Petersen and gung ho Farmer-Laborites felt that it might be possible to get a liberal-radical legislative caucus together. A memo to the governor from Vince Day noted that "the Senate control margin is very close. Hjalmar Petersen believes there is a bare chance of taking control from the conservatives." But Olson took personal charge of the legislative caucuses and delayed them until it was too late to get a combined liberal-radical majority.

Liquor lobbyist Fred Ossanna, who had secured funds from the Minnesota Liquor Dealers' Association, signed the telegram announcing the legislative caucus to select the speaker of the house. Publicist Art Jacobs, who had been convicted of libeling Magnus Johnson in the senatorial campaign of 1924 and was understandably unpopular with old-time Farmer-Laborites, was put in charge of hospitality for new state legislators.[32]

After the election, other Farmer-Labor Party members and editors joined Walter in demanding an end to cronyism and machine politics. The *New Ulm Review,* for instance, charged All-Party officeholders with corrupt practices and seeking personal gain.[33] The *Union Advocate* claimed that the "Olson All-Party Committee was a minus quantity" in the election and that the party carried Olson and not the other way around.[34] In a heated session in St. Paul, the Ramsey County Farmer-Labor Association adopted a resolution flaying Olson's policy of naming All-Party volunteers to important state positions.

Walter was convinced that Olson was creating a political machine on the prairies of Minnesota and determined to keep up his campaign of exposure until Olson was driven from public life. Perhaps, Walter wrote V. F. Calverton apologetically, he could get back to writing his history of the American newspaper "if this damn paper fails."[35]

"My wife and I have lived for several years in New York City under Tammany Hall and are thoroughly familiar with the underworld tactics of professional spoilsmen," Walter wrote in the *Midwest American:*

> That is one reason why we object to the Tammanyization of Minnesota by this All-Party group of racketeers. We knew precisely what to expect when we began our exposé of Floyd Olson and his crew of political hatchet-men.
>
> Knowing them as we do, we will be surprised if they stop much short of assassination. One editor, Howard Guilford, has already been shot down in cold blood by hired gunmen because he dared expose some ramifications of Floyd Olson with the underworld—and to date the much-press-agented State Bureau of Criminal Apprehension hasn't made any headway in tracking down his slayers.
>
> However, I don't think they will have me killed. It wouldn't look good for one thing, and for another thing the whole damned cowardly crew know that they can't find one scintilla of evidence to besmirch my professional reputation in an attempt to justify a cold blooded murder as they did in poor Howard Guilford's case.[36]

The *Midwest American,* not exclusively preoccupied by the break with Olson, continued to cover other local, state, and national issues: Senator Nye's sensational investigation of war profits; the growth of relief rolls in Rochester; Philadelphia residents choosing the broadcasts of Father Coughlin sixteen to one over the New York Philharmonic. At times, Walter joshed the party good-naturedly. He commented, for instance, on the diligence of the state hotel inspector who had spent six weeks in Rochester. Was it possible, Walter wondered, that he could be devoting some time to politics?

Edith's columns were more concerned with the scarcity of women in the Farmer-Labor Party and with the plight of families. "To the mothers of one-quarter of the families in the country today," she wrote on December 7, 1934, "the approach of Christmas has taken on an aspect of dread." After proposing ways to involve children in making gifts and planning celebrations, she wrote:

> There is no sense in telling children we are now in the sixth year of the country's worst Depression, no sense in telling them that we have no idea what life will offer them when they are grown up. The only things we know we can give our children are strong bodies and happy childhood memories. And we must not let even a world collapse or

our own griefs and worries rob a child of celebration which he can help create.

Walter kept writing to possible allies, in state and out, often losing friends in the process. He wrote third-party advocate Howard Williams:

> Your comparison of the Nonpartisan and Farmer-Labor programs... strikes me as absolute balderdash. The prime difference between the two programs is that the men who advocated the Nonpartisan program believed in it—and six months after they assumed power in North Dakota they had enacted it into law. Whereas the Farmer-Labor program in Minnesota is apparently intended, even by the man who drew it, only for conversational and publicity purposes.[37]

When Williams responded with an invitation to attend the Mid-West Legislative Conference, Walter replied that he expected to spend the day of the conference in court "fighting a fraudulent mortgage which state employees put upon my paper in order to frighten me."[38]

Walter sent the *Modern Monthly* an exposition of his views on Olson and Minnesota politics—a "labor of love," he called it. He had stayed up all night to finish it. "It's probably not what you damned Marxians consider cricket," he wrote editor V. F. Calverton, "but it does give the low down on the situation here. Also, it will be read with interest by John Dewey and all his third party group. They think Olson is the second brother of Jesus Christ, whereas he is a damned sight more of a racketeer than he is a radical."[39] Fond though my parents were of Calverton, his *Modern Monthly,* a national forum largely for Marxists, was not the mainstream journal Walter would have preferred. Walter considered Calverton, like other Marxists, to be out of touch with American conditions, while Calverton accused Walter of being a sentimental agrarian reformer.

Olson and Vince Day were also actively pursuing favorable publicity—volunteer and paid—during the winter of 1934–35. And they laid plans to undermine the coming legislative session with unfavorable publicity. "The opposition," Day wrote, "is planning to conduct a great many investigations during the Legislative Session. We need strong offenses to discount their efforts, and I believe Abe Harris...should take a leave of absence and cover the legislative session."[40] Harris, one of Olson's speechwriters, was one of four state-paid editors of a slender monthly newsletter of the state conservation department.

Jack Mackay, the Twin Cities correspondent for the Associated Press, launched an odd story—complete fiction so far as I can tell—in the *St. Paul*

Dispatch: Olson was planning to discharge two hundred state employees for inefficiency and disloyalty, Mackay wrote. This fanciful tale was apparently designed to put pressure on state employees who were opposed to the Olson political machine.[41]

"Mackay," Day wrote to Olson, "was very anxious that you do not embarrass him or his collaborators by an outright denial of the story. He claimed that it would make it difficult for him to serve you as he did in the past, and that his sole purpose...was to aid you by throwing fear into department heads and employees known by him to be disloyal to you."[42]

Other letters in Day's files show a more significant coup: Olson arranged a meeting with Sherwood Anderson, one of America's foremost writers, at which Olson led the talk to the failure of Eastern liberals and intellectuals "to help out." He was so persuasive that Anderson half offered to return to Minnesota in the fall of 1935 to work on the *Farmer-Labor Leader.*[43] In the interim, Anderson provided Day and Olson with a critique of the *Leader* and promised to do his best to get favorable articles into Eastern magazines. He succeeded in getting a three-part series on Olson into *Today,* a biweekly edited by Raymond Moley, of Franklin Roosevelt's brain trust. Anderson himself wrote the third article — an embarrassingly fuzzy eulogy from such a major talent.[44]

7. Move to Danger

Breeding places for crime and sanctuaries for criminals.

—**Homer Cummings, U.S. attorney general, describing Minneapolis and St. Paul**

To carry the campaign against Olson closer to the Twin Cities, our family moved—with printing plant, furniture, and two thousand books—from Rochester to Minneapolis on the last day of 1934.

When we moved to Minneapolis, we moved into danger. Although St. Paul was in the throes of a cleanup, Minneapolis had not cleaned up since Near and Guilford had written about the buildup of a "colossal criminal ring" in 1927. Neither had it cleaned up after Walter wrote about the interplay of liquor interests and political corruption in 1930. More recently, the Twin Cities had made headlines when Homer S. Cummings, the U.S. attorney general, called them "breeding places for crime and sanctuaries for criminals" in February 1934. Senator Royal S. Copeland, chair of the Senate Committee Investigating Crime, called them the poison spots of crime in the United States. After these denunciations, a surprising number of citizens and officials wrote the attorney general's office begging for a federal probe and offering to help, but funds were never made available.[1]

Even from my child's-eye view, Minneapolis was a strange mixture of Scandinavian civic-mindedness and big-city corruption. I loved its lakes and parks. And the schools and libraries seemed up to par. Our West Lake neighborhood, only a few blocks from Lake Calhoun, was a comfortable community of single-family homes; my classmates took me with them to Lutheran Sunday school. Still, there was a seedy and threatening quality to Minneapolis when we drove through downtown at night. I always was glad to get home safely.

My parents planned to establish a neighborhood newspaper, the *West Lake Neighborhood News,* and do job printing to help them support the *Midwest American.* Walter wrote V. F. Calverton in January:

I'm getting out a completely nonpartisan, non-political neighborhood newspaper as a meal ticket, and will start the *Midwest American* again as a state-wide paper in about three or four weeks, mostly as a diversion, since there is no money in it, but lots of fun.... I'm beginning to get this paper organized so that I'll have a little leisure to write after a year and a half of constant work organizing and editing.[2]

In the same letter, Walter asked Calverton to run an ad in the *Modern Monthly* for his pamphlet "Radical or Racketeer: The Truth about Floyd B. Olson." In exchange, he would run an ad for the *Modern Monthly* in the *Midwest American.*

In the twenty-four-page pamphlet, Walter reviewed discrepancies and irregularities in pursuing crime and examined well-known cases. Throughout, he cited docket numbers and specific cases of malfeasance during Olson's ten years as county attorney and used affidavits to back charges of graft and corruption in the state government.

In his attempt to keep leftists informed and get articles published, Walter distributed his pamphlet and the *Midwest American* to newspapers around the state, as well as to Eastern newspapers and journals of opinion. After he sent a copy of "Radical or Racketeer" to Freda Kirchwey of the *Nation,* she wrote Howard Williams, asking his opinion of its accuracy:

I recall Walter Liggett as a rather sensational muckraker as far as his method goes but as an honest and intelligent person.... The *Nation* has of course supported in general terms Olson's program and his candidacy.... We have all heard him criticized and described as a demagogue, but we had never seen any such outright charges of political dishonesty as are contained in this pamphlet.[3]

Williams responded confidentially, and had evidently changed his opinion of Walter. Although he did not challenge Walter's accuracy, Williams called the pamphlet the "work of a man who has sold himself out to the exploiting groups. I hate to say this about Liggett but I know perfectly well that these pamphlets must have been financed by exploiters." Williams asserted that trying economic circumstances had probably led to Walter's downfall.[4]

Still, Williams described Olson as a "brilliant chap, while something of an opportunist.... He told me this week that it has been his political strategy to coast into office more or less kidding the people along and then when he has attained power to use it.... He does go with a cheap crowd ... and accepted campaign contributions from wealthy groups and often is forced to compromise in the nature of paying back political debts."

At first, our move to Minneapolis seemed auspicious. Our new shop was in a storefront on Lake Street, only a few blocks from our rented house on Harriet Avenue, where my room was wallpapered with roses and overlooked a good climbing tree in our backyard. In keeping with the neighborhood theme, my parents displayed the work of my schoolmates in our storefront window; I recall a beautiful, lacy snow scene made from wood and construction paper. Although Wallace and I were used to moving by then, this display window helped us get acquainted in a new school. "Aunt Edith's" children's page reappeared in the *West Lake Neighborhood News,* and some of my new fifth-grade friends were excited about getting published in a real newspaper.[5]

Even the shop arrangement was more to my liking than that of the old stone-cutter's shop that had housed our plant in Rochester. On Lake Street, a counter with an upright partition separated the commercial area in front from the print shop. My parents' rolltop desks were in front, and our job-print paper was stored right behind the counter for easy access. We had all kinds of paper, from news-print to glossy poster cardboard to rag paper in pastel colors. Although our specialty seemed to be advertising flyers, we printed everything from business cards to blotters, posters, and booklets.

Walter enjoyed the minutiae of publishing and job printing. He whistled while he worked at the stones and I recall him smiling with satisfaction at a completed order of blue business stationery decorated with silver scrolls and columns. I thought it looked beautiful; he called it "bootlegger Gothic." And as long as I was careful and didn't use too much, I was allowed to play with our paper; I was given a beautiful little green Corona portable typewriter for my own.

Almost every afternoon during the first few months of 1935, I walked down to the shop in my snowsuit. There, I would use our large counter to weave, draw, type, or fold papers for my parents for a few pennies. Sometimes I splurged and ran across the street to buy a delicious ten-cent hamburger with onions.

Several of our printers had made the journey from Rochester with us. One was our shop foreman, Doug. A slender, courtly man with a gray mustache, Doug thought that our heavy paper cutter was too dangerous for a little girl; he used to cut poster cardboard into strips so that I could weave colorful folders and purses. Though I loved to use the big paper cutter, he was so nice about it that I couldn't complain.

With the advent of spring, a gang of older kids appeared on Harriet Avenue halfway between our house and the shop, five or six boys and girls led by a stringy thirteen-year-old named Marguerite. That always seemed to me a most unlikely name for a gang leader. The gang, tame indeed by today's standards, used to infuriate me by stopping me on my march toward my parents' shop with a mocking "Where are you going, little girl?" and physically turning me around. I never knew what to do. My impulse was to strike out, but they were too many and too old for me to fight. One day, they pushed me so far that I stole a paper-weight from our paper-folding counter—a snow scene, shaped like an upside-down custard—and put it in the pocket of my raincoat. I had decided to hit Marguerite on the side of her head the next time her gang stopped me. Luckily, something about my walk must have given away my determination; they never stopped me again.

The gangs that followed my father were far more sinister. One night in March, shortly after my parents restarted the *Midwest American*, Walter was trailed for twenty blocks by a member of Detroit's Purple Gang, a "notorious gunman and crook," who was, Walter reported, "conveniently holed up in a dive in the shadow of the State Capitol building."

"Are some of the Governor's underworld friends contemplating silencing me as Howard Guilford was silenced?" Walter wondered, but concluded: "It wouldn't be smart to have me killed at this time." Believing that publicity could forestall his being shot, Walter published his account of being tailed by a member of the Purple Gang in the *Midwest American*. Earlier, in *Plain Talk*, he had described the Purple Gang as part of the "organized, ruthless, and efficient" criminal industry of Detroit.[6]

The FBI file on Olson contains a partial corroboration—a summary of a 1937 statement by a state official whose name was, of course, blacked out in the report I received. He told the FBI that in the spring of 1935 Olson had hired "an attorney of questionable character" to have Walter followed by "out-of-town" individuals who were ultimately responsible for his death. The informant claimed that the lawyer prepared three typed copies of reports on Walter's activities; one went to Olson and one to his speechwriter Abe Harris, while the lawyer kept the third.[7]

Walter was not sure whether he was being followed because of his opposition to Governor Olson or because of his vehement opposition to a bill that proposed to legalize pari-mutuel betting—which he calculated would give the state political machine about $200,000 per year. Walter claimed that the bill was supported by the Annenberg gambling syndicate of Chicago and New York, as well as by Minnesota gambling interests and Fred Ossanna's liquor lobby. He believed all of them were part of a national crime syndicate involved in murder, bootlegging, hijacking, extortion, and drugs.[8]

Walter also fought a bill drafted to postpone Minneapolis's city elections to coincide with state elections. He believed that this bill would keep a corrupt city regime in power another eighteen months, and that both bills would strengthen racketeers' grip on the city. His newspaper was successful in both campaigns, but these modest successes led to attempted bribes, then to more persecution.[9]

My parents reported that a man claiming to represent the state purchasing agent had offered state printing in exchange for stopping their anti-Olson campaign. Soon afterwards, an acquaintance who was a friend of Charles Ward, a former convict and substantial financial backer of Olson, visited our plant and thrust three hundred dollars into their hands as he walked out the door. After some hesitation, my parents decided to print the story of the attempted bribe and to use the funds for gift subscriptions. Their account began, "Mr. Ward helps us spread the truth."[10] A political fat cat who lived just across the Wisconsin border and dabbled in politics in both states, Ward apparently was not amused. My parents believed that he later arranged for the distribution in our neighborhood of thousands of pamphlets defaming Walter, and then financed the early stages of a frame-up.

Both the tailing and the attempted bribe occurred when the *Midwest American* focused on state and national, not local, issues — on Olson's role in a national third party, on state legislation, and on state malfeasance. Except for opposing gambling and the postponement of city elections, Walter did not investigate or report on corruption in Minneapolis until the second half of 1935.

Sometime that spring, Doug left our shop — possibly for personal reasons, perhaps from pressure. After that, the print shop ceased to feel like home, even though all the other printers and typesetters seemed decent and kind and glad to be working. But from that time on, it seemed as if my parents couldn't hire a linotype operator or a press operator without the union or the Farmer-Labor Party trying to get him to quit. Although my parents had published a union newspaper in Rochester, Minneapolis union officials refused to recognize the *Midwest American.*[11]

Similarly, advertisers were warned not to patronize either the *Midwest American* or the *West Lake Neighborhood News.* "They used the old pressures," Edith wrote. "They invoked the fire laws and the building laws against advertisers; they found faulty plumbing and dangerous elevators in any establishment that tried to use our paper; they arrested advertisers for fancied traffic violations."[12]

Walter's "Third Parties for Sale" appeared in Calverton's *Modern Monthly* in February 1935. This polemic is a fair summary of Walter's reasons for opposing

Governor Olson, and it may have started the chain of events leading to Walter's death. Directed primarily at third-party advocates outside Minnesota unfamiliar with Governor Olson's record, it predicted, correctly, that the Farmer-Labor Party would be turned over to the Democrats. Walter thought Olson was intermittently supporting President Roosevelt's administration in return for future Democratic support when Olson ran for the U.S. Senate. As evidence, Walter pointed out that Olson's pattern was to soft-pedal Farmer-Labor platforms prior to election and to make radical speeches afterward.

The Farmer-Labor Party had accomplished little during Olson's four years in office, Walter argued, except to create a smoothly functioning political machine. He claimed that state officeholders dominated Farmer-Labor associations, which, responding to pressure from the capitol, elected safe delegates to the state conventions. Meanwhile, independent men and women were expelled or refused membership. At the same time, the governor's friends, especially contributors to his "personal campaign fund," were awarded state contracts for buildings and highways.

In the summer and fall of 1934, Walter reported, more than eighteen thousand people drew pay from the state highway department; there jobs were openly bartered, and membership in the Farmer-Labor Association was a requirement for employment. County road foremen used state cars and state gas to do political work on state time. For weeks before elections, they and state bank examiners, hotel and restaurant inspectors, game wardens, foresters, state police, and other state employees devoted most of their time to electioneering. Unfortunately, this was the only national article Walter was able to publish.

Walter also wrote to Upton Sinclair, who was then active in California politics, about his concerns about the misdirection of the Farmer-Labor Party:

> The Farmer-Labor clubs are mostly controlled by Olson appointees, especially in the Twin Cities, but out in the country many of the old Nonpartisan Leaguers, who were with the Populist party before that, are commencing to see through Olson's dishonesty and hypocrisy. Many of these associations are in open revolt against the Olson "All Party" gang. . . . I believe that a third party based on radical principles is IMPERATIVE if this country is to be saved from the twin threats of Fascism and Communism. I came back to the middle west to work for such a party — only to find to my disgust that the Olson regime combines all the worst features of both the old parties with some new underworld racketeering connections of its own.[13]

Sinclair was equivocal, possibly because of ties between Olson and Sinclair's End Poverty in California movement. He remarked that Walter's account was "very interesting," but he did not investigate Walter's charges or offer an opportunity to publish.[14]

While Walter was having trouble getting published in radical periodicals, Olson's secretary, Vince Day, appealed to Calverton's sense of fair play to publish a rebuttal to Walter's article in *Modern Monthly,* and he contacted Selden Rodman to write it. Rodman—a major proponent of a third party, an avid Olson backer, and copublisher of *Common Sense*—was a one-man industry turning out articles on Olson, the Farmer-Labor Party, and third-party prospects.[15] Rodman's "Walter Liggett for Sale" passionately defended Olson and accused Walter of purveying personal scandal stories about Olson and of being a tool of Republican senator Thomas D. Schall.[16]

Day provided Rodman with background for his supposedly independent interpretation of Minnesota politics, as well as for Rodman's charges. Rodman himself was not convinced. "I am puzzled to know who is really behind this man Liggett," Rodman wrote to Day. "Maybe Schall is only a front. Perhaps it's [newspaper publisher William Randolph] Hearst himself."[17]

Ironically, it was Rodman's article, not Walter's, that printed—as instances of malicious rumors—charges that Olson's health was failing and that he drank to excess and associated with criminals. Although these rumors may have been accurate, Walter's article dealt solely with politics and good government issues.[18] To Rodman's article, Walter replied:

> I have no personal quarrel with Floyd B. Olson. He is intensely human, magnetic, likeable, and very, very clever. Neither, as Mr. Rodman infers, have I ever mentioned any scandals in his private life. . . . My sole objection to Floyd Olson is that he is utterly insincere in his endorsement of Farmer-Labor principles. . . .
>
> My "personal life" may or may not be "unsavory" as Mr. Rodman alleges—in any event I think it would compare favorably with Floyd Olson's—but my public record proves that I fought and sacrificed for Sacco and Vanzetti; that I devoted months of my time in the fight for the Tom Mooney case; that I have fought to prevent the exploitation of Mexico, Nicaragua, Cuba; that for at least 25 years I have been a sincere radical and no one can truthfully declare that I ever sold out a radical cause or accepted a single penny for the expression of my political opinions.[19]

Rodman's article and Walter's reply were published together in the April 1935 *Modern Monthly* with the title "Third Party Free-for-All." Soon Rodman's article, slightly rewritten and without Walter's rebuttal, was reprinted in the *Minnesota Leader.*[20] Later, tens of thousands of copies were distributed in pamphlet form in our neighborhood.

Rodman continued his attack on Walter in another article in *Common Sense*—which declined to print Walter's reply. Walter indignantly wrote to the editor, reiterating his charge that Olson was a "political opportunist whose words can please every liberal while his every action is designed to delight those interested in the status quo.... During better than four years in office, he has worked to perfect an Olson All-Party machine and to graft every cent from the taxpayers that traffic will bear." Walter wrote that Olson's real purpose was to abort a third-party movement while using the movement as leverage to get himself the vice-presidential nomination. He continued:

> And, if Olson continues his friendship with Charles Ward, I wouldn't advise anyone to insure the president's life too high.
>
> Meanwhile, I do not intend to allow your friend, Floyd Olson, to murder me as his underworld friends killed poor Howard Guilford. And I do intend to put Olson and his All-Party gang out of Minnesota politics.... You see, I was present at the conference in 1918 when the Farmer Labor party was founded, unlike Olson who did not hop aboard the bandwagon until all was over but the flagwaving. The radical cause in the Northwest means more to me than political graft.[21]

Around that same time, Walter was offered a less obvious bribe: a job on a state committee headed by Senator James Carley that investigated misfeasance in government—with indifferent success, due in part to heckling from the governor's office. Like the legislative session as a whole, Carley's Senate committee was paralyzed by conflicts between the administration and most legislators. Even the old-age pensions that were voted in were voided by a clerical error in the state printer's office.[22]

The squabbles between Olson and the legislature were reported extensively, if not objectively. The governor subsidized "Rome Roberts" (a clerk named Sylvester McGovern in the state oil inspector's office) to undercut the legislature with radio ridicule. Vince Day had been astute in foreseeing the need for spin control. As he wrote Olson: "Abe Harris believes it would be very important to continue the Merry-Go-Round radio program of McGovern and Seeger. He says $800 will carry this through the legislative session and will do much to laugh off the political investigations of the legislature."[23]

Rome Roberts provided daily, supposedly unbiased, reports on KSTP radio in which he accused Carley's committee of "eavesdropping," called Carley "parrot-nosed," and referred to his "glistening bald pate."[24] On Fridays, the *Leader,* in the person of H. G. Creel, reviewed the legislative week on WCCO radio. Olson himself turned columnist for the *St. Paul News.*[25]

Radicals and third-party advocates around the country expected great progress from this legislative session in this much-touted radical state. Both Gerald L. K. Smith of Louisiana and Socialist Norman Thomas addressed the legislature in February. While Smith described Huey Long's "Share-the-Wealth" plan, Thomas noted that the eyes of the nation were on the pacesetters in Minnesota. But the bony cattle sent to the capital by drought-stricken farmers in February were more effective than these speakers in getting seed and drought relief measures out of the legislature. The governor, however, vetoed both a $10 million relief bill and a $2 million seed loan bill passed by the legislature: Olson did not want the conservative state executive council to control relief administration. The conservatives, in turn, objected to financing relief with taxes on beer and whiskey.[26]

During the course of the legislative session, conservatives delayed confirming some Olson appointees, including Melvin Passolt as director of the Bureau of Criminal Apprehension. And Senator A. J. Rockne, the Finance Committee chair, sponsored an investigation into the Liquor Control Commission and introduced a bill making it a felony to solicit financial contributions from state employees or businesses with state contracts. This was construed as a blow against the Farmer-Labor administration and the *Leader,* which was financed by not-so-voluntary contributions from state employees and by ads from firms that did business with the state government.

The Carley committee investigated political favoritism in the Purchasing Department, the Department of Highways, and the State Emergency Relief Committee and found substantial irregularities in all. One abuse was selling feed grain to speculators when it was needed for relief, and then buying it back at higher prices. The committee also garnered some interesting testimony: when one state employee was asked if it was true that he organized Farmer-Labor clubs at highway department expense, he responded that this was "a free country." Still, while the committee seemed to be sniffing around in the right places, it was not particularly effective.[27]

"The Carley investigation is pretty much fixed," Walter wrote Calverton:

They offered me $125 a week to work for them. And you can guess whether or not I could use the money. But I know there is a pipe line from their committee right into the governor's office, and I don't exactly relish the idea of having my stuff turned over to him or just disappearing from the files. . . . A salary of $125 a week would be a cheap way for them to keep me bottled up. So I'm staying outside and telling what I please and when I please.[28]

Walter was correct about the pipeline. Vince Day's papers contain undated pages that appear to be copies of Carley committee evaluations of prospective witnesses; a few of these pages dealt with Walter. Among other comments, they described him as running a shopping publication that was doing "quite well."[29]

The state official who told the FBI that Olson had delegated a "questionable attorney" to have Walter followed by out-of-town mobsters also reported that an employee of the highway department had managed to steal a briefcase full of evidence at the time of the Carley investigation.[30] This informant thought the FBI might be interested in knowing that letters addressed to Walter were opened by those following his movements, but the FBI merely recorded the information. Walter himself suspected that his mail was being searched. Writing to Calverton, he mentioned problems with our mail:

I assumed you received my air-mail answer to young Rodman. . . . I'm having a great deal of trouble with my mail. Whether inefficiency or because they read it, I don't know.

Right now, the Olson gang are running me ragged to cut down the time and energy I have to promote my little *Midwest American.* You see, I'm financing the *American* from my damn little neighborhood paper, and the dear Olsonites are getting busy tying up my accounts with fantastic suits, generally making me waste time in court that I ought to spend out working for the *Midwest American.*

At that, I believe that I'll be able to get out an 8-page instead of 4-page within three weeks — if I can dodge bankruptcy or gunmen, the two Olson long suits. It's hellishly hard, though, to put up a lone fight such as I've been making, with friends applauding me from the sidelines, but enemies actively going out to ruin me.[31]

One of these lawsuits was engineered by attorney Lindahl O. Johnson, who was also actively working behind the scenes on a frame-up case that was to surface at the end of June. Johnson, a protégé of the Seventh Ward Farmer-Labor

Club, had headed Governor Olson's All-Party Speakers' Committee. Edith described Johnson as an attorney without standing whose partner had kicked him out of his office.[32] In a memo to Olson, Vince Day recommended Johnson as "the best qualified applicant" for the position of secretary to the railroad board, crediting Johnson with "a nice personality" and being "a loyal advocate of your principles."[33] He was probably right on the latter.

According to Edith, Johnson went around in late March to our customers, advertisers, and creditors, attempting to "get accounts assigned to him" by telling them all, quite falsely, that the Liggetts were going out of business and leaving town in April. He managed to get the case of one distributor to whom my parents owed sixty dollars—a bill disputed because of complaints about service. Our bookkeeper discovered that Johnson had managed to attach money owing to us, as well as Edith's bank account. Although the case was dismissed, it became increasingly hard for my parents to distribute newspapers. Newsstands refused to handle the *Midwest American,* while policemen took newsboys up alleys and advised them not to peddle "that rag."

Meanwhile, men and women "weary of the crookedness, the ruthlessness" brought my parents the evidence they needed. A police official's wife used to meet them secretly in the middle of the night. Twice someone brushed by Edith on the street and slipped her pieces of paper containing information on the state pardon racket. At the same time, my parents experienced tapped telephones and sabotaged machines. One afternoon, Edith found a dictaphone inside her desk drawer.[34]

Anonymous phone calls to our office began in April. Callers asked Walter if he wanted "a dose of what Guilford got" and asked Edith if she wanted to collect life insurance on her husband. Later that spring, my parents received a tip from North Dakota that someone was fixing up "a girl charge." Much later, they heard that members of the county attorney's staff had been bragging since May that "Liggett was going to get his."[35]

Time seemed a bigger problem to my parents. Walter wrote Calverton, "I've been so busy lately that about all I've been doing with the *Midwest American* is keeping it in the mails. My equipment is inadequate to the work I am doing, and since the Farmer-Labor group tamper with my printers, offering them jobs at higher pay as soon as they get the run of the shop, I'm kept constantly at the grindstone to keep the place going."[36]

Wallace and I left early that year for another summer at our friends' farm. I had had a difficult siege of measles, and chicken pox was going the rounds. Our parents took us out of school in May. That was fine with us. When we arrived, a few patches of snow still lingered in hollows of the wooded pastures. Along with swimsuits and shorts, balls and bats, I took my little Corona typewriter and masses of copy paper, construction paper, and posterboard. I had ambitious plans to produce a *Wood Lake News* and to teach paper weaving to my friends in Wisconsin. It was one of the best summers of my life.

But in Minneapolis, our parents were experiencing the first rumblings of what Edith called a "crescendo of horror."

8. Framed and Beaten Up

The Olson gang WILL resort to every other despicable method that their underworld minds can invent. I expect baseless suits for libel; I expect long drawn litigation in an effort to freeze me out of ownership of the *Midwest American;* I anticipate frame-ups.

—Walter Liggett, *Midwest American*, November 30, 1934

While Wallace and I were relishing our summer on the farm, our parents — to pay our board and room — moved from our pleasant house on Harriet Avenue into a house on Portland Avenue owned by Republican U.S. senator Thomas Schall. I recall it as a gloomy old house with mailbags in the attic. Our parents had rented it earlier for employees in return for repairs; it was now available for only fifteen dollars a month. It was tolerable, they figured, with a comfortable sleeping porch. They were close to the poverty line then and economy loomed large.[1]

Whatever the economics, it was a bad move politically for both Schall and my parents. In June, the *Minnesota Leader* launched an attack linking Walter with Senator Schall. One article proclaimed that "Schall, Liggett, and scandal sheets are being lined up to save forces of reaction.... With their vested power and limitless wealth vested in them or seized from the people, they are prepared to throw into the coming battle the scathing denunciations of platform oratory of Senator Thomas D. Schall." In truth, our struggling newspapers hardly justified the term "limitless wealth."[2]

"A Weird Case"

On June 23, 1935, a warm Sunday evening, the doorbell rang on Portland Avenue just after Walter and Edith had returned from a family weekend in Wisconsin. When Walter answered the bell, a policeman told him that he was wanted on a sex charge — that Hennepin County attorney Ed Goff had charged him and Austin union organizer Frank Ellis with abducting two minors. Walter couldn't believe what he was hearing and jokingly asked the cop if he didn't also have a warrant for bank robbery.[3]

Unfortunately, the policeman was serious. The supposed abduction had occurred on March 22, 1934, more than fifteen months earlier. Later, when Walter and Ellis checked their records and reconstructed their movements, Walter realized that he had driven from Rochester to Minneapolis that day and had spent the afternoon in Governor Olson's office discussing the *Austin American.* Ellis had driven up separately from Austin to meet Vince Raymond Dunne, a union leader active in the Minneapolis truck strikes of 1934. Ellis had given a ride to two teenage girls, daughters of union members, who had asked him to take them to Minneapolis so they could see the sights and visit with a Mrs. Flagle, the stepmother of the older girl.[4]

Walter and Ellis had both stayed overnight at the Ritz Hotel, in separate rooms and on different floors. They had met by chance in the hotel restaurant, where they had argued about the union, the *Austin American,* and the credibility of O. J. Fosso. The two girls, whom I will call Jenny and Francine (since at least one is still alive, and I consider them victims too), had also stayed at the Ritz, courtesy of Ellis. They had failed to find Mrs. Flagle and were on the verge of hitchhiking back to Austin on a cold night; Ellis had paid for their room and given them money to go to the movies.[5]

At sixteen and seventeen, both girls were what was then known as "wild" or "wayward." Their offenses were minor: underage drinking, public drunkenness, going out with the wrong men, and everything else that goes with looking for excitement in a drab packinghouse town. By 1935 both had acquired suspended sentences and could be sent to a detention center in Shakopee for bad behavior. They were liable to threats and blackmail. And all Austin knew it.[6]

The morning after the policeman's visit, Walter reported to the old courthouse, once a city showcase but now overcrowded, and an underworld hangout where shady characters mingled with court employees. Walter was arraigned before municipal judge Paul W. Carroll, as was Ellis, who was out of town organizing and had not yet learned of the charges. Both were charged with abduction of the Austin girls, an offense that carried a maximum five-year sentence.[7] Although the assistant county attorney demanded five thousand dollars bail, Carroll set Walter's bail at one thousand dollars. Walter requested a preliminary hearing in open court, and Carroll set this hearing for June 28. "It is peculiar," he remarked, "that this alleged offense is said to have taken place fifteen months ago and a warrant is just being issued. It looks like there is some politics behind the case."[8]

That same day, county attorney Ed Goff went to Governor Olson's office to discuss the Liggett case. "Ed Goff is very anxious to meet you immediately upon his return to the city," Vince Day's memorandum states. "I believe that it is in connection with the arrest of Liggett." On the previous Saturday, Goff had filed information that Ellis had brought the two girls into Minneapolis on March 22, 1934, and that Walter had joined them there.[9]

Walter spent most of Monday in the reception room of the Minneapolis city jail, while Edith scurried around the city trying to raise bail money—not an easy task in Minneapolis in the summer of 1935. We were desperately short of money, and under Minnesota law she could not use mortgaged property for bail. When she turned to professional bondsmen, she found that bonding companies had been told not to "go on bond" for a man who was persona non grata with the Farmer-Labor powers. Doors were slammed in her face.[10]

While Joseph Granbeck, Walter's attorney and longtime friend, attended to legal formalities and put up eighty-five dollars of his own money, Edith went to wait with Walter for his release. Sick and dazed, they returned home, glad that Wallace and I were safely in the country.[11] Ellis did not fare as well. He was arrested later that day in South St. Paul and had to spend fifty-six days in jail while fellow unionists raised his bail.[12]

Edith wrote George Calverton that, during the months before Walter's trial, half a dozen times a day, no matter what we were discussing or doing, he would demand like an unjustly accused child, "Edith, do you think anyone really believes that charge about me?"[13]

Distrusting Minneapolis justice and the Twin Cities newspapers, Edith felt that national newspaper publicity was the only way to stop the frame-up. On the morning that Walter was booked, she wrote letters to two men whom she considered advocates of freedom of the press: Marlen Pew at *Editor & Publisher* and Upton Sinclair.[14] Pew broke the news immediately in *Editor & Publisher:*

> There's a newspaperman in jail out in Minnesota, allegedly on a charge which represents a political frame-up. It is something nasty, about "abduction."...He is Walter W. Liggett, and in recent years I have known him as a radical writer, often quite reckless in his stuff, but apparently always on the side of the underdog, against privileged power and public abuses....He is not a scandal-monger, rather a philosopher who writes with a dagger....
>
> I hope that responsible Minnesota newspapermen will look into it and see that an old reporter and writer is not quietly hung up by the heels primarily because he and they differ on political matters.[15]

Minnesota newspaper friends to whom Pew wired inquiries replied that the case was "dark and mysterious" and that "everybody is keeping hands off, pending developments." That only whetted Pew's curiosity. Under Pew's initiative, *Editor & Publisher* investigated the charges against Walter and reported the case as it developed.[16] Managing editor Arthur Robb took over when Pew left for an around-the-world trip in September.

After Pew broke the story, stories and editorials appeared in the *Chicago Tribune* and the *New York Times.* Twin Cities newspapers largely ignored the case in its early stages; the few stories were an inch or two long.[17]

But the Farmer-Labor house organ, now called the *Minnesota Leader,* devoted much of its June 29 front page to the case. A seven-column banner headline read "Liggett, Traitor Arrested at Senator Schall's Home"; a secondary headline asserted "Tie-up with Republican Solon Bared." The *Leader* called Walter an "editor of political scandal sheets" and a "mountebank 'liberal' writer who turned traitor to the Farmer-Labor cause to become a hireling propagandist of a reactionary political plunderbund."[18]

Interestingly, Ellis's name was mentioned only briefly in two paragraphs out of seventeen, while Schall (who had nothing to do with the case) was mentioned eleven times by name, with numerous additional references to "Republican solon" and "solon." Of course, Schall had the Senate seat that Olson craved.

Tens of thousands of copies of this issue of the *Leader* were circulated to voters and prospective jurors, and individual copies were "carefully mailed to judges who might be expected to sit on affiant's case."[19]

The *Leader* could not report on the open court hearing that had been set for June 28, since it had been postponed to July 12; this was the first of four postponements initiated by the county attorney's office. Walter and Frank Ellis were never to have their preliminary hearings in open court.[20]

Walter's old friend Henry Teigan edited this issue of the *Leader,* his first, although he had headed the Newspaper Committee since August 1934. On Wednesday, June 26, two days after Walter was charged with abduction, the Farmer-Labor Newspaper Committee met in the governor's dining room at the capitol. Their main agenda item was to fire longtime editor Herren G. Creel for "insubordination" and to order him to turn in all correspondence, records, files, and office supplies. Creel had apparently challenged the honesty and legality of certain board actions. Teigan was installed as acting editor-in-chief to achieve "greater solidarity" and to "restore confidence in the organ of the Farmer-Labor Association."[21]

Even though Creel was still listed as editor on the *Leader*'s masthead, Walter must have known about the change, since he directed his indignant three-page single-spaced letter to Teigan. Specifying fifteen major libels in the main story —

approximately one per paragraph—he demanded a retraction and an apology, to be given "the same position and prominence as the original" attack. Teigan never answered the letter, and because of the press of circumstances, my parents were not able to pursue their intended libel suit against Teigan and the *Leader*.[22]

Later that summer, the *Leader* ran a massive story about Schall's mailbags and our parents' presence in his house, headlined "Hidden Mail Cache Found in Schall's Home." The house had been ransacked just before the story appeared. In the few months that our family lived on Portland Avenue, the house was broken into four times.[23]

Almost every weekend from mid-May to mid-September in the long summer of 1935, Walter and Edith drove to Wisconsin to spend Saturday and Sunday with us. During the day, we went swimming and rowing together or had family picnics at Spirit Lake or Taylors Falls. Evenings, we watched the northern lights— at their spectacular best that summer—cast their flickering colors from the North Pole down across Wood Lake. I could stand entranced for hours. In that glowing summer at Wood Lake, Wallace and I had few inklings that anything might be wrong at home, although I remember my father looking sad one day when I didn't want to leave a baseball game to join the family. I wish that I could have let my father know how much I loved him and how I looked forward to his visits.

These family visits sustained our parents in their nightmare summer, but it was doubly hard—for my mother at least—to go back to their ordeal in Minneapolis. "When Walter and I used to drive up to see the youngsters every Saturday," Edith wrote Calverton after Walter's death, "we used to draw a deep breath when we crossed the bridge into Wisconsin, and felt ourselves back in America. And I'm not exaggerating when [I say that] we used to feel a pall come over us as we crossed back Sunday night or Monday morning to Olsonland . . . terror."[24]

Fighting Back

Characteristically, Walter responded to his indictment with a counterattack in print. Quoting John Paul Jones's "Surrender? Hell! I have just begun to fight" as his masthead slogan, Walter carried the fight back to Olson in the next issue of the *Midwest American*. In an article entitled "Fighting Olson Is a Dangerous Job," Walter listed harassments he had suffered since breaking with Olson.[25]

Although Walter had raised the issue of impeachment earlier, the June 29 issue was the first to publish "ten reasons for ousting governor by the next legislature"—a special session that Governor Olson had proposed back in April. Olson had just survived a suit for violations of the Corrupt Practices Act. But Walter felt that the governor *could* be impeached "if in the Legislature there are a few men with courage to withstand the Governor's threats ... and with the moral stamina to resist patronage trades." From then on, each issue of the *Midwest American* printed these ten reasons for impeaching Governor Olson:

1. Notorious immorality
2. Protection of vendors of gambling devices
3. Favoritism and graft in dealing with liquor
4. Fraud and favoritism in state contracts and purchases
5. Planned bond steal
6. Improper use of state employees for political purposes
7. Improper solicitation of campaign funds and failure to report contributions
8. Scandals in pardons and extraditions
9. Protection of campaign contributors
10. The sale of public office to persons who are both morally unfit and wholly unqualified.[26]

The July 12 lead story dealt with Olson's sudden announcement that he might not call a legislative special session, although it was needed to authorize the old-age pension law. This issue also reported that Magnus Johnson, an elder statesman of the Farmer-Labor Party, had upset the All-Party group by declaring himself a candidate for governor at a Fourth of July picnic. Walter believed that the All-Party group wanted Elmer Benson to become governor when Olson moved to the Senate.[27]

On July 31, Walter challenged Olson either to call the legislature into special session or to charge him with criminal libel. On September 25, an article pointed out that Floyd Olson had packed a Farmer-Labor conference on patronage. And the *Midwest American* continued to report conflicts within the Farmer-Labor Party in western and northern Minnesota counties.

During the next few months, under indictment and with his business under siege, Walter expanded coverage to explore corruption in Minneapolis and Hennepin County: "Since the Prosecuting Attorney of Hennepin county has seen fit to lend himself to a bare-faced frameup designed to silence this paper by putting the editor in jail, we have decided in the future to devote part of our space to the office of the County Attorney." A front-page article provided details of the return of racket boss Ed Morgan. Another dealt with gambling in the city, where the police, Walter noted, played favorites and protected gamblers friendly to Olson.

And, he suggested, the Hennepin County Welfare Department ought to investigate teenage girls working in gambling dens until one or two in the morning.[28]

Subsequent issues reported on a "wet councilmanic ring" that allowed the Syndicate—felons and former bootleggers—to dominate Minneapolis's retail liquor trade.[29] Through September, Walter detailed the lurid background of Kid Cann and the history of La Pompadour—ostensibly a perfume factory during Prohibition and then the producer of Chesapeake Brands liquors—which he viewed as part of the alcohol syndicate favored by crooked elements of the Farmer-Labor Party.[30]

Walter reported that the Syndicate had been so sure that the city council would approve its bar on Lake Street that its publicity man, Art Jacobs (who also worked for the Farmer-Labor administration), had attempted to buy newspaper advertising at least ten days before the council's vote.[31]

No one charged Walter with libel; instead, "fixers" offered him money and influence to end his attacks. Typically, he responded in print. "I am not a 'shakedown' artist," he wrote on August 7. "Law violators and crooked officials might just as well understand now as later that the *American* does not accept money for withholding or publishing information."[32]

Still, the bribe offers continued. Edith reported on October 30 that the Sixth Street Cigar Store had offered to advertise if we kept its name out of the columns, while an agent for the new Lake Street Liquor Store proposed a series of forty-dollar full-page ads, and a private detective offered Walter three hundred dollars a week to stop his exposés of gambling.[33]

"As a matter of fact," Edith wrote, "the *Midwest American* does not accept liquor ads and neither will we take ads from cigar stores or resorts where gambling goes on. If we wanted to, we could fill our columns with advertisements from various resorts connected with the underworld." Her article mentioned that a prominent politician had telegraphed Walter to contact a businessman connected with the Kid Cann–Bronstein gang. Most likely Schall was the politician involved, since a September 27 telegram from him ("See and talk with Meyer Schuldberg") turned up after Walter's death.[34]

Schall's telegram—his first contact with Walter after the indictment—arrived after a series on the Syndicate in the *Midwest American*. One article, titled "Ex-Bootleggers Seek Monopoly of Rum Traffic," pointed out the connections between Kid Cann and Meyer Schuldberg, who headed both La Pompadour and Chesapeake Brands, and employed Kid Cann as a "salesman."[35]

When Walter met Schuldberg—most probably in late September—Schuldberg pleaded with him to stop the attacks and tried to force a roll of bills on him.

When Walter refused the offer, Schuldberg said, "If you ever need help, call on me." But the *Midwest American* continued its attacks on the Syndicate up to and beyond Walter's death.[36]

In a front-page box headed "Social Notes," the October 2 issue of the *Midwest American* reported that Minneapolis aldermen Henry Banks and Romeo Riley had attended the Joe Louis–Max Baer fight in New York as guests of Kid Cann, "prominent Minneapolis man-about-town," while state liquor commissioner David Arundel was the guest of liquor lobbyist Fred Ossanna. Another article reported that Big Ed Morgan was in the slot machine racket with Art Goff, the brother of the county attorney, and noted rumors that Morgan, who blamed publicity in the *Midwest American* for the hasty—if temporary—removal of his slot machines, had been calmly debating with his gunmen whether to assassinate my father.[37]

It's hard not to admire my father's raw courage, and equally hard for me not to get angry at his intransigence. What about his devoted wife? What about his little daughter? Didn't he think that Wallace needed a father?

Calling for Help: The Radical Response

In that period of turmoil, V. F. Calverton was one of the few radicals to come to Walter's aid. In *Modern Monthly,* he called Walter's case "an obvious and despicable frame-up" that throws "into sharp relief the character of the present State administration and appears to corroborate Mr. Liggett's indictment of the so-called Farmer-Labor Governor." Calverton called on "all radicals and liberals" to "challenge the corrupt practices manifest in this vicious attempt to silence an honest and vigorous editor."[38]

Calverton, who knew my parents well, had kept up with their struggles in Minnesota. He felt that Walter's arraignment clearly demonstrated Farmer-Labor corruption. And he was increasingly concerned about the lack of intellectual honesty in the left. But most of the national radical press, which had been touting Olson as a leading western radical, ignored the story. There was no mention whatever in the *Nation,* the *New Republic,* or the *New Leader.*[39]

Edith had contacted Upton Sinclair early on, but he too declined to write or to investigate. Finally, a month and a half after Edith's first letter, he sent a note to the American Civil Liberties Union, complaining that Edith had been sending him "frantic letters" and asking them to look into the case. But Roger Baldwin at the ACLU, who had learned of the case from Marlen Pew, had written Edith the day before: "What, if anything, can we do at this distance?"[40]

That same day, Ed Goff, the county attorney, again contacted the governor to discuss the Liggett case.[41] While Walter was waiting for his much-delayed public hearing, now set for August 2, Goff had called a special session of the grand jury. In a secret hearing on July 31, Ellis's indictment was modified, although he was still charged with abduction (which carried a five-year sentence). The charge in Walter's indictment was changed to sodomy, which carried a twenty-year sentence.[42]

On August 2, Walter was arraigned and pleaded not guilty, calling the charge "one of the foulest and most perjurious frame-ups ever perpetrated. I will appreciate it if you set the trial at the earliest possible moment that I may show the political animus behind the case." The judge set the trial for September 16 and set bond at two thousand dollars.[43]

Edith responded to Baldwin's letter with a five-page letter. "I have been far more in despair," she wrote, "than I have admitted to Walter."

"In his many years as prosecuting attorney," Edith wrote, "Floyd Olson learned every possible trick of the underworld . . . and he has deliberately set about to make the charge filthy in order to deprive Walter of the support of newspapermen and radicals." They used a frame-up, she thought, because Howard Guilford's murder was still fresh in the public mind.[44]

She heard that Olson's emissaries approached Frank Ellis almost every day, offering to drop the abduction charge if Ellis would perjure himself and say that Walter was guilty, but "he has informed them that he will tell the truth."

"We need an investigator," Edith wrote. She had someone in mind — almost certainly our friend Bill Sheehan in New York City — who would do the job for little more than expenses, but we were too poor to hire him. The *Midwest American,* Edith wrote, "actually [cost] about $25 a week over and above the subscriptions. We have kept . . . going only by some combination of faith, hope, and charity, and now with Walter's trial imminent, it is difficult to see whether we'll be able to keep the shop open."[45]

Baldwin had little to offer except, once again, a suggestion that my parents secure George Leonard as their attorney. Walter sent Baldwin a telegram, politely calling Leonard a "splendid man" whose "close personal and political associations with Governor Olson make him impossible in my case." Baldwin's next list, mostly Farmer-Labor attorneys, included Governor Olson's secretary, Vince Day. Despite Walter's telegram and Jay Near's caustic comments about Leonard in the ACLU files, Baldwin continued to rely on Leonard for his interpretations of what was going on in Minnesota.[46]

Assuming that help was forthcoming, Edith continued to write Baldwin at the ACLU office. They had been warned, she wrote, that the jury panel was being packed with Olsonites and that only five challenges were allowed. They had also heard that the county attorney intended to keep reporters out of court on the pretext that the testimony was shocking:

> Of course, if that can be done, it will be a legal lynching, for without the protection of outside newspapermen, our witnesses will not be allowed to testify. The Twin City papers are completely cowardly and will no more demand their right to report this case than they would insist on Walter's right to a trial in open court. . . . We need a lawyer who can force the court to give Walter his right to a trial in open court.

She ended with a request that Baldwin use plain envelopes: "Some of my mail is being opened if it seems important to the mail clerks."[47]

Baldwin sent Edith a list of out-of-town lawyers, writing, "Don't get the impression that this organization will help. We cannot."[48] Since my parents did not have money for a lawyer, the lists were of little help. Joseph Granbeck, Walter's boyhood friend, did what he could, but his entire practice had been confined to civil cases. Lyle Pettijohn, another boyhood friend, similarly lacked criminal law experience.

In the meantime, the *Chicago Tribune,* which had kept an eye on Minnesota ever since the gag-law case, editorialized that the record suggested that Walter "may be the victim of another ruthless suppression of opinion in Minnesota."[49] *Editor & Publisher* pointed out that it was hard to believe the prosecutor's charge (subsequently changed) that Walter had forced open a bedroom door and assaulted one girl in the presence of the other, and that neither of the girls had complained for sixteen months. (As it happened, the doors were steel; the Ritz advertised itself as Minneapolis's only fireproof hotel.) "We do not know at this distance where the right lies in the matter, but *Editor & Publisher* is never silent when a newspaperman, whatever his political faith or medium may be, cries aloud that he is under a dictator's heel."[50]

When Edith mailed Lucille Milner of the ACLU copies of the *Midwest American* issue that contained my parents' story of the frame-up, asking her to distribute them to ACLU board members, Milner replied that she could not assume that responsibility when Baldwin was out of the country. Edith promised herself never again to contact the ACLU.[51]

Walter, acting as his own attorney, filed a motion to change the venue of the case to St. Paul, in Ramsey County. He said that he could not secure a fair and impartial trial in Hennepin County and wanted to prove his innocence in an "atmosphere untainted by political prejudice and free from powerful underworld interests."[52] In a lengthy affidavit, Walter, calling the charges "false and filthy," charged that Governor Olson had "prior knowledge of the plot and personally directed the carrying out of certain details." He asserted that "state employees using state automobiles were active in rounding up reluctant witnesses," and that in the early stages expenses were defrayed by Charles Ward. In effect, this motion brought the issue of state suppression of his newspaper into the case.[53]

The *New York Times* story covering Walter's request for change of venue was longer than those in the Minneapolis newspapers, and it was the first to report that information leading to the arrests had stemmed from an anonymous letter left on a desk in the Hennepin County child welfare office. *Editor & Publisher* repeated Walter's charge that a witness (Jenny) who had testified against him before the grand jury had "been threatened with a jail sentence if she changes a story which she has since and frequently admitted to be false."[54]

When the ACLU board met on September 9, Walter's case was on the agenda. Although board members had not received the *Midwest Americans* Edith sent, Marlen Pew of *Editor & Publisher* told them he had made a thorough investigation and was convinced that the case was a frame-up. But the board decided to wait to hear from George Leonard.[55]

The board contacted Leonard on September 11, asking him to reply by collect wire. Leonard replied by mail, not wire, on the 14th, advising the board not to intervene. He wrote that he had been given access to the grand jury indictment a month earlier and had access to an affidavit from one of the girls. (This affidavit disappeared from the files before the case was heard in court.) Had it been a frame-up, he wrote, the authorities would have acted earlier.[56] By return mail, the ACLU asked Leonard to complete a full investigation before Monday, September 23, when the board would reach its final decision.

On September 16, the trial date that had been set in August, Walter appeared before Judge Paul Guilford to submit once again his motion for a change of venue and to ask for funds to bring in witnesses. Judge Guilford set a hearing on this petition for September 28.

That same day, Walter telegraphed President Roosevelt, protesting the restoring of citizenship to Charles Ward (convicted felons lost some civil rights at that time). Walter believed that Ward had financed the frame-up, and that he had "constant contacts and close connections" with members of the Twin Cities under-world.[57]

In the meantime, *Editor & Publisher* reported that although it had not asked for funds for Walter, it had received two donations — a money order for $48.28 and a ten-dollar check from a New York City newspaperman who wrote that he had known Walter for many years and did not believe him guilty. This $58.28 constituted about half my parents' defense fund. Walter's sister, Madeleine Moly-neaux Liggett Clarke, had sent fifty dollars; Edith's sister, Caroline Fleischer, sent ten dollars.[58]

Roger Baldwin, back from Europe in October, found that the ACLU board had not heard further from Leonard and consequently had approved Leonard's earlier recommendation not to participate. Troubled by Leonard's letter, Baldwin wrote, "Is there not, in your judgement, some political animus behind the prosecution?" He wondered, astutely, if there were any connection between the child welfare people and Walter's political opponents, and whether political opponents might have taken advantage of irresponsible charges. "It hardly seems credible," he wrote, "that an offense of this sort could have been committed in the presence of another person and that, if any force was used, as I believe the state charges, that both girls should have kept quiet about the matter for over a year." Baldwin was slowly moving toward the idea of helping Walter obtain a fair trial.[59]

Home Life

In September, when Wallace and I returned from Wisconsin to begin school, I was shocked by the dilapidated Schall house on Portland Avenue. Though Edith had told us about the move, I was not prepared for our parents' evident tension. It was not a happy time. I did not like the house, and I worried about the mail-bags in the attic and the hordes of people who had not received their mail. But even though I was a snoopy child, I did not go so far as to open official post of-fice bags. Much later, I realized that the bags probably contained franked letters that Schall had failed to mail.

Two youths — Farmer-Laborite idealists from rural counties who had come to help out with the *Midwest American* — shared the Portland Avenue house with us while Wallace and I were there; they may have been the employees who is-sued the *Midwest American* during Walter's trial, with an apologetic note that it was not up to its usual standard. One of them, a string bean about twenty years old, must have had a young sister of his own. He used to play catch with me in front of the house. When he left for a weekend, my parents gloomily prophesied that he had been "scared off." I innocently reported this to him when he came back from his family visit, and my parents, upset, suggested that I tell him it was my thought, not theirs. I was dismayed. My parents had always told me to tell the truth, and I tried, most of the time. And, while I had told a few childish lies, I knew I couldn't carry that one off.

Friday, September 20, was my tenth birthday—a milestone I had looked forward to. We shared chocolate cake and ice cream that evening with our two boarders. It was a rather subdued celebration, although everyone tried hard. My mother promised that we would go shopping on Saturday for new clothes.

I had hit a growth spurt that summer—I always grew more in the country—and returned to Minneapolis bursting out of my clothes. And, at ten, I had very definite ideas of what I wanted. Poring over the Sears Roebuck catalog at the farm, I had fallen in love with a pair of suede shoes with tongues and tassels—Scottish kilties, I think they were called—and a suede jacket that cost five or seven dollars—a lot of money when I could buy my mother a "lovely lace jabot" from the catalog for nineteen cents. I had not quite decided whether my ideal jacket was rust or golden brown, but the catalog, to help me decide, always opened at the jacket illustrations.

Edith and I went shopping the morning after my birthday. I felt grown-up running in and out of stores with her and enjoyed having her undivided attention. We both felt bad that there were no affordable Scottish kilties in Minneapolis. We had to settle for Buster Browns again. I despised them.

With our poverty, we had little choice of clothing stores. We had an account at an expensive women's dress shop in exchange for printing its advertising brochures. It was, Edith assured me, one of the best in town, and it was—for her. She had an extensive choice of expensive-looking outfits. We decided on a gray shadow-stripe suit with a three-quarter coat and a fitted skirt. She wore it every day to Walter's trial. In back, we found a selection of children's clothes, considerably less glamorous than my mother's options. There were no suede jackets in any color, although we did find a navy skirt and a matching striped sweater and a pretty challis dress with a lace collar. Nice, if not what I wanted. I knew that with all her problems, my mother sympathized with my ten-year-old vanity. And I had seen kids my age wearing dresses made of flour sacks; I told myself that I should try not to be selfish.

At the start of October, we moved to our third and final dwelling in Minneapolis, a solid red brick apartment building at 1825 Second Avenue South. It fronted on a little park whose frost-laden trees looked like glass ornaments that icy winter. In the park, just in front of our building, there was a little hill with an artesian well. Whatever the weather—and it was always cold or wet or both when we lived there—Edith insisted that we get our water from this well. My parents did not trust the city water supply, Mississippi River water loaded with chlorine, and had written editorials and printed articles citing typhoid cases in Minneapolis. They advocated a water supply either from Lake Superior or from artesian wells. We were not alone: sometimes as many as thirty people lined up to get pure water from the well.

Wally and I whined a lot over this chore. He hated waiting in line, but I thought it was worse when I was alone. When people were there, I could always count on someone to pump the water for me. When I was alone, I had to take the mittens off my nearly frozen fingers to pump the recalcitrant handle. It was enough to bring tears to my eyes—even when no one was looking.

Our apartment, on the second floor, faced the narrow alley behind the building where we parked our car. Still, I liked it better than the ramshackle old Schall house, with its peeling wallpaper and feeling of abandonment. Our new apartment was cozier, and it raised my spirits when we moved in.

Aside from the personal and political awkwardness of living in Senator Schall's old house, I suspect my parents moved because the apartment building seemed more secure. What I did not know was that I had been threatened with kidnapping. Criminals wanted to hinder Edith's very active defense of my father; hence the threats. This may be why, shortly after we moved, Edith hired Amanda Ganz as an after-school maid. Amanda, sort of a poor family's au pair, was a bossy teenager who was going to beauty school. I didn't appreciate her presence.

The previous tenants had left behind some furniture too good to throw out and too old to move—a supremely comfortable old chair with a broken leg and a spindly little desk that I claimed as my own. In the desk, I found and also claimed a lovely green fountain pen with a flexible nib, along with a phonograph record that tickled my fancy: "You can tell a man who boozes by the company he chooses—and the pig got up and slowly walked away." Depending upon which books we needed to consult, we propped up the broken chair either with the complete works of Shakespeare or with two volumes of the *Encyclopedia Britannica*. To me the chair seemed just right for our family. We might be poor and shabby, but we were certainly cultured.

During that period, spies watched our family and our visitors closely. One bright October Sunday, Edith wrote, we went for a drive and stopped at the airport so that Wallace could watch planes land and take off. Word went back that Edith had left for the East with us, leaving Walter, trial pending, to his fate.[60]

Friends visiting from Wisconsin were followed when they drove around Minneapolis on a sight-seeing tour. Others — a farmer from Kandiyohi County, a miner from the Iron Range, and a minister from the Dakota line — were questioned reproachfully after they returned home by members of the highway department who wanted to know why they had visited Walter Liggett.

One Saturday, when one of our printers did some grocery shopping, my parents drove him home and Walter helped him carry in the groceries. Three days later, the printer's home was entered and ransacked. Every bureau drawer was pulled out, but nothing was taken. Apparently, the burglars were looking for documents they thought Walter had hidden there.[61]

City Hall and the ACLU

On Monday, October 14, Walter, acting as his own attorney, petitioned again that his trial be moved. He could not expect a fair trial in Hennepin County, he argued, since the charges against him were the result of a political frame-up perpetrated by county officials. Since he was "almost penniless," he also asked the state to pay the expenses for his witnesses. The county attorney's office protested that the affidavits Walter submitted did not constitute legal grounds for removing the trial to another court; the judge took the motion under advisement.[62]

Edith, who had vowed that she would never again ask the ACLU for help, was getting frantic. She wrote a five-page letter to the ACLU secretary, Lucille Milner, urging her to look into ACLU files on Olson and the gag-law case:

> Going back to the records of your own organization, you will find that Walter has always been a radical, that he has aided you in numerous cases. . . . He has never before asked aid from you and would not do so now if we were not so terribly poor that the frameup finds us unable to even afford a lawyer.
>
> The shop makes barely enough to keep going. There are many weeks when, after meeting the payroll and allowing for paper stock for the following week, I have less than ten dollars left for the support of my family . . . two growing children of ten and twelve.[63]

Edith pointed out that Sacco and Vanzetti were jailed not for being anarchists, but were charged with murder. Tom Mooney was in prison not for organizing a street railroad strike, but was charged with dynamiting a parade. Did the ACLU, she wondered, expect the racketeers to acknowledge that Walter was being framed because he was exposing corruption and trying to win the Farmer-Labor Party back to the radicals who founded it?

The question is not whether Walter has committed the weird combination crime of abduction, sodomy, and exhibitionism. . . . It is whether Floyd B. Olson, because he is governor of a state and pretends to be a radical, can disgrace an innocent man, wreck his family and put out of business the only paper in the state which dares expose his corrupt acts in public office, and find the American Civil Liberties Union unwilling to aid his victim.[64]

On at least one occasion, I was dragged along when my parents drove to Austin to investigate the case. I remember being sent outside to play with Jenny's younger brother. We agreed, silently and amicably, that we did not want to play with each other, but stood side by side, munching cookies and staring at our parents as they stood on the porch, shaking their heads and commiserating over young people nowadays.

George Leonard was still writing Roger Baldwin that he did not believe that there was political enmity behind the prosecution, and that the prosecuting attorney had told him there was no opposition to Walter's motion for change of venue. In truth, the assistant county attorney had just opposed it.[65]

Further, Leonard wrote, the two social workers involved, Florence Davis and Mabel Whipple, were Republicans. But Davis, interviewed by a reporter from the *Chicago Tribune,* called herself a longtime friend of Governor Olson and said she had worked closely with him when he was county attorney.[66]

As a clincher, Leonard wrote that it was hardly conceivable that Ellis, a leading Farmer-Laborite, could be framed. But the bitter controversies within the Independent Union of All Workers and on the *Austin American* were unraveling in the governor's office. In June, the Newspaper Committee of the Farmer-Labor Association had supplied money to Ellis's opponents at the *Austin American,* while unionists loyal to Ellis threatened to boycott the paper. Only two days before Goff filed charges, the IUAW Action Committee had demanded that O. J. Fosso, Emil Olson, and Frank Prochaska be fired from the Newspaper Board.[67]

Vince Day's files were filled with denunciations of Ellis, supplied by union opponents. And Day, who spent the evening of October 5 meeting with Ellis's enemies in Austin, had referred to Ellis's "irresponsible leadership" of the union in a memo to Governor Olson just the day before.[68]

On October 21 Edith sent another long letter to Baldwin, telling him that the county office had made excellent use of time while the case was being delayed: Two friends of Jenny's, who had been ready to testify that she had told them that there was absolutely nothing to the story, had vanished from town.

Several other witnesses had had their lips sealed with state jobs. Francine, the supposed assault victim, had been kept incommunicado since her return from California. Edith wrote:

> Now that Goff's office has discovered that Jenny was talking and that her parents do not believe the story, they [Goff's office] have taken her into custody also. In order to keep both girls properly intimidated, there is a two-year suspended sentence over Jenny's head, and a secret indictment for sodomy — with a possible twenty-year sentence — over Francine.
>
> If I had been able to have an investigator on the job three months ago . . . there would be affidavits from all these people, so at the trial they could be confronted with their sworn statements. . . . When I hunt out any person, it is merely proclaiming to the Olson forces what I know — and they can rush in with a job to silence the man or woman.[69]

That same day, the judge granted Walter's request for a change of venue and ordered the trial to proceed immediately. My parents still had no funds for a lawyer or an investigator.[70]

Although Leonard continued to counsel noninvolvement, Baldwin was slowly making up his mind to help. "Whatever the facts," he wrote Leonard, "you will, of course, agree that Liggett is entitled to the services of a lawyer and investigator. Even a common criminal should have that much protection."[71] Edith wired V. F. Calverton, asking him to find out whether Baldwin really would help. Her follow-up letter to Calverton continued:

> Walter will win the case, even unaided, but if we have no aid now or during the trial, I'm afraid it will mean that the *Midwest American* will be put out of business. That is what Olson wants, and what Roger [Baldwin] with his deep feeling for the freedom of the press, doesn't choose to protect. . . .
>
> Where Roger Baldwin has done Walter a terrible injustice was by his refusal when I first asked aid, to pay for an investigator. The Olson gang have had four months to bribe with jobs and intimidate — it makes it much harder for us.[72]

Assault and Battery

On Thursday morning, October 24, Walter once again appeared before the court asking for funds for twenty-three witnesses.[73] That evening, he went to a meeting at the Radisson Hotel. He arrived home around 2:00 A.M., severely beaten and nearly unconscious.

There were even more accounts of this beating than there were participants, since several of them changed their stories. Some accounts were screened through the Minneapolis police and through newspapers, both partisan and nonpartisan. Everyone had a story; everyone had an angle.

All stories agree that Walter was introduced to Isadore Blumenfield—Kid Cann—by Annette Fawcett in her suite at the Radisson Hotel. Annette Fawcett was the divorced wife of magazine mogul Captain Billy Fawcett and a former mistress of Governor Olson. Many believed that the affair and the divorce were related. The Fawcetts had often entertained Olson at their resort, Breezy Point on Pelican Lake, which featured roulette, slot machines, illegal liquor, and fly-in starlets as well as the lure of the outdoors.[74] Now single, Annette Fawcett ran a sort of Twin Cities salon at the Radisson, where she entertained politicos, lawyers, businessmen, newspapermen, labor leaders, and, apparently, gangsters. (Edith wrote that the salon was frequented by Floyd Olson, Chief Justice John Devaney, Gil Carmichael, and other members of the All-Party gang.)[75]

Accounts of how Walter came to be at Annette Fawcett's apartment differed. My parents said she had asked Walter to come; other newspapers initially quoted her as saying that Walter had invited himself over. My parents reported that Kid Cann had attempted to bribe Walter and then led seven gangsters to beat him up when he refused the bribe. The Minneapolis police were quoted as saying that Walter had solicited Cann for a bribe and then started a drunken brawl.[76]

Edith's account appeared as the headline story in the *Midwest American* of October 30, 1935: "Police Protect Kid Cann after Attack on Liggett: Gangsters Beat Editor When He Refuses Bribe." Edith's story, which provided detailed accounts of other attempted bribes, was probably unjust in assuming that Annette Fawcett had set Walter up to be beaten; she does not seem to have been vindictive, but only a person ready to do favors for friends. Edith wrote that Fawcett had repeatedly phoned the *Midwest American* asking for Walter and had finally left her telephone number on Wednesday, October 23. When Walter returned the call, Fawcett told him that she had vital information on his trial and asked him over to her suite to discuss it. He made a tentative appointment for Friday. Next day, he recalled that he had planned to attend a local newspaper banquet on Friday. When he phoned to cancel, Fawcett urged him to come to the Radisson that evening. Apparently, it was a pretext to introduce him to Cann at Cann's request.

When Walter arrived at the Radisson, it turned out that Fawcett had no new information but was very sympathetic, saying she knew the case was a frame-up.

She suggested that Walter needed an attorney. Walter told her that it would cost fifteen hundred dollars, and he had no way to raise that sum. Fawcett indicated that she could get him counsel for nothing — from a firm of attorneys that he did not trust. Shortly after Walter's arrival, Fawcett received a telephone call from Kid Cann. Walter heard her say "The gentleman is here now" before she turned to tell him that Cann was on the phone. When she asked Walter if he wanted to talk to Kid Cann, Walter replied that he had nothing to say to Cann then or any time.

In the meantime, two men arrived: Fawcett's secretary, Felix Doran, and a Democratic politician whom Edith did not name because she considered him an innocent bystander. Walter discussed politics with the politician while Fawcett talked on the phone. Around eleven o'clock, Kid Cann made his appearance; it was the first time that Walter had met him. Soon afterward, the politician left.

In Edith's account, Kid Cann asked Walter why he was attacking him in the *Midwest American.* It was nothing personal, Walter replied, but he was tired of seeing a gang of crooks run the city of Minneapolis, and he intended to expose Floyd Olson's connections with the Syndicate. Kid Cann suggested that if the *Midwest American* would "lay off," Walter would be "taken care of." Walter laughed and told Cann that he did not accept bribes. If he took money from racketeers, he declared, he would be worse than the racketeers.

Suddenly, with no warning, Kid Cann tried to strike Walter while he was seated in a chair. Not wishing to cause a disturbance in Fawcett's apartment, Walter merely shifted his head and grabbed Kid Cann by the elbows and set him back in his own chair. Shortly after this, Walter announced that he was leaving, and Kid Cann, who had apologized profusely, offered to drive him home. "Very foolishly," Edith wrote, Walter accepted his offer. As they drove out Hennepin Avenue, Cann suggested that they have one last drink and forget their hard feelings. The two men, along with Felix Doran, stopped at a nightclub where bootlegger Brownie Bronstein was sitting at a table. Bronstein repeated Cann's bribe offer, and Walter again turned it down.

At that point, Cann and Bronstein attacked him, with several others joining in. Walter was knocked down but had regained his feet when the proprietor and waiters intervened. When he went outside to catch a taxi, a group of men swarmed out of the café, yelling, "It's Liggett — the fellow who is giving us all the heat. Let's beat him up!" When Walter tried to enter a parked cab, the gang shouted to the driver not to open the door. Walter next tried to get into a passing cab, with the same result.

In the alley outside the café, at least seven men attacked him. Backed into a doorway, Walter defended himself as well as he could, managing at least to keep on his feet. A heavyset man ran up shouting, "I am your friend, Liggett. Come on, we'll clean up these s.o.b.'s," but as Walter turned to face another attacker, the supposed rescuer knocked him to the pavement. Then the entire gang started kicking at his prostrate body, jumping on his chest, kicking his groin, head, and face. A crowd collected, and Walter thought a policeman appeared on its outskirts. Regaining his feet, he staggered into a cab. The driver drove him home without charge and left him at our apartment door, nearly unconscious.[77]

I heard my father come home from this beating. I had developed a habit of lying in bed awake, eavesdropping on my parents. An intermittent insomniac, I was on some level aware of my mother's worries. Around two, I heard my father come in and my mother exclaim, "My God, Walter, what happened?" After that, they dropped their voices to a murmur and I went back to sleep. Edith later wrote that she telephoned three times for an ambulance and was told each time that the only available ambulance was out on another call. Finally, almost two hours later, one arrived and took Walter to Swedish Hospital.

I did not hear him leave, nor did I see him until just before the trial, when he still had a black eye and moved as if he were in pain. All stories agree that Walter, a trained boxer in good physical condition, was badly beaten about the neck, chest, and face. No one disagrees that he came home with a black eye, an ear nearly torn off, a split lip, a tooth kicked out, his head and face battered, and his ribs severely bruised.

Years later, going over the clippings in the Minneapolis Public Library, I saw a picture of him in his hospital bed—bandaged, pugnacious, with a black eye—and, fifty-one years after the fact, felt sick to my stomach. He was such a big man and had seemed so invincible. How could they do this to him? And I was surprised to see my father characterized as a drunken brawler. Both he and Uncle Bob were gifted amateur boxers; both taught boxing. When my dad showed me how to box, his emphasis was on the rules. And although he liked to have a drink after work with friends and newspaper buddies, we hardly had liquor in the house, and for long periods of time he didn't drink at all.

The first two detectives who came to the hospital seemed sympathetic and honest, Edith wrote. They took Walter's statement, asked if he would sign a complaint, promised to return with one for him to sign—and never came back. Edith surmised that when they returned to headquarters, they had been instructed to do nothing.[78]

Indignantly, Edith called police headquarters and managed to arrange an interview with the captain of detectives, who seemed sneering and unsympathetic.

He told her that Walter was the aggressor in a drunken brawl and claimed that Walter had solicited a bribe and repeatedly attacked Kid Cann in Fawcett's apartment. The police told Edith that both Cann and Bronstein denied attacking Walter on the street. And, despite her pleas, the police refused to bring a complaint to the hospital for Walter to sign.[79]

Kid Cann had a different version. The police told reporters that he claimed Walter had asked him for fifteen hundred dollars for trial expenses, but the internal police write-up told a different story. In the internal interview, Cann said he had met Fawcett recently and asked her to help persuade Walter to stop attacking him. Fawcett, he said, had arranged for Walter to come to her hotel room.[80]

The police also interviewed Fawcett; the *Chicago Tribune* reported that she told the police Walter had asked to come to her apartment at the Radisson. Still, in a police interview after Walter was murdered, she testified that Cann had asked her to introduce him to Walter. She and Cann agreed that Cann phoned and was invited to come up. Then, she said, the two men had a long, sometimes heated conversation and a few drinks. Finally, she had asked both of them to leave. Neither Cann's written interview nor Fawcett's interview mentions any bribe proposed by Walter.[81]

According to the *Chicago Tribune,* Walter first told his story to night captain Frank Rickman, then to police captain James Mullen — who later investigated Walter's murder. And Cann was interviewed by his old friend Joseph Lehmeyer, the former police chief who had been demoted in 1933 after testifying for Cann.[82]

The *New York Times* repeated Walter's story, adding that he planned to swear out warrants for Cann and Bronstein when he got out of the hospital.[83] The *Minneapolis Star* evenhandedly published both Walter's account and the denials and countercharges.[84] The *Minneapolis Tribune,* apparently quoting Cann, claimed that the fracas began when Walter annoyed other customers in the Hennepin Avenue café by offering to display his pugilistic prowess.[85]

The *Minnesota Leader* had its own gaudy interpretation, featuring multiple headlines studded with quotation marks: "Liggett Beaten Up after Attempting 'Shake-Down': Again Charges 'Frame' — Story of 'Attack by Foes' Disproven; Asks $1500 for Editorial Silence." It began: "Walter W. Liggett, Minneapolis publisher and Tom Schall's latest hurler of invective against Governor Floyd B. Olson, has been 'framed' again. He has a very sore jaw, lacks a tooth or two, and suffers from sundry bruises and contusions, as the police reporters say, all because he butted in on someone else's party." This account stated that Walter had invited himself to the apartment of a "prominent woman writer in the Radisson hotel one evening . . . not at all in accordance with her wishes," and ordered a quart of liquor sent up. He became abusive and lunged at Kid Cann, who was able to ward him off.[86]

"Finally," the *Leader* continued, "they 'got down to brass tacks,' witnesses, in signed statements, declared Liggett demanded $1,500 from Blumenfeld [*sic*] as a price for which he would cease editorial attacks upon the latter." Although these signed statements have never emerged, this article seems to be the Farmer-Labor source for the allegations of blackmail that linger on.

By this time, the *Leader* claimed, Walter had drunk most of the quart of liquor. Although Fawcett's secretary was instructed to take him home, Walter insisted on leaving with Cann, and, once they were in the car, wanted more to drink. He ordered Cann to stop at the Hennepin Avenue café, where he forced himself on a party of revelers that included Bronstein. Bronstein objected to Walter's approaches to his female companion and beat him up. "Liggett wended his way home, then three hours later went to the hospital for treatment and a place to tell his story of being attacked by seven men."

Editor & Publisher reported that Walter was still in the hospital with pleurisy and that the police had cleared Bronstein and Cann. A lengthy statement by Walter read in part: "The failure of the Minneapolis police to arrest Isadore Bloomfield [*sic*], alias Kid Cann, and 'Brownie' Bronstein, the leaders of the gang of thugs who attacked me, is precisely what I might have expected. Apparently, the only activity of the police to date has been to aid my assailants in cooking up a weird tale of an attempt to solicit a bribe and a drunken attack they claim I made upon a gang of seven gangsters."[87]

A *New York Times* story pointed out that both Cann and Bronstein were bootleggers who had served time in prison and were barred by federal, state, and city liquor regulations from the liquor industry. Still, Walter noted, Cann and Bronstein controlled at least six retail outlets in Minneapolis and were gaining control of the local retail trade with the connivance of the Farmer-Labor majority on the Minneapolis city council and the assent of the Olson-appointed state liquor controller. Walter claimed he was beaten because he had exposed this situation in the *Midwest American,* and he urged a legislative inquiry into liquor control.

"If the decent civic organizations of Minneapolis will not act and the state legislature's leaders sidetrack the investigation," Walter said, "I intend to appeal to [U.S.] Attorney General Cummings to send federal investigators into this city — as was done in Chicago — so that the local underworld may be cleaned up just as the United States government wiped out the Capone gang."[88]

From his hospital bed, Walter sent an SOS to old newspaper friends to come to Minneapolis to help Edith run the *Midwest American.* Frank Orsini came from Cleveland with a friend, but after they learned what Walter was doing, declined to help: "We simply did not have the kind of courage for a battle of that kind. We also said we thought he was a damned fool to keep on with it himself, for he had no chance of really getting anything done. He laughed and said he didn't agree with us."[89]

Walter remained in bed until his trial, leaving Edith to raise funds, investigate the case, and manage somehow to produce the *Midwest American* and the faltering *West Lake Neighborhood News*—and, of course, to look after me and Wallace. Somehow, Edith managed to dig up and mail to Roger Baldwin at the ACLU a comprehensive record of Kid Cann's criminal career. She had researched it "at intervals between doing housework, taking care of Walter, getting out a paper, and assuring all and sundry that the *Midwest American* would come out as usual."[90]

Walter's beating seemed to be the jolt that Baldwin needed. "Will endeavor to raise fund of $500 next week among personal sympathizers," he wired. "Cannot guarantee anything. Try to get further postponement in view of Walter's injuries. My sympathy."[91]

"I do hope that you will be able to raise the fund," Edith wrote. "I'm waiting to hear from you almost prayerfully."

9. On Trial

You, of course, know what it is to be poor — but to be penniless, as we were almost continuously when in this state, never to know when or where rent was coming from, and yet to run a paper fighting a ruthless political machine — I still marvel that it could be done.

— Edith Liggett, letter to V. F. Calverton, January 3, 1936

Since Walter was too ill to get out of bed, his friend Joseph Granbeck went to court on October 31 to ask the judge to postpone the trial to December 2 and to postpone a hearing on witnesses until November 9. Granbeck brought a letter from Walter's doctor, who wrote that Walter was "badly bruised and battered up," had great difficulty breathing, and was "confined to bed most of the time and should remain quiet for several more days." The judge merely asked the county attorney to respond on November 2.[1]

The next day, after Edith secured another statement from the doctor, she telegraphed Roger Baldwin that "now Walter is injured, Goff's office is trying to force immediate trial."[2] The ACLU files of November 1935 contain a flurry of telegrams between Edith and Baldwin, telegrams from Baldwin to George Leonard, and Leonard's leisurely replies. As always, Leonard was absolutely the wrong person to consult; he saw Olson at least once a week, and on October 29 had helped Olson answer queries from a national correspondent.[3]

On November 2, Granbeck again asked the judge to delay the trial to allow Walter time to recover, and to provide travel funds for character witnesses (the state had spent substantial amounts of money transporting and maintaining prosecution witnesses).[4] The judge declined to postpone the trial and denied the motion for funds, but said Walter could renew his motion before the trial judge.[5]

Judge Albert H. Enerson of Marshall, Minnesota, who worked half-time out of the county, offered to handle the case if the governor approved. A strict Methodist and a Prohibitionist, Enerson was reputed to be a convicter. Edith had heard that he had told two reporters he believed Walter was guilty.[6]

When Walter appeared before Judge Enerson to renew his motion for a postponement, his ribs and chest were still so sore that he could not stand up straight. His face was badly bruised and he still had a black eye. But Enerson ordered the trial to start immediately. Although he offered Walter a lawyer, the lawyer would have had only two hours to prepare. Walter declined.[7]

Walter, acting as his own attorney, asked prospective jurors if they had any business with the state or knew anybody on the state payroll or connected with the state government. On the first day, he asked if they knew Governor Olson or Charles A. Ward. The next day, he added the names of Vince Day and state purchasing agent Carl Erickson.[8]

In New York City, Baldwin finally began to raise funds for Walter's defense.

By noon the next day, selection of the jury — nine men and three women — was complete. Edith described the jury as "unusually intelligent, yet one that represents every walk of life."[9] Walter told the judge that "unless the jury is locked up you may as well save the state the expense of a trial and sentence me now. This is a political case and unless I have a locked jury, I am doomed."[10] The judge agreed to sequester the jury each night.

Although the prosecution objected strenuously, Judge Enerson also agreed to allow reporters into the court. Edith's efforts to get out-of-town reporters to cover the trial were fairly successful: *Editor & Publisher,* the *New York Times,* the *Chicago Tribune,* and the Associated Press were there. While the *St. Paul Dispatch* covered the case well, coverage in the other Twin Cities papers was scanty. Except for the *Minnesota Leader,* union and radical papers did not touch it at all. From her seat at the defense table, Edith, wearing her new shadow-striped suit and a black velvet beret, took notes for the *Midwest American.*[11]

Prosecuting attorneys Arthur Markve and Howard Van Lear of Hennepin County and Mike Kincaid of Ramsey County argued that Walter had committed a statutory offense in Frank Ellis's hotel room on March 22, 1934. At first, the *Chicago Tribune* reported, it seemed to be an "open and shut case."[12] As the trial proceeded, the state's case proved to be replete with lost documents, false identities, and missing witnesses.

The first state witness, Eleanor Newton, assistant cashier at the Ritz Hotel, verified the hotel register, which showed that Ellis, Francine, and Jenny had registered in adjoining rooms on March 22, several hours after Walter had registered at a distant room on another floor. On cross-examination, over the objections of the state, Newton testified that Walter had visited the hotel two or three days a week for months prior to the alleged offense, and that he came to the hotel approximately once a week for nearly a year afterwards. (Until we moved from

Rochester to Minneapolis, Walter traveled to the Twin Cities every week to keep up with state political news.)[13] When Walter asked whether anyone at the hotel had ever complained at any time of his conduct, the prosecution's objections kept Newton from answering.

Francine, now nineteen and the supposed victim of an "unnatural act" at the age of seventeen, was the next witness. Edith, in sob-sister tradition, described her as a "well-developed blonde . . . of an obvious type" who told her story "with an affectation of simpering modesty that created amused snickers among newspapermen attending the trial."

Francine said that she had asked Ellis to take her to Minneapolis to spend the night with relatives, but when she and Jenny arrived at the Ritz sometime between 8:00 and 8:30 P.M., she made no effort to get in touch with these relatives. After Ellis registered them, the three went up to their adjoining rooms, washed up, then went to the hotel restaurant, the Spanish Village. They spent about forty-five minutes there and then went back upstairs about ten o'clock. She and Jenny bathed together while Ellis was in the adjoining room. Francine put on a pair of pajamas and went into Ellis's room with the fully dressed Jenny. At that time, Ellis told them that Walter was coming up to visit.

According to Francine, Walter arrived at 10:30 and drank wine from a quart bottle that Ellis had picked up en route. He talked about stories he had written for the *Saturday Evening Post* (a magazine for which he had never written). Then, Francine continued, he asked her to go with him into the girls' room, where he spoke to her poetically of the delights of "unnatural love" and performed an indecent act. "Shocked and horrified," she returned to the room a few minutes later and tricked him into performing the act again so that Jenny could witness it. She claimed that she and Jenny spent the night in the same bed as Frank Ellis, but, since they were sound sleepers, Ellis left sometime in the morning without waking them.

Jenny testified next. Edith described her as tall and dark, "pathetic and even appealing . . . torn between distaste for the lies she was forced to tell and fear of going to prison." Jenny's wrists still bore the marks of a suicide attempt three weeks earlier. Edith, who had talked to Jenny three times in Austin, wrote that the prosecution had brutally used Jenny's earlier indiscretions to force perjury. Jenny, Edith wrote, had told her that nothing improper had happened to her and that she had never heard any complaints from Francine. When Edith asked why she lied to the grand jury, Jenny had looked at her in terror and said, "I've got to tell that story or go to jail for years and years."

Jenny's story echoed Francine's in every detail; in fact, they used identical phrases. But while Francine had smirked at the jury and winked at acquaintances,

Jenny sat quiet and downcast. During cross-examination, Jenny kept looking toward Mabel Whipple and Florence Davis, as if seeking answers. She proved to be less adept than Francine under cross-examination, admitting that she had never mentioned the incident to anyone until a "total stranger" confronted her in March or April 1935 as she was hanging clothes out in her backyard in Austin. This stranger accused her of being "on a party with Frank Ellis and Walter Liggett" and threatened to tell her parents "all about her" unless she signed a statement. He said he was a bill collector and that Walter owed "someone a lot of money."[14]

At first, Jenny identified the persons who took her to the Hennepin County attorney's office as Mr. and Mrs. Johnson. Walter's cross-examination revealed that "the Johnsons" were really Emil Olson, the state oil inspector at Austin, then on the board of the embattled *Austin American,* and his sister. Jenny admitted that the Olsons registered her at the Nicollet Hotel in Minneapolis under an assumed name.[15] Although Emil Olson had been subpoenaed, he was not present, so Jenny could not identify him. At this point, Jenny recalled that the man who called himself a bill collector was actually Per Larson, an assistant Hennepin County attorney.

Jenny testified (her account varied somewhat in the subsequent Ellis trial) that they met attorney Lindahl O. Johnson on a street corner and moved to a café, the Covered Wagon, where she had a few drinks. Then she was taken to Johnson's office. There, at his request, she signed an undated affidavit (which she told my parents she had not read). Johnson told her that the purpose of this affidavit was to get Walter to pay his bills.[16] Lindahl Johnson was the All-Party attorney who had engineered a suit against my parents in April 1935 and whom Vince Day had recommended for state employment in June.[17]

Walter was not able to lay the legal groundwork to show that this affidavit (which disappeared sometime before the trial) had been used to bully Jenny into perjuring herself. The judge similarly overruled his efforts to introduce testimony that she was under a two-year suspended sentence for delinquency.[18]

A few weeks after she signed the affidavit, Jenny said, two Hennepin County social workers — Whipple and Davis — came to Austin claiming that they were "wealthy society women" looking for a maid. Her father refused to let her go with them then, but they returned soon afterward and took her to Minneapolis. My parents believed that the social workers and the county attorney's office used Jenny's first affidavit to force her to sign a statement that became the basis for Walter's arraignment. Later — after the social workers brought Francine back from California — the story and the indictments were altered.[19]

Walter launched a twofold defense, denying the charges and declaring that he could show why "certain powerful political enemies have sought to destroy me and stop my newspaper."[20] As Walter tried to outline his case, the prosecution objected repeatedly, interrupting almost every sentence. Judge Enerson sustained most objections and told Walter to limit his questions to the matter of his defense.[21] Throughout the trial, Walter was never permitted to introduce evidence that state officials had participated in a frame-up and never succeeded in his attempts to subpoena either Emil Olson or Lindahl Johnson, although both worked for the state.

Mattie Fairbanks, Walter's first witness, had known the girls well when she was Austin's police matron and probation officer, but Walter was not able to lay a legal foundation for her testimony, and it was stricken from the record.[22] Finally, after the judge had reprimanded him several times for his lack of knowledge of legal procedures, Walter asked for help. Judge Enerson was exasperated. "At the beginning of this trial and several times since," he complained, "I have offered you counsel at the expense of the state. I have named men and said you might have your choice, but you felt you didn't need an attorney."[23]

Walter asked the court to bear with him and to appoint Lyle Pettijohn as his attorney, though Pettijohn didn't fare much better with the next witness, Stella Rochford, the current police matron and probation officer in Austin. Asked what she knew about the two girls' reputation for veracity, she replied, "May I tell what I know about the case?" Markve and Van Lear objected vigorously, but she did manage to testify that the two young women had poor reputations.[24]

Next morning, one of Jenny's brothers testified that he heard Jenny tell Ellis that "nothing improper" happened at the Ritz Hotel. He recalled that Edith had talked to his sister three times and that he was present once.[25] Jenny's mother testified that her daughter had never complained to her, nor had she ever told her that the story was true. Jenny's father said that he knew nothing of the case until he was called to Minneapolis and asked to sign a complaint. At that time, Jenny told him it was true, but he had never asked for details.[26]

Frank Ellis testified that he went to Minneapolis to attend an evening union meeting on March 22, 1934, and that he gave Jenny and Francine a ride at their request. They arrived at the Ritz Hotel around 6:00 P.M. and the girls left the car to telephone relatives while he parked the car. When he joined them, they told him that they could not locate their relatives and would have to hitchhike back to Austin. By then it was dark and getting cold, and Ellis felt responsible for their welfare. He suggested that they stay all night and ride back with him the next morning. Their rooms were on a different hall, he testified, and he did not know theirs adjoined his through a common bathroom until he went upstairs with the girls and a bellboy. At that time, he gave the girls a dollar and told them to get something to eat and go to a movie.

Ellis went down alone to eat dinner at the Spanish Village, where he unexpectedly met Walter and got into a stormy argument with him about O. J. Fosso, the head of the Independent Union of All Workers. Walter accused Fosso of betraying the union, while Ellis defended Fosso, whom he then considered a friend. Ellis left for a union meeting. When he came back an hour later, Walter was still in the Spanish Village. They briefly resumed their argument, then agreed to meet in Ellis's room, where he had some papers that bore on the argument.

Ellis said that Walter came to his room about 9:30 and that beer was served. While they were talking, they heard a knock on the door and the two girls — neither in pajamas — entered from the hall. The men poured some beer for the girls and resumed their argument. After about an hour, Ellis told Walter he was tired and asked his three visitors to leave. Jenny and Francine left through the bathroom around eleven o'clock, and Walter left through the hall a few minutes later. Walter had never been out of his sight.

Ellis and Walter ate breakfast together in the hotel dining room the next morning. While they were eating, Jenny and Francine came in and sat down with them. Shortly after breakfast, Ellis, Jenny, and Francine left for Austin. They stopped at the capitol, where Ellis talked to Fosso for a few minutes, and arrived at Austin around noon.[27]

Prosecutor Arthur Markve took the tack that Ellis had been trying to frame someone by taking the young women to Minneapolis. During cross-examination he asked, "Had you talked with anybody and told them Liggett and the girls would be there?" and "Have you been framing with anybody [sic] in having the girls there?" Ellis responded, "Absolutely not!"[28]

Pettijohn put Walter on the stand to testify in his own defense. After briefly reviewing his career as a newspaperman and political investigator, Walter told of the events of March 22, 1934: He had spent nearly all afternoon in the governor's office discussing the *Austin American*. Around six o'clock, he had returned to the Ritz Hotel and read in his room until about 7:30, when he went to the dining room. He was sipping his drink and reading the paper in a booth when Frank Ellis came up behind him and slapped him on the shoulder. He thought this was about 7:45.

His testimony confirmed Ellis's exactly. He described the girls chatting and laughing at one end of Ellis's room while he and Ellis discussed union matters at the other end. He denied that he had ever left the room with either Francine or

Jenny, that either wore pajamas, and that he ever "touched either of the girls in any way, shape, or manner."[29] He did not see the young women again until the next morning, when they came down to the dining room where he and Ellis were still discussing the union and the *Austin American* over breakfast.[30]

Markve's cross-examination was brutal and, Edith wrote, "insulting." He "seemed to delight in rolling filthy words and phrases under his tongue." He tried to insinuate that since Walter was a writer, he had made up an alibi just as he would compose fiction. Walter defended himself vigorously, calling the charges against him "an unqualified falsehood." Several times Walter responded to Markve's questions with forceful statements: "That's a lie." "No, that is emphatically not true." "I did not." "No, no." "I was not and the answer applies to your whole list of assumptions."[31] Walter denied that he had told Ellis to "tell your story here in court just as I published it in my paper." But his statement that "I just wrote the truth of what happened" was stricken from the record.[32]

Midway through the trial, Baldwin wired Edith fifty dollars — the first money from the ACLU.[33]

On the final day of the trial, the defense opened with two new witnesses: a dietitian from St. Paul and a farmer from Baudette who had happened to be in the Spanish Village on the evening of March 22, 1934. The dietitian, Helen Orth (whom Edith described as a devout Catholic) testified that she arrived at the Ritz around 7:30 P.M. to meet her cousin, Harry Biesiot, who asked her to wait for him while he went upstairs to talk to friends. She sat down in a booth in the Spanish Village opposite the one occupied by Walter and saw Ellis come up and slap Walter on the back. Almost immediately, they began to argue. She heard swearing and the names of Fosso and Emil Olson. When Biesiot came back, she asked him if he knew the two men in the booth; he told her they were Walter Liggett and Frank Ellis. Ellis got up and left for a time, then returned and resumed the argument. Later Ellis left again, and shortly afterward Walter too left the dining room.[34]

Harry Biesiot, court commissioner of Lake of the Woods County and a farmer long active in Farmer-Labor politics, corroborated Orth's story and added that when he went up to his room, he saw Ellis going up alone on the elevator. Both Biesiot and Orth testified that they were in the Spanish Village until Walter and Ellis left the restaurant and that no women were with them at any time.[35]

That day, the judge allowed Joseph Granbeck to join Lyle Pettijohn as associate counsel for the defense. Walter had known both of them since boyhood, when they played on the same baseball team.[36]

Although Walter had not been able to obtain funds to bring in out-of-state character witnesses, the spectators' section of the courtroom was half filled with volunteer witnesses—so many that Judge Enerson ruled that only a limited number could appear. Walter's brother was the first. The others were Laurence Hodgson, five-time mayor of St. Paul; William A. Anderson, former Farmer-Labor mayor of Minneapolis; Roy Dunlap, managing editor of the *St. Paul Dispatch* and *Pioneer Press;* Sheldon R. Wilcox, an editor of farm publications; T. Howard Dolan, former secretary to Senator Henrik Shipstead; Dr. Ernest S. Powell, a St. Paul osteopath and civic leader; Sam Haislet, former secretary of the Minnesota Editorial Association; and Al Westerhagen of the Western Newspaper Union. Walter had worked with many of them in newspapers or as a Farmer-Labor publicist. Barbara Ritchie, the young reporter who had lived with us in Rochester and Red Wing, was the only woman to testify.[37] Although much of their testimony was stricken, Edith felt that collectively they had some impact on the jury.

Van Lear began his address to the jury by emphasizing that Walter was a writer and that writers throughout history had been addicted to sexual abnormalities. He compared Walter to Oscar Wilde, who died of a venereal disease after a life of dissipation. Pettijohn asked Van Lear to confine his remarks to the record.[38]

In his own hour-long address to the jury, Pettijohn reviewed the changes in the charge against Walter, which had started out in June as abduction and was changed in July to sodomy. Pettijohn declared that the state's case was based on "deliberate falsehood":

> It is easy to teach anyone to speak a piece, and these two girls were just repeating what they had been taught on the witness stand. . . . If it were not for the filthy nature of these charges, knowing Mr. Liggett as I do, and as the character witnesses who appeared for him do, I would be inclined to look upon the matter as a joke.[39]

Judge Enerson told the jurors to confine their deliberations to the testimony. He said there was no evidence of a frame-up or conspiracy before them. Then he added, "I want to say, however, that perjury has been committed in this case."[40] After he had read the indictment and defined the nature of the crime, Enerson looked sharply at the jury and remarked, "Offenses of this nature are not usually committed in the presence of eye witnesses."[41]

Edith collapsed in her chair when the jurors finally left the courtroom at 5:45 P.M. on Friday, November 8. She had supported Walter for five days at the defense table—even when gangsters had telephoned threats that they would kidnap me. Walter himself was barely able to rise from his chair.[42] Judge Enerson released Walter on his own recognizance until the verdict.[43]

The jury was out for more than twenty hours. When the jurors returned, Edith had her hand on Walter's shoulder. When the judge read the verdict—not guilty—she put her arm around Walter.[44] There may have been a flicker of a smile on the judge's face, and he assessed all trial costs against Hennepin County. My parents celebrated with friends—spied on by government officials—and Walter announced that he would ask for a grand jury investigation of the whole affair.[45]

The *Chicago Tribune*'s half-page story, subheaded "Case Goes Back to Bitter Political Break," included two paragraphs on the murder of Howard Guilford and a seven-paragraph history of Minnesota's gag law. The *Tribune* noted that Walter had never been charged with libel and that "the *Minnesota Leader*, organ of the Farmer-Laborites, has run flamboyant stories of Liggett's case in which he is referred to as a 'traitor' to Olson, indicating that some at least of the Olsonites were not at all displeased to have found him in such serious trouble."[46]

Editor & Publisher called the trial a "brazen use of political power to silence a free editor" and the charge "a palpable frameup from its start."[47] The *Minnesota Leader* reported only that Walter had conducted his own defense and that the telephone operator had testified that he was a frequent visitor at the Ritz; never did the *Leader* report that he had been acquitted.

Ironically, the first newspaper reviews of Sinclair Lewis's *It Can't Happen Here* had started to appear during Walter's trial. This political thriller transplanted fascist persecution of newspapermen to American soil in a gripping and believable account of a demagogic American dictator-president confronting a liberal Vermont editor in 1936. The editor, a man with the usual quota of human frailties and an instinctive fighter for a free press and a free society, was threatened, intimidated, and jailed under the most humiliating circumstances.[48]

Third-Party Overtures

While Walter was recovering from his injuries and Edith was struggling to keep our print shop alive, they learned that Governor Olson was planning to tout the third-party idea at the first public meeting of the Commonwealth Federation of New York. Edith wrote to V. F. Calverton:

> That damned arch-hypocrite, Floyd B. Olson, will be in New York November 15th as the guest speaker of Alfred Bingham's Commonwealth Federation. Part of the old game to round up the Third Party sentiment with radical speeches—then safely deliver it to Franklin D. next year.

He'll make a grand speech—he always does. I remember here last April, the day after he vetoed a bill—which had passed both houses of the legislature—... whereby crippled children would be given rehabilitation training; he got on the radio with an eloquent speech about the fact that youth must have its chance, and that he wanted a co-operative commonwealth in the future.

For the love of fair play, will you see that the s.o.b. has a bunch at the meeting to ask him about his record?... Since you've been getting the *Midwest American,* you know what to ask him about—and demand why he framed Walter.

Calverton underlined these last words.[49]

Alfred Bingham, editor of *Common Sense* and a strong advocate of a third party, regarded Floyd Olson as the American Commonwealth Federation's best asset in launching a third party.[50] The Commonwealth Federation and its New York affiliate went all out to promote Olson's visit, contacting every conceivable relevant organization from the Swedish Chamber of Commerce to the railroad brotherhoods. From Minnesota, Vince Day, striving for the maximum political advantage, sent a series of suggestions that included having New York Mayor Fiorello La Guardia greet Olson. One wire announced that the Minnesota Federation of Labor had endorsed the governor for any office that he desired.[51]

In his main speech to the federation, Olson declared that "the economic order we know as capitalism is no longer capable of supplying the vital needs of our party." Advocating a third party and a "completely new economic order," he predicted that the American Federation of Labor would soon become a unit in the third party. "When the time comes, in 1936 or 1940," he declared, "we will have a fighting force in the United States to elect members of Congress and possibly a President of the United States."[52]

As both Olson and the *New York Times* pointed out, a new party would require that all radical groups and factions unite—but the Socialist Party had voted that very week to expel all its left-wingers, many of whom had joined the party to subvert it.

Walter's editorial ultimately proved to be correct:

Olson, who can make marvelous speeches between elections in which he will picture a coming co-operative commonwealth in glowing terms, turns practical when election time rolls around. All he can gather of the Third Party movement will be led around the block with speeches, cheers and singing and then neatly delivered to Roosevelt on the eloquent plea that the New Deal is really the cooperative commonwealth and that now is the time for all good men to fight the Republicans.

Olson is an ambitious man. He wants to be Senator. Beyond that he wants to be in the cabinet, to become vice-president.

And, as he took what had been a splendid popular radical movement in Minnesota and wrecked it in order that he might build up a personal All-Party machine, Floyd Olson is now anxious to side track the Third Party movement in the United States—so that he can 'be taken care of'...if the Minnesota voters fail to send him to the Senate.[53]

Checking the Records: A Historical Aside

Researching the origin of the frame-up, I found the transcript of Ellis's trial and appeal, and I used Freedom of Information queries to get copies of Ellis's records from the Minnesota Bureau of Criminal Apprehension, the Board of Pardons, and the state prison system.

I suspected that some participants might be found in Austin. Surprisingly, it took only five phone calls and a few letters to locate one of the original complainants. I thought that historian Larry D. Englemann, a professor at San Jose State University who had written an article on the Hormel strike for *Labor History,* might have tapes of an Ellis interview. He didn't, but he recognized Walter's name and offered me his mother's address and telephone number in Austin, with the assurance that she knew just about everyone there. When I read her a list of Ellis's character witnesses, she referred me to John Winkles. At eighty-six, he was exceptionally alert and had a remarkable memory for detail. He told me that O. J. Fosso, whom he called "a company man who wanted to take over the union," had framed Ellis with the help of Emil Olson, whom he called an "oil smeller." They had had the help of a man named Hoffman, Winkles said, "the head of highway maintenance in Owatonna."[54]

After Ellis was convicted in a separate trial, Winkles and a co-unionist uncovered the Ellis-Liggett frame-up and helped get Ellis's jail sentence commuted. One hot summer day, Winkles and others talked to Hoffman. Sitting outside next to an open window, they tricked him into spilling the story while a stenographer inside the building wrote it down. They took their notes to the governor, then Elmer Benson, and ultimately the Board of Pardons commuted Ellis's sentence.

Winkles gave me Jenny's brother's telephone number, and he told me where to find her. I did not call Jenny for several months. In part, perhaps, I was afraid of what I might learn. In part I hated to intrude.

But Jenny was expecting my call. Now in her seventies, a mother and a grand-mother, Jenny did not particularly wish to discuss her testimony against Ellis and my father. Her husband did not want her to talk to me at all.

In our five-minute talk, Jenny told me regretfully that she felt bad that some-one had gone to jail because of her testimony. When I asked for details, she replied, "I just don't want to get into it. I was a kid at the time and didn't know what I was getting into."

"What was behind the story?" I asked again. She answered, "Nothing hap-pened; it was all political." Before she hung up, she repeated once again, "I can truthfully say that nothing really happened."[55]

Part II. Death in an Alley

10. Crescendo of Horror

Well, I suppose I will have to stay here on the firing line until after the next election at least. I have determined to drive Olson and his gang out of public life if it is the last thing I do. It will be a tough job — but I have already weakened his popularity and in another year I think I can finish him off — that is, if he doesn't have me shot in the meantime as he did poor Howard Guilford. There is always that danger.

> **—Walter Liggett to V. F. Calverton, who received the letter a few days before Walter was murdered**

My parents were almost giddy with relief after Walter was acquitted. As Edith put it, "With this hideous frameup off our necks, [we have] nothing to worry about but the ordinary matter of running a business without any capital in the midst of a depression."[1] They hoped that Harry Peterson, the state attorney general, would bring the frame-up before a grand jury. Walter still aspired to clean up the Farmer-Labor Party and supported Peterson as a candidate for senator.

"As you can imagine," Edith wrote Roger Baldwin at the ACLU on November 21, 1935, "in view of Walter's illness, the trial, and the fact that for days afterwards I was almost in a state of collapse, our business is a mess."[2]

Edith's letters to Baldwin show our poverty; my parents allowed themselves only $80 to $125 per month for personal expenses. Listing the trial costs, Edith wrote Baldwin of their trips to Austin to investigate the frame-up. Attorney Lyle Pettijohn had put in four days of trial work and had also gone to Austin to investigate. Joseph Granbeck had advanced $250 for bail bond fees and had not charged for three months of general assistance. And they still had to pay the hospital and the doctor who had cared for Walter when he was beaten up.[3]

The phone bill, too, worried Edith. After Walter's beating and during the trial, when she was struggling to keep the business going, they were forced to rely on the phone for investigations. Their telephone and telegraph bill — mostly calls to Austin — came to $110. Edith feared that our telephone would be shut off.[4]

Baldwin wrote back that he had collected a total of $175.50, minus clerical expenses. He refused to let Edith use the fund to pay Granbeck, since the money had been raised for investigation and lawyer's aid—not for general defense. Baldwin did send Lyle Pettijohn a sixty-dollar check for trial work, and, after assurances that the calls were related to the investigation, authorized a fifty-four-dollar check to the telephone company. Still, our telephone was disconnected on November 18.[5]

Edith wrote Baldwin asking him to mail the telephone company check to her: "If you mail it directly to them, they may keep it and try to insist that I make a new deposit of $100 in order to reconnect the phone. This is illegal, but the Railroad and Warehouse Commissioner is an Olson employee." Having powerful enemies complicated every transaction.[6]

The post office held up the November 22 issue of the *Midwest American* until Walter deposited an additional penny for each copy. The local postmaster claimed that part of our subscription list was subsidized; some Minneapolis clergymen did get the paper free. After Walter threatened to take the issue of suppression of a free press to friends in Congress, the postmaster reluctantly agreed to mail the papers. As Walter pointed out, the postmaster had taken no action against the *Minnesota Leader*, which had fewer than 30,000 subscribers but mailed out as many as 500,000 copies.[7]

Walter suspected that Hennepin County attorney Ed Goff was behind the postmaster's action. He believed that Goff wanted to suppress a story headlined "Rackets Run Wide Open Under Goff and Latimer" in this issue. The article charged that Ed Morgan of the "Combination"—a rival of the Syndicate—boasted that his friendship with Art Goff and William Appelt gave him an "in" at city hall. Walter frequently asserted that Art Goff, the county attorney's brother, headed Minneapolis's slot machine racket. G-men had told him, Walter wrote, that approximately one-quarter of the "take" went into protection, with small amounts to police captains and patrolmen but most to higher-ups.[8]

As Walter continued to expose connections between Minnesota politics and Minneapolis's rackets and grafts, nearly every page of the *Midwest American* contained something to annoy the power structure. Walter asked why the Farmer-Labor city council allowed ex-bootleggers like Kid Cann to be connected with the liquor industry. He kept tabs on the actions of David Arundel, head of the state liquor commission. Above all, he challenged Governor Olson.[9]

Walter probably annoyed labor groups with his interpretation of the Strutwear strike, which went completely counter to the conventional wisdom of the labor and radical press. He claimed that the strike stemmed from an effort of St.

Paul financiers—friends of Olson—to purchase the Strutwear Knitting Company at a bargain price. Just before the strike, he reported, the major stock owner, the widowed Florence Struthers, had been approached by a St. Paul broker to sell her stock at one-third of its value. When she refused, she was threatened with labor trouble.[10]

The Strutwear plant was singled out, Walter reported, although dozens of Minneapolis clothing plants operated nonunion shops. The strike took place, he wrote George Calverton, "with the connivance of crooked labor leaders—some of whom doubtless do not know what it is all about." Governor Olson ultimately used National Guard troops to close the plant and keep would-be workers out.[11]

Carl Beck, an old friend, remonstrated with Walter shortly after his trial, when Walter still bore visible scars from his beating. Beck and Walter had known each other back in Nonpartisan League days, and Beck was one of the out-of-town friends Walter had wanted as a character witness.[12] Since Walter suspected that he was being watched by gangsters and wanted to protect Beck from them, they met in Beck's car.[13]

"The crooks and racketeers are hell-bent after me to stop my newspaper exposures," Walter told Carl, "but they won't be stupid enough to have another shooting right away. It would arouse the public too much. They won't dare shoot me so soon after bumping off Guilford."

"Why do you feel it necessary to take the chances you are taking?" Carl asked. "Do you have to go against this game? You are exposing not only yourself, but your family. What can you hope to gain? You certainly aren't going to get rich."

"All you say is true," Walter responded, "but I suppose it is in my blood to attack corruption wherever I meet it. I belong to that breed which wants to improve society. My wife is of the same species of human being. We understand each other and will fight together, side by side, to the end.

"Of course, they have tried to bribe me. The gang sent an emissary to me not long ago. They offered me real money, but I flatly refused, as you know I would."[14]

That may have been the last bribe Walter was offered.

That fall, the campaign against my parents had taken another tack; my parents heard that politicians and underworld characters were circulating rumors that the *Midwest American* was a "Nazi paper" and that they were anti-Semites, a ridiculous charge to anyone who knew them. These stories were apparently based on the fact that many—certainly not all—of the gangsters Walter denounced were

Jewish. The gangsters and ex-bootleggers in the Syndicate happened to be largely Jewish, while the Combination, headed by Ed Morgan, had an Irish core.[15]

My parents responded with two editorials in the *Midwest American:* "Jewish Racketeers Dishonor Race" and "Rats Have No Nationality." The latter ended: "Whatever the race of the parents they shame, rats are without nationality."[16]

For the only time that I recall, my parents argued that fall—dramatic scenes that were shocking to me. My mother stormed out one day, head up but with a trembling mouth, saying that she was going back East and taking the kids. My father lay on the sofa, looking hurt. I didn't know where to look. I respected my father and loved him deeply, but sensed that he was leading himself—and perhaps our family—into danger. My mother, I felt, was trying to protect us. If she wanted to take us back East, I would go without fussing.

Then they reached a compromise. Edith agreed to stay in Minnesota until after the 1936 election. Walter agreed to look into publishing in a less dangerous city. They were considering Fargo, North Dakota where they could publish and distribute in two states—and would not need to be on guard every minute.[17]

Family life limped on. We still occasionally went to Saturday matinees. Evenings, in the dining room overlooking the alley, my father and I used to play a football board game with spinners and markers. I learned about football from that game, but was, from my dad's viewpoint, overly dependent on the forward pass. I did not then know that someone was spying on us. After Walter's death, cartridge shells were found in an apartment across the alley, and one person reported that a gray car with three men and a machine gun was parked in the alley three weeks before his death.[18]

It is hard to say how seriously my parents took the dangers of the situation. During the last week of Walter's life, they carefully told each other of every telephone call, of where they were going and when they would be back. It seems they half-realized, but didn't truly believe, that Walter might be killed. Still, Edith later heard he had told friends that by January "either Governor Olson will be impeached, or I'll be full of holes."

That winter, Wallace and I split up after school. Wallace, perhaps less susceptible to cold than I, loped home through backyards to avoid bullies and fierce dogs. Once he was home, he took comfort in hot chocolate with marshmallows and listened to *Jack Armstrong, the All-American Boy* on the radio.

I found a refuge in the public library down Lake Street. Our new apartment was perhaps a mile from my school, too far for me to walk comfortably that icy winter. The buses seemed to go in convoys; I always had to wait at least twenty minutes. And by then, our newspaper office seemed more tense than inviting. So each day after school, until my parents came to take me home, I spent my after-noons reading my way through the fairy-tale shelf; I was especially drawn to Scottish fairy tales and others like them where wit and courage conquered evil. Even little girls like Molly Whuppie, if they were brave and clever, could outwit giants and save their families.

The *Midwest American* reported the demise of the *Austin American* on November 22 under this headline: "Charley Ward's Paper Suspends after Frame-up; Union Men, Loyal to Ellis, Repudiate Subsidized Olson Organ." Although the paper had recently been given financial aid by the Newspaper Committee of the state Farmer-Labor Association, union men had refused to accept it after Frank Ellis was framed, and they boycotted merchants who advertised in it.[19] The following week, the *Midwest American* reported that both Emil Olson, still working for the state as oil inspector, and O. J. Fosso had been dismissed from the Mower County Farmer-Labor Association.[20]

The continuing factional hostility may have been the reason that county attorney Ed Goff pursued Ellis's trial for abduction. After Walter's acquittal, most reporters and attorneys had assumed that the case against Ellis would be quietly quashed, but he went to trial over the Thanksgiving Day weekend. He had an experienced labor lawyer, Neil Hughes, who did not attempt to change the venue or prove conspiracy. And, instead of capitalizing on Walter's acquittal, Hughes implied that it didn't matter whether or not Walter was guilty. Ellis was innocent.

Goff's office seemed determined to replay Walter's case. Twice it altered the indictment. On November 18, prosecuting attorney Arthur Markve struck out Jenny's name as a complainant. And on November 26, after half the jury was chosen, the prosecution dropped the charge that Ellis had personally committed any offense against Francine. The charge was changed to read that he brought her to Minneapolis so that she "should then and there have intercourse with one Walter Liggett, a male person." Hughes protested that Ellis had been indicted on one charge and was being tried for another, but the judge accepted the changes.[21]

The jury panel was "wretched," Edith wrote — so wretched that Hughes used up all his challenges before the jury was half picked. The final jury included a night watchman from the Radisson Hotel, which Edith considered a hangout for gangsters, and Hughes later learned that another juror was the brother of a special deputy in Austin.[22]

Ellis's trial did not have the safeguards that my parents had managed to achieve for Walter's trial. It was held at the corrupt Hennepin County courthouse, and, since it encompassed the Thanksgiving weekend, the judge declined to sequester the jury.[23] Walter wrote Calverton that "Ellis would be acquitted in jig time if the jury had been locked up, but that was refused and the Olson-Goff-Latimer gang will do their damnedest to try to fix some members."[24] Perhaps worst of all, no out-of-state reporters covered the trial. The *Midwest American,* in fact, seemed to be the only newspaper to report the trial fully, although the case was mentioned in the conservative *Austin Herald.*

In theory, at least some of the labor press should have covered the trial, since these papers typically provided detailed coverage of labor martyrs, sluggings and frame-ups of union organizers, and real and imaginary plots against labor. Yet the Farmer-Labor press, the labor press, and the radical press all stayed away. The *Northwest Organizer,* official organ of the Northwest Labor Unity Conference, had frequently reported on the Austin packinghouse workers, and its first issue had contained two front-page stories on Ellis and the Independent Union of All Workers, calling Ellis "honest, courageous, and faithful."[25] The *Organizer* would extol him again later, but at the time of his trial Ellis may have been too hot to handle. Both Local 574 and the Trotskyists who controlled the Teamsters' newspaper might have wanted to stay in Olson's good graces.

The Communist press was equally silent, though the local paper *United Action* had written about the packinghouse workers and the IUAW as recently as early October. Up until October 18, *United Action* and the Minnesota Communist Party had been urging the Farmer-Labor Party to transform itself into a class struggle party, and had criticized Olson severely. In fact, from September 16 through October 18, *United Action* carried a historical muckraking series on Olson, purportedly written by "one of the founders of the F-L party."[26] Although the series was marked "to be continued," it stopped abruptly, leaving an exposé of Olson's political career unfinished. Earl Browder, head of the Communist Party of the USA, met secretly with Olson on October 18; afterwards, the Minnesota Communist Party reversed itself and became a strong proponent of Olson's.[27] In November, near the time of Walter's trial and acquittal, Clarence Hathaway, a Minnesota native then editing the national *Daily Worker,* came to Minnesota to make the about-face more palatable. He had known Olson since 1923 and had worked with him before.[28]

The prosecuting attorney began Ellis's trial with a lengthy exposition that repeated the charges against Walter. It was difficult to determine whether Markve was indicting Ellis as a pimp or a blackmailer. He claimed Ellis had said to the girls, "I want to use this, if I have to, in order to make [Walter] do what we want him to do."[29]

Francine, the first witness, who was being held at a Minneapolis detention center, was considerably more demure than at the first trial. She testified that she had known Ellis since the early days of the union and that Ellis had taken her and Jenny with him several times when he drove to union meetings in Albert Lea. Both had continued to take out-of-town rides from Ellis after the purported assault.

In this trial, Jenny and Francine embellished their stories a bit in ways that discredited Ellis. Francine testified that he talked of "unnatural love" on the way to Minneapolis and that he actively discouraged them from looking for Mrs. Flagle. In response to a leading question about whiskey, Francine testified that "it seems to me like he drank some whiskey" in the car.[30] But the young women disagreed on many details. Walter wrote that Ellis's attorney caught the girls in lie after lie.[31] Under cross-examination, Jenny admitted that Emil Olson, the state oil inspector at Austin, drove her up to Minneapolis to sign a complaint.

Vincent Ray Dunne of Local 574 testified for the defense that he had called for Ellis in a cab to take him to a union meeting. Helen Orth and Harry Biesiot again testified that they had seen Walter and Ellis arguing alone in the hotel restaurant. Walter again testified that he had come to Minneapolis completely independently of Ellis and that he had spent the afternoon in the governor's office.[32] And once again, state employee Emil Olson could not be located to testify.

Summing up on December 4, Arthur Markve took an unctuous tone, portraying Francine and Jenny as country innocents led astray. Markve claimed that Ellis had brought the young women to the Ritz because he knew Walter stayed there when he was in Minneapolis, and that Ellis's purpose was to blackmail Walter.[33]

The judge reminded the jury that they were the sole judges of the truthfulness of the witnesses and told them, "If you do not feel morally certain that the defendant is guilty as charged—it is your duty to give the defendant the benefit of that doubt and find him not guilty."[34] But after twenty hours of deliberation, the jury convicted Ellis of the diminished charges. Ellis greeted the verdict with a rueful smile, but my parents were horrified. They had thought the judge would direct an acquittal. At worst, they had expected a hung jury.

Next day in the *Midwest American,* Edith's report on the Ellis trial ended: "Because he refused to perjure himself in my husband's case to save his own skin . . . today Frank Ellis lies in the filthy Hennepin County jail, waiting sentence for a crime he did not commit." A separate boxed editorial by Walter appealed to union members to organize a statewide protest, and for "workers everywhere" to contribute toward Ellis's bail and defense and to help expose the "foul political plot behind his persecution."[35] My parents went to see Ellis in jail, and Walter was scheduled to speak in Austin to raise funds for Ellis's bail.[36]

That was the last issue published by my father. My parents had given up the *West Lake Neighborhood News;* the *Midwest American* was now the *Midwest American* and (in small type) the *West Lake Neighborhood News.*[37] Walter had continued to write about ties between the Syndicate and the political structure. In an update on the prospective license of the Minnehaha Liquor Store on Lake Street—which Walter strongly opposed—he noted that the proposed liquor store was within two hundred feet of two schools and that it was illegal to give liquor licenses to former felons.

He did see a few helpful signs: Sheriff John Wall had started a county-wide campaign against beer parlors and nightclubs with gambling devices, and was working with the county commissioners. Federal agents were making arrests for liquor law violations. Best of all, the Hennepin County grand jury was investigating vice violations. This same grand jury would follow up on Walter's murder.

In his final issue of the *Midwest American,* Walter listed twelve, rather than his usual ten, reasons to impeach Olson. The two new reasons were "Use of state officials to engineer frameup" and "Governor exceeds powers in labor troubles while his friends and supporters try to confiscate plants." In his major story, five columns wide with a two-line head that read "Impeachment of Olson Is Justified by Record, An Open Letter to the Legislature: Either Olson Should Be Impeached or I Should Be Indicted for Libel," Walter pointed out that he had been listing his charges against Olson for twenty weeks. If they were false, they were criminally libelous; if they were true, they were grounds for impeachment.[38]

The much-postponed special session of the Minnesota Legislature finally got under way, overlapping Ellis's trial. A headline in the *Midwest American* predicted "Olson Is Facing Fight When Legislature Meets." The article stated that Olson was facing opposition both from the conservative majority in the House and Senate and from Farmer-Labor Party members who had been asked by the Farmer-Labor Association's state central committee to back radical tax and social legislation that the governor did not approve.[39]

Ironically, at the very moment that third-party activists were looking to Minnesota for leadership, conservatives once again took control of both houses of the Minnesota Legislature.[40] The day after the conservatives were chosen, Governor Olson made a stirring radical speech, proposing that state unemployment insurance be funded by employers and that the old age pension be funded through taxes on public utilities, iron ore, chain stores, and excess profits. Whatever the rhetoric, the conservative legislature was not likely to adopt these proposals.

Olson was out of his office on December 5 and 6; he had gone to Rochester for a medical examination that was, the *St. Paul Dispatch* wrote, "carefully concealed": "His own employees did not know where he was." An alarmist report "was met with statements that Governor Olson is in good general health and the operation which may be decided upon later is not a serious one."[41]

Meanwhile, the Minnesota District Committee of the Communist Party met to steer the Minnesota Communist Party into supporting pro-Olson, pro-third-party positions. With mea culpas for some past efforts against the Farmer-Labor Party, the Minnesota Communist Party reiterated its collective belief that the common people of the United States were finally beginning to recognize that the New Deal was against their best interests. In a lengthy resolution, the Minnesota Communist Party accused capitalist parties of trying to disrupt the Farmer-Labor Party from within and declared that "the Minnesota Farmer-Labor Party and its progressive leadership can and must become the leader of all progressive movements in the country.... The Communists will support the Farmer-Labor State Administration." The Minnesota Communist Party had transferred its support from radical insurgents to the cliques trying to run the Farmer-Labor Party from the top.[42]

The week before Walter's murder, local merchants spotted a green sedan parked for several afternoons opposite the Rite-Spot Cafe in front of 313 West Lake Street, about two blocks away from the *Midwest American;* two men sat in the front seat of the car looking up the street toward our print shop.[43]

Quite probably, other cars came closer to our apartment. In the basement of the Minnesota Historical Society, I found a long-buried file from the attorney general's office that contained testimony by Sally Baker Mairovitz, a practical nurse who was working on our block in December. Mairovitz said that on Friday evening, December 6, 1935, she went to the theater with Ray Appeal, whom she had known since July 1934. (In August 1935, on another date, he had pointed out Kid Cann on the street.) Near midnight on December 6, she showed Appeal our apartment, where she could see Walter by the window talking on the telephone. That same evening, she said, Appeal gave her three dollars for "information."[44]

Two days later, she saw Appeal standing on the sidewalk opposite a green car. Later that evening, he telephoned and wanted to come over to her apartment, but changed his mind when she told him that her employer was home. The day Walter was murdered, she saw Appeal once again, around 2:30 or 3:00 P.M., sitting in the green car with another man. The two men walked up the street to our building with something bulky in a brown sack, then turned around and walked back to their car with their bundle.

My parents, as it happened, were working at home that day.

11. Last Day: Family Recollections

Walter's last day was — like his last three years — full. After driving Wally and me to school, he spent most of the day at home with Edith working on the next issue of the *Midwest American* and polishing a speech recommending Governor Olson's impeachment. My parents did not go to the newspaper plant until late in the afternoon. Our apartment was a quieter place to work, and the plant telephone may have been shut off a few days earlier.

Our telephone figured heavily in Walter's last afternoon. Edith recalled that evening that our home telephone seemed to ring every eight or ten minutes during the afternoon, making it difficult for her to proofread. One of Walter's last acts was to call the sheriff to request that Frank Ellis be moved to a cell where he could exercise.[1]

Two other calls may have had some bearing on Walter's death. One was with former governor William Langer of North Dakota, Walter's old Nonpartisan League colleague, who had been accused of extorting campaign contributions from federal relief workers; his trial was coming up. Langer proposed that Walter move the newspaper to Bismarck and continue his campaign against Olson, and he stated that Walter had agreed to testify in Bismarck as a "star witness" in the trial — possibly on Minnesota relief practices that Walter regarded as thoroughly corrupt.[2] Another — after three o'clock — was with Meyer Schuldberg, Kid Cann's employer.

My father was in a relaxed and smiling mood when he came to pick me up at the library a few minutes before five o'clock. I remember that I was reading the *Green Fairy Book* that afternoon; I carefully returned it to its spot on the shelf. "Bundle up," he told me, shivering dramatically to make me smile, "it's gotten cold again." It was cold and blustery, with a slight flurry of snow as we drove companionably down Lake Street to the newspaper plant, where my mother was waiting with A. B. Gilbert, an old friend of Walter's from Nonpartisan League days, who had dropped by late that afternoon to pick up some printing and to chat.

Walter and Gilbert had maintained their friendship through political disagreements. Gilbert, who marched to his own drummer, was a perpetual letter writer and political gadfly who supported himself through subsistence farming.[3]

I recall a bustle of action as my parents introduced me to Gilbert and closed down the office, snapping shut their rolltop desks and turning off the lights in front. A couple of printers were still working in back, and my parents called out cheerful good-byes as we left for home and evening errands.

I vaguely recall my father insisting to Gilbert that it would be no trouble to drop him off at the bus stop. It always felt good to be driving home with my parents at night. My mother chatted with me in the back seat while my father talked to Gilbert in front. They were commiserating over hard times; my mother was scolding me gently about some now-forgotten childish act of thoughtlessness. She was so soft and sweet that her gentle reproaches felt like love.

First we drove to Swenson's Market at Lake and Lyndale, where we got groceries in exchange for printing advertising flyers. A big labeled box of groceries was waiting for us inside. While my father double-parked, I located our groceries and Gilbert put the box into the back seat. We dropped him off at a bus stop downtown before picking up the Sunday edition of the *New York Times* at Sixth and Hennepin. My parents, to my way of thinking, were strangely addicted to this dull, heavy newspaper with few pictures and no funnies. We drove down Sixth Street to Third Avenue South, then entered our alley from Nineteenth Street.[4]

Dusk had just fallen as we turned up the well-lit alley behind our apartment house. The sky was almost a navy blue; on our way home, I had glimpsed the full moon rising, dodging around our car as we changed directions. The snow had stopped, but the streets were wet, and a light powdering of snow lay on top of the parked cars. It seemed that everyone had just gotten home from work and turned on their lights.

From the alley I could see the lights in our apartment, where Wallace was listening to *Jack Armstrong* on the radio. We parked, as always, on the left side of the alley, just below and about ten feet away from our second-floor apartment. As soon as we had parked, I noticed a dark car turn purposefully into the alley and head toward us. Somehow, it seemed ominous even as it turned. But my father seemed unconcerned. Because of the high curb on the left, he had gotten out of the right-hand door and was bending over to pick up the groceries from the back seat, joking with me that he'd bring in the *Times* and let me carry the groceries.

When he saw the car, he motioned us to stay inside. I remember that he smiled at us before he straightened up and moved close to the front fender to allow the other car room to pass. Suddenly, I saw a hand with a gun at the window of the moving car; I ducked without thinking and heard five quick shots at the same time. When I looked up, my mother was half out of the car and my father lay stretched out in the alley.

Our family recollections of the murder night vary; possibly all are correct. My mother remembered me shouting "Don't die, Daddy, don't die!" I remember yelling "They killed Daddy!" as Wally peered, frightened, from our window. He remembers me bursting into the apartment, yelling "Daddy's been shot!" Neighbors, listening from above, heard children's voices crying and screaming. I ran to our apartment manager for help. My mother ran to my father's body.[5]

In no time at all, the alley, which had seemed so empty, was swarming with neighbors, reporters, and policemen. My father lay on his back, next to the car. My mother was holding his head in her lap. She couldn't seem to believe that he was dead. He was so warm, she said. But five bullets, fired by an expert gunman, formed a tight crescent around his heart. Any one of them would have been fatal.

The reporters and police who descended on our family that night still seem to me to represent the dregs of their professions. Indifferent or impervious to our loss, detectives and reporters dominated our living room — laughing, cursing, and smoking smelly cigars and cigarettes. They seemed keyed up and excited and said things like, "Well, whatever you can say about him, he was a good writer." Framed photographs disappeared from our bookcase only to show up later in newspapers across the country. One was our only copy of a studio portrait taken of me two years earlier.

"Get the kids together," someone suggested, and the photographers told me to put my arm around Wallace, who was whimpering. I put my arm around him, more for his sake than theirs. At that moment, whatever the squabbles between us, I felt truly sorry for him. He was somehow less prepared than I.

I even felt sorry for our teenage maid, Amanda. Though I could tell she was trying to be brave and adult, she seemed badly shaken. Her voice, usually brassy, was subdued, and I saw her hands trembling when she brought a glass of water to a photographer. I wanted to put my arm around her, too, and to protect my mother out there in the cold alley, waiting for the coroner and besieged by photographers who kept taking picture after picture of her leaning over my father's body.

I wanted to yell at the photographers to stop, and to order the reporters out of our house, but I was only a child and had no authority. Our family badly needed to be alone together, to cry together over our loss, but we were not to have that luxury.

The detectives and reporters became noticeably more civil after the arrival of our uncle, Bob Liggett, an advertising man with the *St. Paul Dispatch*. The reporters who appeared over the next few days were considerably more civilized; some from out-of-town papers even seemed kind and concerned.

The police who showed up that evening seemed a bumbling crew who stumbled over each other and did not know what to do. Some, it turned out, were personal friends of Kid Cann, the gangster my mother identified as the killer. They spoke to my mother in harsh, accusing voices, without a trace of sympathy. They didn't want her to telephone her mother. I wanted to scream at them: "Don't you know my father's been killed?"

12. The Cops Arrive, a Little Late, with Their Notebooks

"Absolutely true, 100 percent."

—Isadore Blumenfield, alias Kid Cann, alias Harry Bloom, alias H. Lee, of his deposition after Walter was shot

Between 5:43 and 5:45 that evening, the police telephone operator had received three calls. The first caller shouted that he thought a man had been shot in the alley behind 1825 Second Avenue South; the second said, "A man has been shot!" and the third, "Liggett has been killed." Three detective cars were dispatched: number 30 with Schroeder and Higgins, number 8 with Duffy and Hamilton, and number 10 with Fabriz and Seidenstricker. Higgins and Schroeder heard the first call around 5:45 and another around 5:49. Detectives Art Olson and Charles Wetherille, out in a car with their radio open, answered the call without being dispatched and arrived earlier. Patrolman Ralph Jacobson was probably the first on the scene, followed by Patrolman Richard Miller, who said he arrived eight or ten minutes after 5:45, when Jacobson was in the alley with my mother. By the time the police arrived, Walter was covered with a blanket.[1]

Some of these policemen wrote up or dictated reports to stenographers at police headquarters. Some interrogated the neighbors. Overall, the Minneapolis police did a workmanlike job of interviewing nearby apartment dwellers that first week, although there were conspicuous omissions: no one ever interviewed Amanda, and no one interviewed our apartment house manager until well after Kid Cann went on trial for the murder. On December 13, three days after the shooting, inspectors from the county attorney's office redid the task. Neither the police nor the county agents followed up some interesting leads.

Marguerite Van Wold, who lived on the third floor of our building, gave Inspector A. E. Crummy a good description of the murder car. She had been standing by the window when she heard the shots and had looked out to see the car racing down the alley, its engine roaring as though in second gear. She described the car as gray-green with a black top and black fenders; it looked dirty, with dried mud on it. She remembered thinking that it would be difficult to see the license number.[2]

Across the alley, Catherine Straightoff heard a commotion even before the shots and my scream. It sounded to her like "things moving about, things being pushed aside." She thought that someone got into a car. Then, after the shots, she looked out her window and saw an excited woman come out of an apartment and walk toward the body. By the time she got downstairs, there were six or eight people, and Edith was sobbing, "They murdered him."[3]

While more details emerged over time, these initial witnesses confirm and amplify my memory of the murder, the well-lit alley, and the behavior of the police and reporters. All of Edith's statements, as reported in newspapers and recorded by police investigators over the next few days, are completely consistent with the signed statement she gave at 7:30 on the evening of the murder.

Harvey Meyers, from the rear of 214 East Nineteenth Street, first heard shots that sounded like a machine gun. When he heard a child scream, he ran out and saw Edith kneeling down. When he asked what had happened, she answered, "They have shot him." He ran to phone the police, and when he came back, he saw a hatless woman in a housedress who told him that the murder car almost hit her as it sped out the alley. He described her as about thirty-five years old, 125 pounds, about five feet four inches, with blond hair. He was able to give this detailed account, he told the police, because "the alley is very much illuminated there."[4]

Nell Wilkinson, at 214 East Nineteenth Street, heard a sound like a shot but thought it was a car backfiring. A few seconds later, Meyers rushed in to use her telephone to call the police. Looking out of her living-room window, Wilkinson saw Edith down on her knees saying, "Don't die, Walter." Then, she said, "I shut my window, as I could not stand the sight." She left for a movie to get away. Like most witnesses, she described the alley as being "very well illuminated."

One of the first to be interviewed was William F. Hartman, the janitor at 1810 Third Avenue South, who told the police that the murder car struck the rear door of 1810 just as a tenant he called Isaacson opened the door into the alley. The tenant—actually Wesley Andersch—called to Hartman, who was sitting down to supper with his wife, that a man had been shot.[5] When Hartman reached the alley, only two people were there—a woman standing six or eight feet from Edith, who was leaning over Walter calling for someone to get the police and an ambulance. Hartman took Walter's right-hand pulse while his wife phoned the

Walter Liggett as a baby, 1887.

As a youngster, Walter (*second from left*) spent most of his summers in the country.

Edith's family, around 1907: Ida and Charles Fleischer, Caroline, Edith (with big bow), Walter, and Erna.

Walter, with Wallace, around 1925.

Edith Liggett, twenty-eight, in Washington, D.C.

Marda, in Washington, D.C., four years old.

Edith's favorite picture of Walter, around 1930.

Walter in November 1929, after testifying on corruption in Washington.
Underwood & Underwood photograph; reprinted courtesy U.S. Library of
Congress.

Floyd B. Olson, ca. 1936. Photograph reprinted courtesy Minnesota Historical Society.

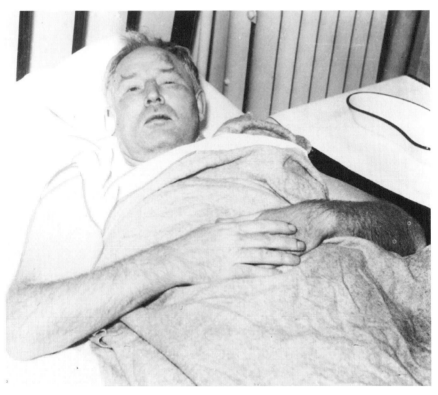

Walter in Swedish Hospital, Minneapolis, October 1935, after being beaten
by gangsters. Minneapolis Collection photograph; reprinted courtesy
of Minneapolis Public Library.

Edith sat at Walter's side each day at his trial for sodomy, November 1935; his eye was still black from his beating in October. *Minneapolis Journal* photograph; reprinted courtesy *Star-Tribune.*

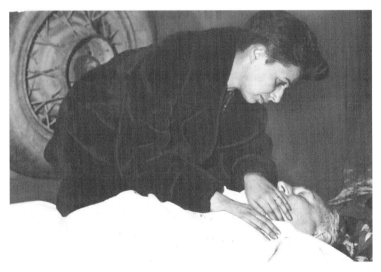

Edith at Walter's body on the night he was murdered. *Minneapolis Journal* photograph; reprinted courtesy *Star-Tribune.*

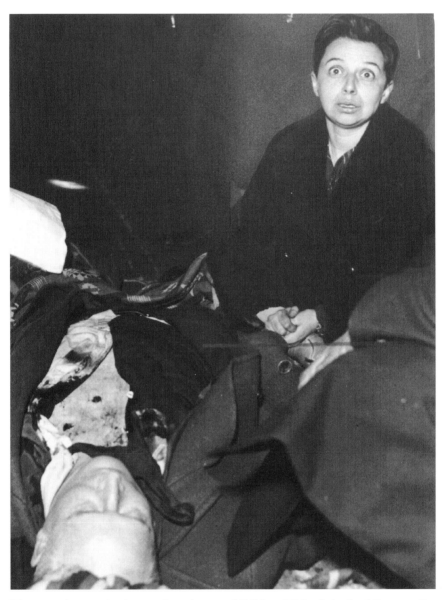

Photographers took picture after picture of Edith at Walter's body. *Minneapolis Journal* photograph; reprinted courtesy *Star-Tribune.*

Murder alley on the evening of December 9, 1935. The Liggett car has a blanket on the hood; people are looking out of apartment windows. Minneapolis Collection photograph; reprinted courtesy Minneapolis Public Library.

Wallace, Edith, and Marda the day after Walter's murder. Minneapolis Collection photograph; reprinted courtesy Minneapolis Public Library.

TWINS OF THE TWIN CITIES.

A cogent Fitzpatrick cartoon appeared in the *St. Louis Post-Dispatch* on December 13, 1935. Reprinted courtesy of the *St. Louis Post-Dispatch* and the State Historical Society of Missouri, Columbia.

At Kid Cann's trial, Edith had to enter and leave court through back elevators or through mobs of the curious. *Minneapolis Journal* photograph; reprinted courtesy of the *Star-Tribune*.

Dapperly dressed, Kid Cann (Isadore Blumenfield) at times appeared bored
at his trial for murder. Photograph reprinted courtesy of Minnesota
Historical Society.

Marda and Wallace were brought in from Wisconsin to testify at Kid Cann's trial. *Minneapolis Journal* photograph; reprinted courtesy *Star-Tribune.*

On February 4, 1936, Marda marched down the aisle to testify on her father's murder. *Minneapolis Journal* photograph; reprinted courtesy *Star-Tribune.*

police. Walter's heart was still beating. When Hartman's wife came out to the alley, she felt Walter's left hand; he was still alive. His shirt was open and Hartman could see one bullet hole. Dashing up to our apartment, Hartman pulled two blankets off a bed to spread over my father. When he came down, he felt the pulse again and knew that my father had died. The police arrived a few minutes later.

Alice Delaney, our apartment manager, who stayed with Edith most of the evening, gave one of the most detailed accounts, although it was not recorded until February.[6] Alice said that just before the murder, during a furniture delivery around 5:20 or 5:25, she had noticed smoke in the hall. It turned out that Wallace had burned some marshmallows while he was toasting them over our stove and had then opened the door between the kitchen and the hall to clear out the smoke. Alice went into our apartment and helped him open the kitchen windows to let the smoke out into the alley. While she was there, she noticed that our curtains were raised and our lights were on.

A few minutes later, she heard someone running down the hall. The doorbell rang just as she got to the door, and I burst in half-sobbing, "My daddy has been shot, come quick!" She asked where he was and I said out in back. She told me to stay in the apartment and hurried to the alley, where Edith was leaning over Walter's body. She put her arms around Edith and asked what had happened. "A terrible face, a grinning face," Edith said.

"Do you know who it was?" Alice asked.

Edith replied, "Kid Cann."

At 5:49, Alice went in to call the ambulance, which still had not come. The dispatcher told her that it would be there in about five minutes. I followed her out to the alley, and, when Edith asked her to telephone Walter's brother, Alice again took me with her into her apartment. She reached Aunt Frida.

Back in the alley again, Alice saw a uniformed officer kneeling at Walter's head. Edith, still not convinced that Walter was dead, kept saying, "If only they would hurry. They want him to die, they want him to die!" The Hartmans, as well as the woman in the housedress, had told Edith he was still alive.

Two plainclothesmen arrived a few minutes later and began questioning Edith out in the alley, where a crowd was gathering, pushing up toward the body and trying to talk to her. Alice suggested that they question Edith in our apartment.[7] Inside, Alice asked Amanda to take Wallace into the bedroom while Edith telephoned my grandmother in Brooklyn. Even while Edith was trying to phone her mother, the detectives kept asking who shot her husband. "Kid Cann," she answered. "I saw his terrible, grinning face."

Meanwhile, the doorbell kept ringing. Alice tried to keep reporters out, letting in only a newspaperman from the *Journal,* who insisted he knew Edith, and a young fellow from the *Tribune.* Until 1988, when I read Alice's account of her efforts to keep out newspapermen, I assumed that the surly, cigar-smoking men in derby hats were reporters. Now, having read the police dispatch record, I believe that most were police detectives.

Police accounts indicate a certain impatience. Fred Higgins called Edith "hysterical" and complained that she would only say that it was Kid Cann:

> I asked her, how do you know Kid Cann? Do you know Kid Cann? She said: I have never met him, but he has been pointed out to me. I asked her what description could she give us of his face. I said: What complexion has Kid Cann got? And she said: He has the same complexion that I have. I got a good look at him and he had a grin on his face. I said: Did you see anyone else in the car, and she said: No, I didn't get a good look, but I think there were three in the car. We asked her what kind of car it was, and she said she wasn't sure, but she thought it was a Dodge car, sedan or a coach.

Higgins's partner, Fred Schroeder, reported that Edith said, "Well, what's the use of telling you who done it, you wouldn't pick him up anyway. And we told her we wanted to do all we could, and then she finally said: 'Well, it was Kid Cann.' She said that Mr. Liggett got a call that afternoon from Schuldberg... and they argued."

When the doorbell rang once again, Alice tried to keep out yet another intruder, but the police told her it was the coroner, Gilbert Seashore. He questioned Edith, and when he asked who shot Walter, Edith repeated once more that it was Kid Cann. "She asked the coroner where they were taking her husband, if she could see him; and he was unusually kind. You and he were the only ones who were kind to her," Alice Delaney told John Hilborn, supervisor of detectives.[8]

Still, according to Alice, a patrolman did bring up the groceries from our car, and a reporter went out with Edith to help her find the car keys, which Walter had dropped or left on the back seat.

After Walter's body had been removed to the morgue, Detectives Olson and Wetherille reported back to their captain that Edith had named Kid Cann as the killer, and had told them that Walter had quarrelled with Schuldberg over the telephone around 3:30 that afternoon. All the police reports—from Marxen, Higgins, Schroeder, Olson, and Wetherille—agreed on these two points.

Wally, Amanda, and I were left alone to cope as best we could with the sweating policemen and rambunctious reporters who swarmed through our apartment when John Hilborn—the supervisor of detectives and one of the few Minneapolis policemen Edith trusted or respected—escorted Edith down the hall to talk to her in the apartment office. A police stenographer took down her statement.

"She was grieved and shocked," Alice reported, "but she had full command of her senses. The only time I heard her raise her voice that evening was right after the officers got there and they were all shouting questions to her at once, but I wouldn't say she was hysterical then. When her statement was taken in my apartment, she was calm and collected, and sat on the sofa and drank a cup of tea that was offered to her."[9]

In her statement, transcribed in question-and-answer format, Edith told of our evening errands and our route home; she described the murder car as dark with individuals in both the front and back seats. She identified Kid Cann as the man who did the shooting. She saw him plainly, she said: he had "a snarling smile on his face I will never forget."[10]

Edith told Hilborn that Cann had been pointed out to her at the Radisson Hotel several months before and again on the street within the past three weeks. She said that she could not recognize the driver of the car. Around 3:30 that afternoon, Edith told Hilborn, she had overheard a heated telephone conversation between Walter and Meyer Schuldberg, Cann's employer and the proprietor of Chesapeake Brands. She was sitting on the sofa in the living room, reading proof, while Walter talked on the telephone about twelve feet away in the dining room. Trying to concentrate on the proofs, she had paid little attention to Walter's phone calls, but she noticed that Schuldberg shouted in a strong foreign accent, threatening to sue. Walter replied, "Go ahead if you think I can't prove what I say." Schuldberg answered, "Well, I'll stop you some other way then."

The only other threats had come from a man in Ed Morgan's gang, Edith said. Asked for additional clues, she said that it was well known that Walter had mailed the current edition of the *Midwest American,* which listed twelve reasons to impeach Governor Olson, to every state legislator. Further, she said, Governor Olson knew that her husband was slated to speak before the legislature to demand impeachment.

One thing in her statement puzzled me as I read it fifty-odd years later. She thought the murder car was parked thirty or so feet down the alley from us before the shooting, while I distinctly remember a car rounding the corner.

When Hilborn was through taking Edith's statement, Alice went up to our apartment and found that Uncle Bob had arrived. She brought him in and introduced him to Hilborn. A few minutes later, Wetherille and Olson returned and told Alice that Kid Cann had been picked up.[11]

Kid Cann was a picture of composure when he was brought into police headquarters, chewing vigorously on a wad of gum and greeting several police officers with a wide smile and a wave. He took off his overcoat to make himself comfortable, then picked up the most recent issue of the *Midwest American* and scanned an article on himself, chewing gum rapidly as he flipped the pages back and forth.[12]

Schuldberg was questioned first—at 8:15 P.M. In the presence of Detectives Kramer and Eisenkramer, Kid Cann, attorney Charles Bank, and a police stenographer, Schuldberg gave Al Marxen, the night captain, a detailed statement of what he said was his only meeting with Walter, eight or ten weeks earlier, and claimed that Walter had tried to shake him down at this meeting.

Schuldberg said that Walter had contacted him using Senator Schall's name, and their encounter took place in an automobile in front of Schall's Portland Avenue house. Schuldberg honked three times and Walter came out of the house and offered to "lay off" in return for $1,500 for his upcoming trial. Walter accused Schuldberg of running a cutting plant for doctoring liquor and being illegally connected with the retail liquor trade. Schuldberg told Walter to go jump in the lake.[13] He hadn't seen Walter since then, he said, although Walter had phoned him around 3:30 that day to say that he was starting a new series on Schuldberg. Schuldberg said he had hung up on Walter.

One flaw in Schuldberg's account—subsequently offered as proof that Walter was a "shakedown artist"—was that we had moved from Portland Avenue by the time the shakedown was supposed to have occurred. Although both the police stenographer and newspaper reporters recorded the date as "eight or ten weeks ago," the next day Schuldberg moved the date of this supposed encounter back to August. At Cann's trial, he testified that it was "July or August." Still later, he signed a new deposition changing the date to September—September 1934 on one page, September 1935 on another.[14]

Marxen questioned Cann in the presence of Detective Kramer and Charles Bank at 9:00 P.M. The police reported that Cann offered an "ironclad" alibi and that his time was fully accounted for. Whether or not his alibi was airtight, Cann did make a few misstatements. He gave the police a false address (his mother's, not his own) and claimed that he was the sales manager of Chesapeake Brands. (Schuldberg had said he was a salesman.) He said he had been married for eight years, when in fact he did not marry until August 1936. And his testimony about his first meeting with Walter—he said he met Walter by chance at the Radisson Hotel—contradicted his earlier statement, in which he had acknowledged asking Annette Fawcett to introduce him to Walter.[15]

In this "absolutely true, 100 percent" deposition, embellished at his trial, Cann provided yet another account of the earlier assault on Walter. According to Cann, they stopped off for an amicable drink, after which Walter "disappeared and walked outside." "That," Cann declared, "is the last I saw of him until I understood that he got slugged outside. This is the last I saw or heard of him until I heard of his being shot."

Cann's alibi was a circumstantial and redundant account of his working day, replete with details of where he had been and to whom he had spoken at what times. It was roughly, if not completely, consistent with later testimony at his trial. For a person making five hundred dollars a month during the Depression, Cann had an easy working day. He went downtown at ten and stayed until noon. And, although Cann and his "wife" had two cars, including a company car, he drove Meyer Schuldberg's 1935 green Dodge sedan for all errands. (He said that his brother, Harry Bloom, had his car.)

At noon, he drove to Northwestern Terminal to collect $2,040, then was back at the office until he went to lunch with Schuldberg and a Chesapeake Brands officer at 12:30 or 12:45 at the East Side Restaurant. He shot dice at the cigar counter until 1:30 or 1:45 before heading back to the Chesapeake plant. Around 2:00 he drove over to the Northwestern Bank, then on to the Keystone Bar, where his brother Harry sometimes worked, to pick up a heater for a Chevrolet. Then, Cann said, he went over to the American Fruit Company until about 3:45 P.M., then to the Colonial Warehouse for twenty to twenty-five minutes. He left at about 4:30 for the office and stayed there until 5:05. During that time, he said, Schuldberg told him Walter had phoned.

Apparently Cann left Schuldberg's green sedan at the office, for, he said, Schuldberg asked a boy in shipping to drive Cann downtown in another car, a black coupe with red wheels. He took a Chevrolet heater for his wife's car to St. Anthony Motors around 5:15 and was there until 5:30, when he went on to the Liquor Mart at 12 South Fifth Street. At the Mart, he met Lou Galinson, who walked part of the way with him to the Artistic Barber Shop on Hennepin between Fifth and Sixth Streets. He stayed from 5:45 until 6:25 P.M. at the Artistic Barber Shop, where he had the works: a shave, his spats cleaned, a shoe shine, and a tonic.

Cann's attorney left the room before he had completed his statement.[16] Marxen lodged Cann in the city jail. In the meantime, Hilborn returned with

Edith's statement. Next, Marxen called morgue keeper John Anderson, who reported that Walter had been shot five times and that he had found a fully loaded .38 revolver on Walter's body.

Marxen left a sealed envelope for Captain James Mullen containing the depositions of Edith, Schuldberg, and Cann and his own chronology and summary of police testimony.

Meanwhile, Nell Wilkinson, back from the movie, glanced out her window and saw Edith sitting with her head on her arm leaning on our window, looking down at the alley.

13. The Word Goes Out

I thought how each of us might hold a . . . crowd spellbound with a recitation of what we'd be writing.

—Cedric Adams, *Minneapolis Tribune*, December 10, 1935

In newspaper headlines the next morning, Walter's murder had replaced the kidnapping of the Lindbergh baby and the Italian assault on Ethiopia. Most of the first few pages of both the *Minneapolis Star* and the *Minneapolis Tribune* dealt with my father's life and death. In New York, my great-grandmother screamed when she saw the *New York Times,* and my thirteen-year-old cousin Eda became aware for the first time that evil could reach close to her.[1]

In papers large and small, from Seattle to Alabama, the story made headlines and inspired editorials: in small-town papers in Minnesota and North Dakota, where Walter had worked for the Nonpartisan League; in Chicago, where the *Chicago Tribune* had covered Minneapolis in depth ever since the 1927 gag-law case; in New York, where Walter had worked on the *Sun*, the *News,* and the *Times;* in Washington, where reporters remembered the Prohibition exposés in *Plain Talk* and his testimony on Prohibition.

In the next issue of *Editor & Publisher,* Walter's murder was the lead story. An editorial by the president and publisher appealed to the nation's newspapers to raise funds for a thorough investigation of the slaying, a "subject of national concern." The lead story reprinted commentary and editorials from newspapers around the nation, reporting that "a wave of indignation over the assassination of Walter Liggett . . . swept through the American press this week. . . . Influential editors characterized the murder of the crusading editor as a challenge of the right to criticize of the whole press of the United States."[2]

Ironically, the out-of-town reporters Edith had hoped would cover Walter's trial arrived from all over the country to report on his murder. The *Chicago Tribune,* the *New York Times,* and other papers sent reporters. The *New York World-Telegram* sent its heavy gun, Forrest Davis (Franklin Roosevelt's favorite reporter), who

141

covered the case for the Scripps-Howard newspapers in a series of five widely syndicated stories. The out-of-state reporters quickly confirmed my parents' evaluation of the interplay of politics and crime in Minneapolis.

"Behind the murder of Walter W. Liggett," the *St. Louis Post-Dispatch*'s staff correspondent wrote, "lies an incredible condition of officially tolerated vice and crime, which has existed in this city for many years. . . . Today, even after repeal, this city's nightlife is still on a 'speakeasy basis.' . . . Establishments which are 'in right' never close—although the man across the street may be compelled to do so. Three truckloads of liquor have been 'hijacked' in true pre-repeal style this month."[3]

In the *New York Times,* Herbert Lefkovitz reported that "the bullets of the assassins are now ricocheting back on the underworld": Walter's death had "closed" the town, something Walter had not been able to do when he was alive.[4] The flamboyant *New York Daily Mirror* account reported that "the five shots that mowed down Walter W. Liggett . . . echoed yesterday in the hasty closing of scores of Minneapolis dives and in a demand for a Congressional investigation."[5]

Many newspapers had to make do with dispatches from the wire services, all of which had their own angles. United Press called Walter a national literary figure as well as Governor Olson's most outspoken foe, and reported that he was the second Minneapolis editor to die by assassins' bullets.[6] The Universal Service account, perhaps the most succinct, reported under the headline "Liggett 'Targets' Seek His Assassins" that "the gun blast that closed the stormy career of Walter Liggett, firebrand editor, echoed wildly in political circles today and sent underworld characters scurrying from the cities as State and local authorities the crusading editor had bitterly attacked sought his assassins."[7]

Then, as now, Associated Press reports dominated the nation's newspapers. Jack Mackay, the AP Twin Cities correspondent, was favored by Governor Olson and distrusted by my parents. The AP story called Walter a "storm center of numerous political and other controversies here for several years." The AP wire was responsible for spreading the poignant, inaccurate, and much-reprinted detail that groceries spilled from Walter's arms as he fell dying. In reality, the groceries, unlike my father, were safe in our car. Most accounts derived from the AP wire included these sentences: "Three pistol shots ended his variegated career" and "Always a vigorous foeman in his writings, Liggett had earned a variety of enemies and police began a close check of all phases of his career to seek a motive for his death." Some papers did not reprint AP's references to "unconfirmed reports that Liggett had 'double-crossed' liquor interests in Minneapolis."[8]

In Cleveland, Frank Orsini, who had traveled to Minneapolis to help Walter after his beating, wrote an indignant letter to the *Plain Dealer* protesting the tone and implications of the AP dispatch and a *Plain Dealer* editorial.[9]

Orsini was not the first to object to the bias of certain media accounts. A. B. Gilbert, who had been with us in the car before the shooting, heard the news on WCCO radio just after he arrived home. WCCO apparently implied that Walter was a blackmailer or associated with the underworld or both. Gilbert responded by calling Walter "one of the finest men I have ever known. . . . The suspicion of underworld connection as a possible explanation for the crime is unjust. He had nothing to do with the underworld except as a crusader for clean government."[10]

Across the state line in North Dakota, newspapers that had fought Walter in the Nonpartisan League's heyday also objected to the WCCO broadcast. Walter's old political opponents on the *Mandan Pioneer,* the *Bismarck Tribune,* and the *Fargo Forum* all quickly wrote editorials countering radio statements that apparently used the word *blackmail.* The murder, the *Bismarck Tribune* wrote,

> serves to illustrate the penalty a man can pay for independence. Liggett was a professional exposer of the ills of the body politic. He had a talent in that direction and he used it. . . . Whether Liggett's death was due to his attack upon a political ring or upon a gang of bootleggers, it demonstrates that a cancer exists in the public life of Minnesota, which should be destroyed before it consumes the honor, the independence, and the decency of our neighboring state."[11]

The *Forum,* once a strong political adversary, put it this way:

> There is nothing in the record to show that Liggett was a blackmailer, that he was anything but a crusader who believed sincerely in what he was about. . . . The underworld had challenged Minneapolis and the nation, in this killing of an editor who exercised those rights guaranteed to him by the Constitution of the United States. . . . The Minneapolis underworld knows who killed Liggett, as it knows who killed Guilford. The underworld knowing, the police can find out.[12]

The *Times* of London similarly looked to politics in an article titled "Middle West Journalist Murdered: Politics in Minnesota" that stated, "Mr. Liggett became prominent in the later years of Prohibition when he exposed the abuses of the Liquor Laws and alleged official complicity. Recently he attacked the administration of the Governor and demanded his impeachment."[13]

Delbert Clark of the *New York Times* Washington bureau, who had assisted Walter on *Plain Talk,* wired his comments to the *Times:*

> The assassin who struck down Walter Liggett in Minneapolis removed from the American scene one of the last of the old-school crusading journalists, miscalled "muckrakers," who for personal integrity, stood head and shoulders above the common ruck.
>
> As a former editorial associate of Mr. Liggett, I wish to pay my small tribute to a man whose principal fault, if it can be called that, was his disinclination to look out for his own interests — the rash courage which made him an easy target for the guns of the underworld.[14]

The *Christian Century,* a liberal religious monthly, zeroed in on the third-party issue with characteristic acumen:

> Every practical proposal for the formation of a national third party with genuine political importance has involved participation by Governor Olson and his party.... But before there is the slightest chance of such a movement acquiring importance, Governor Olson and the Farmer-Labor party leaders of Minnesota must now absolutely clear themselves and their party of the slightest responsibility for this assassination.[15]

The *New Republic* also addressed this quandary:

> Though Liggett was a bitter foe of Governor Olson, he was also the enemy of bootleggers, gamblers, and other rulers of vice and crime in that state.... All evidence now available points to the conclusion that Liggett's death came from the gangsters he was engaged in exposing. Liggett also charged, however, that these gangsters were protected by Governor Olson, and unless the latter can demonstrate that these charges were without foundation, it will jeopardize his future political career.[16]

Twin Cities columnist Cedric Adams, who stopped off at the morgue on his way to an informal meeting of the Newspaper Guild, wrote that it was a strange feeling to see a man he knew on the slab there. "The incident electrified our party," Adams wrote. "Photographers straggled in, fresh from the scene of the slaying, to bring the newest bits in detail."[17]

Uncle Bob stayed at our apartment late into the night talking to Edith, then went to the offices of the *St. Paul Dispatch* and, using my mother's words as he recalled them, wrote a story that he attributed to her.[18] The story stirred the Minneapolis press to belated action. The *Journal, Star,* and *Tribune,* which had barely covered Walter's accusations or his trial, reported the murder in depth. For the first time, they summarized his charges against Cann and Schuldberg, and they gave fuller accounts of his beating and trial than had appeared originally. One paper reprinted the first page of the last issue of the *Midwest American.*

An editorial in the *St. Paul Dispatch* proclaimed:

> Not the least part of the disgrace is the cool arrogance of the crime. Howard Guilford exposed the underworld and political corruption of the city and was murdered. Fourteen months later, Liggett goes the same way. Not a hand was turned to clean up the city of which these men wrote. It was thought enough to dismiss the charge by impugning their motives.
>
> The police never acted against the racketeers, but Liggett was framed, then slugged, and is now murdered. The whole state will watch with profound interest to see how Minneapolis and Hennepin county meet this challenge.[19]

Most national radical publications ignored the murder, although many of the editors were acquaintances or had published Walter's articles.

In Minnesota, over the course of the next month, Farmer-Labor spokesmen and the *Minnesota Leader* did their utmost to defame both Walter and the outside press.

In the *Union Advocate,* A. J. Lockhart, no friend of Walter's, called Walter's journalism a policy of "rule or ruin" and claimed he exaggerated everything that might be detrimental to his foes. Still, Lockhart wrote, Walter had both physical and moral courage:

> It remains for the prosecuting attorney, who worked so strenuously to convict Liggett of a trumped-up statutory charge, to run to earth the perpetrators of this brutal murder.... Any half-hearted attempts to solve this crime will only tend to convince the world at large that some of the charges made by Liggett during his hectic career were more of truth than ordinary yellow journalism.[20]

Governor Olson, for his part, called the slaying "an outrage" and offered the aid of the state Bureau of Criminal Apprehension, which had signally failed in its investigation of Guilford's murder. Questioned about charges that Walter had made against him, Olson replied, "I haven't read them. I didn't read his paper."[21]

County attorney Ed Goff, who had done his best to put Walter in jail, said it was "an outrage that anybody should be shot down the way Liggett was. I shall do everything in the power of this office to see that the killers are brought to justice."[22]

In Washington, Senator Schall was not surprised: "I suspected something like this would happen to Liggett judging from what happened to that other editor [Guilford] last year," he asserted. "It is pretty hard to live in that town and tell the truth."[23]

In Boston for a conference, Roger Baldwin of the ACLU heard of Walter's murder and announced that the assailants were "undoubtedly connected with the political and underworld rings which Liggett had so vigorously attacked in his paper":

> We have long been familiar with the political attacks on Mr. Liggett. He was repeatedly threatened with death . . . [and] he had often predicted what would happen to him. Whatever freedom of the press includes, certainly one of its aspects is the right of editors to publish without fear of death for what they say. For that reason, the Civil Liberties Union will go to the limit in uncovering the situation in Minneapolis which brought both Guilford and Liggett to their deaths.[24]

As was his wont, Baldwin telegraphed both Edith and George Leonard. He wired Edith that he was "shocked and grieved," and that he had "wired Governor Olson asking what official investigation undertaken and whether state will offer reward for arrest and convictions. If not, we will." And, typically, Baldwin asked Leonard for his interpretation of events.[25]

Frank Ellis, in the county jail, hoping that the murder might expose those who had framed him and Walter, urged the union to step up its own investigation. "Dear Friend," he wrote Beatrice Chase, the IUAW secretary in Austin, "I guess you have read all about the murder of Liggett by this time. Tell Joe to get his intelligence committee on the job, find out where Fosso-Emil Olson-Johnson and Larson were about six o'clock Monday P.M. . . . This is our missing link that will prove that the charge . . . was a frame up and may also reveal who killed Liggett."[26]

My brother and I, sitting on our living-room floor, read the papers carefully, going through all the stories about our father before we read the funnies. Reading somehow validated our experience. It was easier to read the newspapers than face the reality. Even though I had hated the reporters who had come to our house the night of the murder, I took comfort in the fact that my father's story dominated the newspapers. I hoped the attention would solve the crime and convict the men who had killed him.

14. No Time to Mourn

As if by magic, Aunt Caroline was there the next morning: she had taken the plane from New York. It was good to have her with us, despite her Christian Science determination to view things positively.

At Caroline's instruction, I called Lyndale School to tell them we weren't coming. "The Liggett children won't be in today," I started, "because, because..." I couldn't go on. I wanted to cry, to wail, to dramatize. Caroline took the phone from me. "The Liggett children won't be in today," she stated crisply. Her emphasis had always been more on correct behavior than on feelings.[1] We never attended school in Minneapolis again.

Except for the newspapermen who besieged us, and the police, barely civil, it was a lonely time for us children, and probably worse for Edith, haunted by the vision of Kid Cann's leering face. Wallace and I moped around the house, reading the newspapers, while Edith, too shaken to go to police headquarters, took a trip to the morgue to see our father's body.

After announcing that Kid Cann had a "watertight" alibi, the Minneapolis police assigned two detectives to investigate it. These detectives seemed more than a bit slow. When the *St. Paul Dispatch* interviewed Dave Garfinkle, proprietor of the Artistic Barber Shop and the linchpin of Cann's alibi, late on December 10, the reporter found that the Minneapolis police had not yet questioned him.[2]

In both news and police interviews, Garfinkle said that Cann was in the barbershop at the time of the murder. Indeed, all employees at the Artistic Barber Shop enthusiastically confirmed Cann's alibi. In one police interrogation, three barbers, the shoeshine "boy," and the manicurist all stated independently, with circumstantial detail, that Cann arrived sometime between 5:15 and 5:20 on the evening of the murder. Cann himself had told the police that he arrived around 5:45; he had a different alibi for his time between 5:00 and 5:45.

The *Dispatch* noted that police activity finally began popping around 6:00 P.M. on December 10, after a day when practically nothing developed. Shortly after six that evening, county attorney Ed Goff appointed inspectors Andrew

Crummy and Ed Comstock and lawyers Peter S. Neilson and Arthur Markve to the case. The four appeared in Captain James Mullen's office asking why the police had not presented evidence or reports to the county attorney's office. "The newspaper says here that Mrs. Liggett can identify Kid Cann," Neilson asserted, slapping the paper with his hand. "Why doesn't it say she does identify him? You have him in jail, don't you?" But neither Edith nor the Minneapolis police wanted to confront Cann.[3]

The next morning, Louis H. Gollop of the *St. Paul News* and Charlie Granger of the *Minneapolis Star* interviewed Edith in our apartment. They captured its atmosphere perfectly. Walter's typewriter was still on its stand, near a table stacked with books, telegrams from all over the country, and back issues of the *Midwest American.* When Uncle Bob, whom Gollop knew, opened the door, Edith was sobbing on the telephone in the next room, while Wallace and I, "restless, but unnoticed by [our] griefstricken mother," played in the bedroom and eventually came out to read the funnies.[4]

Edith, who distrusted both the police and the county attorney's office, wanted an independent ballistics expert to examine the three bullets that the coroner held. She thought that if the county attorney's office had anything to do with the investigation, the assassination would never be cleared up.[5] When Gollop told her about Senator Schall's proposal for a congressional inquiry, Edith replied that while she would welcome a federal investigation, she felt Schall was trying to make political capital out of Walter's murder.

"If he wanted to help Walter," she asked, "why did he wait until now?"[6]

A few minutes later, she, along with Uncle Bob and Walter's lawyer and friend Joseph Granbeck, left for the city jail. Wally and I stayed with Aunt Caroline. Although the police had pressured Edith to bring me to the jail to try to identify Cann, she refused. "I won't take Marda down there to the police station. . . . A child like that? I don't want her to see that man!"[7]

They had to take a circuitous route to avoid reporters and photographers. In the police "showup" room, Cann stood on an elevated platform with six other men. Captain Mullen had ordered the jailer to "get some fairly well-dressed fellows in there." Neilson, who witnessed the lineup, noted that Kid Cann did not stand out distinctly.[8]

Edith, quiet but "visibly restraining an outbreak of nerves," looked the men over closely as they were commanded to give her a front view, a side view, and finally a rear view.[9]

Detective supervisor John Hilborn broke the heavy silence. "Do you recognize anyone there as the man who killed your husband?"

"I do," Edith replied, her voice breaking a little.

"Go over and point him out," Hilborn requested.

With shaky steps, Edith advanced close to the platform and (as Neilson described it) "without any hesitancy" pointed at Kid Cann. "That's the man," she said. Hilborn characterized her identification as "very cool."[10]

At that point, Cann burst out angrily, "Oh, yes, you saw my picture in the papers." At a jail interview, he said, "Sure, she identified me, but I'm innocent and can prove it."[11]

Edith left through the county jail elevator to avoid newspapermen, then, escorted by Hilborn, went to the Bureau of Identification to look at photographs. Hilborn hoped that she could identify the driver of the murder car, but although Edith looked at approximately fifty photographs, she could not identify the driver. She did recognize Philip "Flippy" Share, a local gangster, whom she had seen driving around our newspaper office and glaring at the office from across Lake Street.

Before Edith left the building, she stopped off once more at the county jail to talk to Frank Ellis; she felt she had to carry on Walter's fight to free him. Her final errand, mercifully not accompanied by newspapermen, was to take one of my father's suits to a mortuary in St. Paul. His funeral was set for Friday, December 13.

Part III. Edith's Story

15. Aftermath of Murder

My husband was slain, but his work will go on.

—*Midwest American* headline, December 13, 1935

Widowed and without funds in a hostile city during the coldest winter since 1912, Edith acted with courage, dignity, and grace. Even in these circumstances, she thought of others. Without success, she pressured the ACLU to help Frank Ellis, and she wrote Roger Baldwin suggesting that the ACLU's proffered reward money be used to repay Joseph Granbeck for Walter's bail.[1] The debt, she wrote, "was on Walter's mind at the end."

Although the Minneapolis city council and even Meyer Schuldberg had offered rewards, Baldwin responded that the ACLU could not make an outlay for past services. He essentially withdrew his reward offer after receiving wires from George Leonard and Governor Olson.[2]

Because Walter had borrowed on his life insurance policy to meet the payroll of the *Midwest American,* his death left our family in dire poverty. He had not been able to repay the loan and the policy had lapsed. My mother didn't even have enough money to pay the electric bill.[3] After newspaper colleagues learned of our plight, *Editor & Publisher* raised a small fund—enough for us to eat.

A week later, Monte Bourjaily of United Features (whose syndicate was soon to capture Eleanor Roosevelt's famous "My Day" column) concluded that Walter's murder was a bona fide story of freedom of the press and offered to syndicate a six-article series by Edith. Bourjaily declined to take a commission and told publishers to pay Edith directly. "Mrs. Liggett's story," he said, "is not only a good human interest story, it is a story of the dramatic fight for freedom that the press of America constantly has to wage. . . . It's a great story of an authentically brave woman."[4]

The period between Walter's murder and our return to New York three months later was a watershed not only for our family, but also for Minneapolis crime and for Farmer-Labor politics: the investigation, trial, and acquittal of Kid Cann took place; the Communist Party aligned with the Farmer-Laborites; Governor Olson underwent an operation for cancer; and two inconvenient candidates for Minnesota senator and governor were knocked out of the race.[5]

The ruling Farmer-Labor clique knew that it was time for damage control. The dirty politics underlying Minnesota crime continued. Although Farmer-Labor officials denied that Walter's murder had any political aspects, they consistently tried to discredit my parents, the out-of-state press investigating the murder, and ultimately the grand juries that explored the relation between Minneapolis crime and government. They called Walter a blackmailer and Edith hysterical, and they stated that Cann's alibi was "perfect."

Edith's tasks were made much more difficult by her isolation in Minneapolis, by the grandstanding of politicians, and by foot-dragging by police and prosecutors at all levels. The *Chicago Tribune* reported that an aroused citizenry, discovering that Edith was not guarded by the city police, insisted that a bodyguard be posted. Edith wondered aloud: "Who will guard me from the police?"[6]

Although Edith was a warm and gregarious person, she had sacrificed her personal life to Walter's crusade and had few friends in Minneapolis. One evening about a week after the murder, Helen Orth, earlier a defense witness in Walter's frame-up trial, came by hesitantly with a cake for Wallace and me. Helen, who had not known my parents before, had grown to admire my mother. When I saw my mother and Helen settle down with a pot of tea for an evening of talk, I realized suddenly just how lonely my mother was and how distant from her friends.

My father's funeral, on the afternoon of Friday, December 13, was conducted without a minister, in accordance with his wishes. Two longtime friends, Joseph Granbeck and Dr. Ernest Powell of St. Paul, spoke, both calling Walter a courageous idealist who sacrificed his life for a free press. "The challenge has been given to those of us who believe in those principles, that he and other crusaders . . . shall not have died in vain," said Powell.[7]

The Sunday after my father's funeral, Dr. Ernest C. Parish, pastor of Central Park Methodist Church, paid a glowing tribute to Walter in his sermon, comparing him to John the Baptist. The Reverend George Mecklenburg of Wesley Methodist Episcopal Church also chose Walter for the text of his sermon: "Liggett," he told his congregation, "must have had the dope or he would not have been killed. He knew too much. . . . Anyone who speaks his mind is apt to be shot down."[8]

The next day, the Twin Cities Baptist ministers conference unanimously adopted a resolution demanding that the murderers "be uncovered and brought to . . . justice." Pointing out that both Guilford and Liggett "were bitter critics of [Olson's] principles and policy," the resolution asked the governor to allay suspicions that the murderers enjoyed "either his sympathy or . . . his clemency."[9]

The day of the funeral, Edith had wired Homer Cummings, U.S. attorney general, asking for a federal investigation; it would be impossible, she felt, to obtain a fair investigation through county or state authorities.[10] President Roosevelt already had received a telegram suggesting that "G men get the killers of Liggett and clear up the underworld rumor that Governor Olson suggested his murder." After newspapers published Edith's telegram, the Justice Department received letters and telegrams of support from all over the country. These ranged from postcards from old Leaguers to a petition signed by 7,800 veterans in Brooklyn.[11]

For their own reasons, Governor Olson, Minnesota attorney general Harry Peterson, and Minneapolis police chief Frank Forestal joined Edith in asking for federal aid to track down the slayers. Forestal requested aid under the National Firearms Act, prohibiting unregistered possession of a machine gun, and noted that he was "hampered [in his investigation] by circumstances and conditions in Minneapolis." Edith was pleased; she had always believed that Forestal was personally honest.[12]

By this time, Minneapolis police, who had originally thought the murder weapon was a Smith and Wesson automatic .45, decided that it was a Thompson machine gun. The FBI analyzed the bullets (the only job the bureau was willing to undertake) and reported that the five slugs were of different types—some steel-jacketed, some copper-jacketed; obviously, they came from a large supply rather than a single box.[13]

Cummings declared that he had no information to indicate that the murder was a federal offense. (He had a rather narrow view of federal responsibilities; he had refused to act earlier when Ohio union leaders were kidnapped and taken out of state.) Instead, he notified Olson that "the burden of enforcing state and local criminal laws rests on the state and communities in which infractions of such laws occur" and invited the governor to supply grounds for intervention. But Olson, in one of the many public sparring matches he indulged in after the murder, claimed that this refusal to become involved proved Cummings wrong in labeling Minneapolis a hotbed of crime.[14]

Even though the FBI decided not to investigate, rumors persisted that its operatives were active in Minnesota, and it collected hundreds of pages of incidental information, mostly newspaper clippings, which for the most part it did not share with other investigative jurisdictions. Even its ballistic report arrived late.[15]

Edith wrote Governor Olson as well, asking him to take the case out of Goff's hands and name a special prosecutor:

> Since the brutal murder of my husband Monday evening I have seen in the press your statement regarding this terrible crime. I was particularly interested in your expressed desire that the murderers be brought to justice. If you are sincere in this statement...may I suggest a concrete action that will prove it....I ask you as chief executive of Minnesota...to supplant the Hennepin county attorney and his staff with a special prosecutor...a man who will be able, honest, fearless and above influence by the many liquor, racket, business and political interests that are certain to be affected by a full and honest investigation.[16]

In response, Governor Olson appointed two Farmer-Labor functionaries, Frederick A. Pike and Roy C. Frank, as special prosecutors. Pike was a scholarly seventy-one-year-old lawyer with a long history of involvement in Farmer-Labor politics but no experience in criminal law. While he seemed to want to convict Cann, he did not seek a wide investigation. Worse, Roy Frank seemed hostile to Edith.[17]

When Ed Goff suggested assigning his assistants Neilson and Markve — who had prosecuted Walter on false charges — to the team, the attorney general immediately made the appointments. In fact, Neilson and Markve were still prosecuting Frank Ellis.[18]

The Hennepin County grand jury, meeting in special session, closed its doors on Ed Goff and demanded that a special assistant attorney be named immediately and that a corps of investigators be appointed at once to dig into the entire Minneapolis underworld situation. Although this grand jury never got a special attorney, it did investigate Walter's charges of widespread vice. When it ended up indicting liquor industry figures, it drew a lot of flak from Farmer-Labor publicists. The other quasi-independent state assistance was a solitary investigator from the state Bureau of Criminal Apprehension.

The out-of-state newspapers following the case noted that both the county attorney and the attorney general seemed reluctant to take over. The Hennepin County chapter of the Minnesota Law and Order League called for someone to be held responsible, lest this investigation, like the one that followed Guilford's murder, "die a natural death."

In spite of everything, Edith persisted in publishing the *Midwest American.* Before the funeral, besieged by calls, letters, telegrams, reporters, and visitors, she checked proofs for the *Midwest American,* which went to press shortly before the services. The lead headline read: "My husband was slain, but his work will go on."[19] Recounting the history of Walter's persecution in Minnesota, Edith vowed to fight "until honest men and women can walk the streets again without fear of gangland guns":

> They tried to persuade people to sue us. They garnished our bank account. They tampered with our employees. They used every method including award of state purchases to make our advertisers leave us and take away our job printing. They sabotaged our machinery. They tried to have our paper thrown out of the mails. They intimidated newsboys with our paper. They framed up a filthy charge against my husband. They tried to keep me away from the trial by threatening to kidnap our children. They had Walter beaten by gangsters. When these methods of intimidation failed, Walter was murdered.

For the twenty-first time, the *Midwest American* reprinted its reasons to impeach Olson. The masthead still showed my father as editor and publisher; it was not until the December 27 issue that he was listed as founder.

Ironically, the newspaper's circulation went up immediately after his death, and Edith had offers of assistance. She wrote V. F. Calverton: "What makes it so ghastly is now that Walter has been killed . . . people who turned him down when he asked for help in his lone wolf fight against the Olson machine are offering to co-operate with me."[20] Edith managed to get out eight more issues before she was forced out of business.

With the help of Calverton and Charles Abrams, Edith attempted to sell the newspaper and the job-printing business to Farmer-Labor dissidents who would carry on Walter's work. She wrote Calverton that perhaps the paper could be moved to North Dakota, but "I believe that since this is an election year, and since, despite all the work of the Olson All-party gang, Walter had a loyal following in both states, that it would be best for the paper if I were associated with it until after the election."[21]

Forrest Davis, a Scripps-Howard newspaperman, had heard rumors that some Farmer-Laborites had had a scheme to buy out the *Midwest American.* He surmised that they had decided to kill Walter when they realized he could not be bought out and that Walter was killed because of his last conversation with ex-governor William Langer about moving to North Dakota.

While the police and the prosecution dithered, the local and visiting press turned detective. After the funeral, a reporter showed Edith a picture of Frank Nitti, Al Capone's enforcer, who bore a strong facial resemblance to Kid Cann. She identified the picture as someone who might have been the gunman, and then she broke down. Both the *St. Paul News* and the *Chicago Herald Examiner* reported that Nitti and several other Chicago gangsters had been seen in Minneapolis immediately after Walter's acquittal. Supposedly, Nitti had contacted several big shots in the Minneapolis underworld.[22]

Police reports indicated at least one other witness to the murder. Reporters from the *Journal* and the *Tribune* identified Wesley Andersch and traced him to his father's farm near Kimball, Minnesota. Andersch, called "Mr. Isaacson" in police notes, had seen the shooting from across the alley, from the rear door of his fiancée's apartment building. After the murder, Andersch went home and told his parents what he had seen. Later he talked to an attorney who advised him to go to the police. Instead, Andersch, who had recognized Cann, hid out with his fiancée on his father's farm. After he was located, both he and his fiancée asked to stay in jail for their own protection.[23]

Although Ed Goff moved toward indicting Kid Cann, most reporters doubted that county and state authorities who had ignored the *Midwest American*'s attacks would probe the conditions that had led to Walter's murder. The *Union Advocate* predicted, in a scathing editorial, that after a routine investigation "the corrupt forces of the Mill City, whose rule apparently has never been challenged by the law, will regain some of their old self-assurance."[24]

Fred Pike announced on December 17 that the state's case was ready to present to the grand jury. That morning Kid Cann, in jail since the night of the murder, awoke to face reporters. "I know I'll be indicted," he mumbled through the bars of his cage, "but when it comes to trial, I'll beat the rap. My witnesses are all right. I can account for every minute of my time."

He was right. Immediately after Edith identified Cann as "a face I'll remember to my dying day," Goff declared that "plenty of other angles will turn up before this is over." His office had examined twenty-one witnesses, looking for weak spots in Cann's alibi; witnesses obligingly put Cann in the barbershop about twenty minutes before he said he had arrived.[25] The police were slow in impounding Schuldberg's green Dodge, the car Cann had been driving on the day of the murder; when Markve finally impounded it nine days after the murder, it had a mark on the sill, while the upholstery still smelled of gunpowder.[26]

Wesley Andersch told the grand jury that on the evening of the shooting, he was just going out of his fiancée's back door when a car came rushing up the alley and almost struck him. He turned to shout at the occupants. In our headlights, shining on the moving car, he could see two men in its front seat, one hunched over the wheel, the other with a gun. A few seconds later, he saw Kid Cann lean out of the car window and begin shooting, and he saw Walter reel and fall into the glare of our headlights as the murder car sped away. (Andersch had been jailed for eight days in 1934 for defrauding an innkeeper; Kid Cann had been in the same jail—one of the few terms he ever served.)[27] Andersch's story was completely congruent with my memory, except that he said he saw a third car throw a spotlight on Walter, as though marking him for the killers.[28]

The next day, Edith also identified Cann as the gunman.

That evening, a prowler jimmied the doors of the attorney general's office and sprung the side door with a chisel, apparently in an attempt to get the records of the case. Fortunately, they had been secreted in a vault.[29]

Meanwhile, in the state legislature, Representative Marius Waldal, an anti-administration leader, introduced a resolution asking for an investigation of the murder and of vice in Minnesota. He proposed a joint legislative interim committee with full investigative and police powers and a $50,000 budget. Senator Mike Galvin of Winona, calling Walter's murder "a challenge of the underworld to the government," proposed a $100,000 fund for a joint investigative committee. Attorney General Harry Peterson drafted two bills asking for $50,000 and the power to call witnesses and demand testimony. The Senate Rules Committee decided that these bills did not come within the limits of the special session, which was supposed to be limited to issues of relief and social security, and refused to reconsider its decision.[30]

" 'Liggett is dead,' said the Governor, 'hence we may not speak ill of him.' " Forrest Davis, in the second installment of his Scripps-Howard newspaper series, described his interview with Governor Olson in St. Paul. Widely known as a newspaperman who refused to take handouts, Davis had worked on the *New York World-Telegram* with avid Olson champion Heywood Broun and had arrived in Minneapolis as an Olson supporter. His research soon convinced him that political entanglements with gangsters were even worse than they were portrayed in the *Midwest American*.[31]

In his December 19 story, Davis noted that the governor had "proceeded with finesse, shrewdly, legalistically, to extinguish the reputation of Liggett." The "official theory" was that Walter, pressed for funds, had solicited money from the same liquor dealers he had been attacking. "A fable is being constructed of Liggett the blackmailer, the underworld chiseler," Davis wrote. "Visitors to his apartment and his printing office find it difficult to accept this view." Davis noted that Olson, who had earlier professed sympathy to Edith, ignored the usual gestures in this interview: no expressions of regret or community outrage, no avowals that the criminal must be run to ground.

"I suppose Liggett was the victim of what the Marxists call economic determinism," the governor said. "He had to have the money, and he went out to get it."[32]

Although Davis, like most hands-on journalists, did not buy this fable, it was more plausible to distant radicals and third-party advocates, who wanted desperately to believe in Olson. They and most state officials stuck with the official story. Certainly Olson's supporters pushed it: Vince Day wrote a friend that Walter was "in desperate need of funds and had tried to secure aid from the leader of a liquor syndicate whom Liggett was bitterly attacking in his paper,"[33] and third-party organizer Howard Williams wrote a North Dakota friend that although Walter had been a "pretty good progressive" over the years, his murder was a case of "economic determinism": "He just could not finance his paper and unquestionably sold out to Senator Schall."[34]

George Leonard attended to radical opinion in the East through a series of missives to Roger Baldwin at the ACLU. He sent, "in confidence," a five-page, unsigned, single-spaced, not-for-publication report, hastily prepared on yellow copy paper by HZ of the Federated Press. This fanciful account, mailed nine days after Walter's murder, did not even get the murder date correct; it contained only one accurate sentence in its five pages. Throughout, Walter was portrayed as a heavy drinker and an inveterate blackmailer who lived "most of the time" at the Ritz Hotel rather than at our apartment. Walter's newspaper articles, which cited specific names, crimes, and connections, were called "attempts at blackmail."

Both in this report and in his dispatches for the Federated Press, HZ claimed that Senator Schall, "a foul and bitter enemy of the Farmer-Labor party," had hired Walter to "find some dirt" on the Farmer-Labor leaders and, "it is presumed, promised Schall information which would enable him to defeat Olson in the coming senatorial campaign and destroy the Farmer-Labor movement." In reality, Walter supported Harry Peterson for senator and wanted to rebuild the Farmer-Labor Party.

Leonard's own December 18 letter to the ACLU (also marked "not for publication") was equally damning, if slightly more persuasive. Leonard depicted Walter as a man whose "mental deterioration [was] traceable to his excesses.... His drinking and what generally goes with it made great demands on his purse

and developed an insatiable urge for funds." He claimed that "Liggett, while doing the dirty work on the one hand for Schall, who could not satisfy all his
needs, was seeking sources of revenue from the alleged bootleggers, whose enmity he easily incurred."

Leonard and his son appeared before the ACLU on December 23 to attest
that Walter's murder was merely a gangland revenge for blackmail. Although
Baldwin relied on Leonard, he found it hard at first to believe Leonard's con-
tention that there was no political motive for Walter's murder.[35]

The day after Christmas, Roger Baldwin contacted Robert McCormick of
the *Chicago Tribune* to help resolve the divergent interpretations of Walter's assassination. Baldwin had read that McCormick was personally pursuing the case.
McCormick responded:

> When I consider that the state went to great lengths to obtain evidence
> to prosecute him but made no effort to detect and punish the people
> who assaulted, and later assassinated Guilford, and who still later as-
> saulted Liggett, it seems reasonably clear that he was murdered with
> the approval, certainly implied if not expressed, of the authorities.
>
> The suggestion that he was trying to blackmail gangsters does not
> seem reasonable. Why blackmail men addicted to crime and protected
> by the authorities when there are always a number of harmless indi-
> viduals who can be shaken down by a crooked newspaper?

Baldwin forwarded McCormick's reply to Arthur Le Sueur, a Farmer-Labor
attorney thoroughly out of touch with Walter. Le Sueur responded confidentially
that he knew "from the lips of persons in whom I have every confidence" that "Mr.
Liggett was trying to shake down people in the liquor business here. . . . The man
who is under indictment for the murder of Liggett was 'boned' about a week before the murder for $2,000. . . . I know nothing about it first hand."[36] (It would be
interesting to know who Le Sueur's confidential sources were. Kid Cann himself, though certainly not a man of truth, had insisted to the police that he had not
seen Walter since the evening in October when Walter was beaten up.)

Baldwin seemed to accept Le Sueur's appraisal, to which he replied, "You
confirm what others have already told us. We are not involved at all now."

In Edith's second edition of the *Midwest American,* which came out the day the
grand jury indicted Kid Cann for first degree murder, she reprinted a rousing
Editor & Publisher editorial on Walter's murder and excerpts from eighteen other
editorials from around the country. She reported that federal Treasury Department

agents had come to the Twin Cities and confirmed Walter's charges that a cutting operation put creosote in Scotch whiskey in Syndicate liquor stores.[37]

Forrest Davis, whose series in the Scripps-Howard papers was making him unpopular with the Farmer-Labor oligarchy, noted in his third article that the "indictment of Isadore Blumenfield [Kid Cann] by no means resolves the question" whether Walter was killed by gangland or political enemies. "The line between politics and crime is not clearly marked." He next reported that he had had to hire a bodyguard, pack hastily, and move to St. Paul, leaving a false forwarding address. A former G-man advised him not to leave his new hotel except on business.[38]

On December 23, Kid Cann, dapperly dressed and with a fresh manicure, applied for bail. Fred Pike, the special prosecutor, told the judge that if bail was granted, mysterious "influences" would "handicap the investigation." Pike claimed that investigators had already experienced difficulties in talking to persons who knew or were supposed to know something about the crime. The judge denied bail.

We children coped as best we could. It was hard to remember that our father was dead. I recall feeling bewildered while I was shopping for gloves with Edith's aunt Flora Rosenblatt, a woman I hardly knew. Wallace recalls sliding on the ice and laughing with our cousins, then suddenly remembering our father's death.

We drove to Wisconsin for Christmas Eve. I remember painting turkey wishbones silver and gold for the Akermark family's Christmas tree and waking up Christmas morning in their familiar living room with a feeling of peace. After Christmas, Wallace and I stayed on in Wisconsin at our friends' cottage. Edith wanted to protect us from the press and from possible kidnapping. It was a welcome haven for us, but it left her completely alone.

When she got back to Minneapolis, Edith found that our newspaper plant had been robbed once again—on Christmas Eve. This time, the thieves took Walter's files, a mass of private correspondence, and his address book. For the first time since the murder, Edith lost her cool in print.

"Please," she wrote in the *Midwest American,* "return the letters.... Certainly the first scrawled letter of our little girl, letters from old friends of Walter's dead these many years, concerning the history of the Populist movement which always interested him; correspondence dating back twenty years, can have significance only to me, now he has been assassinated.

"Copy anything you want, clip signatures if you want ... but ... as the loneliest woman in Minnesota, I appeal to you, please return the letters."[39]

16. Hard Times

Cop Show

I beg of you to appoint...a man who will be able, honest, fearless and above influence by the many liquor, racket, business and political interests that are certain to be affected by a full and honest investigation.

—Edith Liggett, letter to Governor Olson, December 12, 1935

At least five separate Minnesota agencies—the Minneapolis police, the Hennepin County attorney's office, the attorney general, the Bureau of Criminal Apprehension, and the Hennepin County sheriff—investigated Walter's murder in a routine that suggested the Keystone Kops. They seemed reluctant to go below the most trivial level, and they seldom trusted each other or exchanged information—perhaps with good reason.

While Edith believed that Chief Frank Forestal was honest and John Hilborn, supervisor of detectives, was sympathetic, the Minneapolis Police Department was riddled with corruption and ties to gangsters. Captain James Mullen, in charge of the voluminous but unproductive investigation, called Edith "that Liggett woman" and had sneered at her when she tried to get an arrest warrant for Kid Cann after Walter was beaten. Other Minneapolis policemen were hostile from the start and declined to protect her after she announced that she would continue to publish evidence of corruption.[1]

The police investigation quickly bogged down. Though the police had interviewed our neighbors, and the county attorney's investigators repeated the job, neither group analyzed its notes, which clearly showed that there had probably been two eyewitnesses—Wesley Andersch and Sally Baker Mairovitz—to the murder besides my mother and me.[2] And the police usually dropped the ball when other jurisdictions sent information. When the Los Angeles police forwarded an anonymous letter suggesting two men from Kansas City as hitmen and Jack Davenport, a local mobster, as payoff man, the detective assigned to investigate did not question Davenport or contact Kansas City police. Similarly, no one followed up when a Chicago deputy coroner asked that a bullet be sent to compare with bullets used in Chicago's gang shootings and unsolved murders.[3]

The police took down but never investigated the excited report of a cabdriver who told them that two weeks after the murder he had picked up two men carrying a machine gun at 214 East Nineteenth Street—Mairovitz's building, whose back door opened on our alley. He described the men carefully, and they did not sound hard to find; one had a deep scar under his right eye.[4]

And the police were amazingly slapdash in checking out automobiles seen near the time of Walter's murder. At least two and probably more were implicated, since several witnesses had heard sounds indicating that someone had gotten into or out of a car shortly before the murder. Confusion about the various cars possibly related to the murder would come to characterize the police investigation and the subsequent trial.

One car was the dark car that I remember rounding the corner.

Several witnesses, Edith included, noticed another car parked in the alley just before Walter was killed, with its windows open, lights on, and motor running. Andersch claimed that this car marked Walter with its headlights. Two witnesses—state senator Walter W. Wolfe and thirteen-year-old Robert Bressler— gave good descriptions of this car.

Wolfe, who was driving east on Eighteenth Street, saw a car enter our alley just after 5:30. Wanting to park in our alley, Wolfe had just pulled out of a tight parking space when a dark sedan turned into the alley and honked loudly at him. He saw three men in the car—two in front, one in back. Not liking the look of the men, Wolfe went around the corner instead of through the alley for his errand. When he came back out, he saw that their car had moved further down the alley toward Nineteenth Street and was standing still, at an angle, with its motor running and lights on. Despite the snow, the car's windows were open. He noticed a dark man in the right front seat wearing a soft felt hat.[5]

Robert Bressler also saw this car. Riding his bicycle home, Robert entered the alley from Nineteenth Street at about 5:40 P.M., just after our car pulled up to the rear of our apartment; my dad was still in the front seat. Further up the alley, on the same side, Robert noticed a large dark blue or black sedan with its lights on and motor running. Unlike Wolfe, he did not pay attention to the men in the car, but noted, as boys will, the license number. He remembered that the first part was B396 or B398.[6]

The car Robert described must have been the blue LaSalle sedan, license number B393–370, that had been stolen around five o'clock that evening. The police recovered this sedan the next afternoon and returned it to its owner, C. D. Crisp, with two Kleanmore twelve-gauge shotgun shells in the rear. Crisp called the police about the shells and a policeman picked them up for the property room, but the police did not check the car for fingerprints or show the car to Wolfe or Bressler.[7]

Marguerite Van Wold, our upstairs neighbor, probably gave police the best description of the murder car. She said it was a dirty, mud-covered, gray-green sedan with a black top and fender. Meyer Schuldberg's car, a green 1935 Dodge, license B372–490, sounds similar. When the police impounded his car on December 17 — more than a week after the murder — it was muddy and the seat smelled of gunpowder. Arthur Markve noted a nick on its right front windowsill that "might have been made by a crowbar or some other fairly heavy instrument and superficially it appears to have been caused by a metal object thrust at a right angle across the sill."

The Minneapolis police called in an amateur criminologist from St. Paul to compare the height of the Dodge's left front fender with the scratches the murderers' car had left on the back door of Andersch's fiancée's apartment building.[8] After inspecting Schuldberg's parked car and the alley with rules and micrometers, he concluded: "The license plates on the auto in question are too high, front 18 [inches] and have not been changed recently." Apparently it did not occur to him that the fender and license plate of a swerving car might be lower than those of a parked car.[9]

Sally Baker Mairovitz told Fred Pike that she had seen a green Dodge parked in the alley behind our apartment on the Saturday, Sunday, and Monday before the murder. Although the Minneapolis police had talked to Mairovitz briefly on the night of the murder, they did not realize that she was an eyewitness and did not question her about the car.[10]

Hyman Adlin, whom journalist Forrest Davis considered a possible suspect, also drove a 1935 Dodge coach with a dented front left fender and running board. Adlin and Harry Goldie (alias Harry Goldberg) had left Minneapolis immediately after the murder, but the police did not check the pair's alibis, even after they were picked up for questioning in Minot, North Dakota. Adlin, then on probation, had a long record of arrests for bootlegging, larceny, burglary, and disorderly conduct in Minneapolis. (Interviewed in Minot on December 20, he could not remember where he had been on December 9 or 10.) Even though a Dodge agency in Minneapolis worked on the car, the Minneapolis police did not bother to look at it.

Indeed, the police did not check either the cars or the alibis of any of the gangsters who had threatened Walter or whom he had denounced. When detectives interviewed Art Goff, William Appelt, Harry Weisman, Jack Heavey, Jack Doyle, and Sammy Goldman on December 14, they took these hoods at their word that none knew Walter and did not ask where they were on the evening of December 9.

The police also failed to check out the suspects' cars. When Lillian Lee, Cann's future wife, was finally interviewed on January 9—a month after the murder—she told the police that Cann had a work car in the garage on the evening of December 9. From police records, it appears that the police didn't even ask its license number, nor did they inspect Cann's personal auto. Lee said that Cann's brother, Harry Bloom, had borrowed it sometime before the murder.

Neighbors told police that three men with a machine gun had been parked in a gray car in the alley three weeks before Walter's death, but the police failed to follow up this lead. Another car that might have been involved belonged to Joe Baker, a former liquor runner for Kid Cann. Baker sold this car two days after the murder. On January 16, assistant county attorney Peter Neilson recounted a story he heard: a week before the murder Cann had called at the Baker home and gotten three fur coats. A week after the murder, Baker, nervous and drunk, kept saying, "That son-of-a-bitch wanted me to drive the car to kill this man in front of his family for only $18.00."[11] But, so far as records show, Baker was never questioned.

Despite Governor Olson's declaration that he was putting the entire power of the state into the investigation, the Bureau of Criminal Apprehension sent only one man—agent Fred L. Witters.[12] Witters started with a hidden agenda from Melvin Passolt, the bureau chief who had been Olson's personal investigator. The bureau file contains three copies of an order to locate two telegrams supposedly exchanged between Walter and Senator Schall and/or Meyer Schuldberg on December 9.[13] This particular order appeared to be more fully checked out than any aspect of Walter's murder except the driving times.

Although no one—not Witters, Western Union, the telephone company, or the Minneapolis police—could locate these elusive telegrams, the police obtained numbers for numerous phone calls that Schuldberg and Chesapeake Brands had made to and from Chicago shortly before the murder. Even though the Minneapolis Police Department had suggested that Chicago gangsters were imported for the murder, they did not investigate the callers or the recipients of the calls.

When the attorney general's office entered the case late on December 12, Edith hoped that they would solve the case. (She confided, for example, that Ed Goff's brother Art was seen in the alley just after the murder.)[14] Pike wanted to convict Kid Cann but did not want to push the investigation. Sally Baker Mairovitz told him that she had seen a car — a car she could describe and one of whose occupants she knew — waiting in the alley on the three days before the murder. Ray Appeal had pointed out Kid Cann to her on a date and had asked her to point out our apartment. Pike did not share this information with anyone. No one looked for Appeal or checked out Mairovitz's story.

Pike's assistant, Roy C. Frank of the attorney general's office, had signed the respondent's brief asking the Minnesota Supreme Court to deny Frank Ellis a new trial. While Ellis hoped that tracking Walter's murder might uncover more details about his own frame-up, Roy Frank was not about to pursue this angle, although Agent Witters made a stab at investigating the Austin and Albert Lea angles involving Ellis.[15]

Early on, Federal Bureau of Investigation head J. Edgar Hoover and his assistant both telephoned the bureau's St. Paul office and told the staff not to be drawn into the investigation "under any circumstance whatever."[16] Quite a few individuals who did not trust the Minneapolis police attempted to give the FBI information, but the FBI held to its line. When a volunteer came in on January 10 to say he knew the hiding place of the machine gun used to kill Walter, the FBI refused to take down the information and told him to contact the Minneapolis police or the Internal Revenue Bureau. (The man had just confided that he did not trust either the Minneapolis police "controlled by Olson" or the Internal Revenue Bureau.) An anonymous letter suggesting that Olson's chauffeur, Maurice Rose, was a friend of Kid Cann's and "knew more about the killing than anyone" was passed on to the St. Paul FBI office but not to the Minneapolis police. On the rare occasions when the FBI *did* pass information to the Minneapolis police, it was not acted on.

The U.S. Department of Justice similarly declined to get involved, but did accept one interesting phone call from a man calling from the Minneapolis YMCA who said he knew the man who killed Walter. An agent for the Department of Justice in St. Paul verified that the call was made from and charged to the YMCA, but neither he nor the police could locate the caller.[17]

Politics, Politics

The death of Liggett, man of a thousand enemies, had become within 24 hours, a certain factor in the turbulent politics of Minnesota.

— *New York Mirror*, **December 10, 1935**

While Farmer-Labor Party spokesmen tried to defuse charges of corruption, Senator Thomas Schall leaped into the fray. He raised the issue of press suppression as soon as he learned of Walter's death. Schall, a caustic critic of the New Deal, had always been a heated advocate of press freedom. The morning after Walter was killed, Schall asked Congress to authorize an inquiry into the murder. Next, he proposed that statues be made of Walter and Howard Guilford as the "first martyrs to the cause of American Freedom of the Press since the Civil War."[18]

To become senator in 1936, Governor Olson would have had to defeat Schall, a formidable contender. Although they had worked together when Schall was first elected to the Senate in 1924, the two were at odds in 1935.[19] Schall opened his senatorial campaign by charging Olson with corruption. On December 14, he joined Robert McCormick of the *Chicago Tribune* in decrying Minnesota's "terrible alliance between crime and politics" and called on the American press to unite to restore freedom of the press. The investigation of Walter's murder, he said, should not end with finding "the weak tool who fired the gun"; rather, "the political gang behind the gun should be the main objective to achieve justice and lasting results."[20]

On December 16, Schall wrote Homer Cummings, U.S. attorney general, an impassioned letter urging that the Justice Department get involved: Walter's murder was a federal case, he said, because the assassins were members of an interstate crime syndicate, because the murder was an attack on freedom of the press, and because Walter, as a publisher, "depended upon the facilities embraced by a recent Federal Act — the Communications Act of 1934."[21]

His crusade did not get far. On December 19, just ten days after Walter's death, the blind senator was struck by a hit-and-run driver as he crossed the Baltimore-Washington highway near Cottage Grove, Maryland. He had left his office with his secretary, Orell Leen, and Harold Birkeland and James Laughlin, political friends from Minnesota; Laughlin had attempted that year to oust Olson on corrupt practices charges. The group had been en route to Schall's home in a car driven by Birkeland when Schall suggested they stop to buy groceries for lunch.

For seven years, Lux, Schall's Seeing Eye dog, had led him safely through traffic. On this day, however, Leen guided him across the street while Birkeland and Laughlin waited in the car. Leen and Schall reached the center divider and then, Leen said, after they dodged a speeding car, they were hit by a car coming from the other direction. The driver, Lester Humphries of Hyattsville, kept going, but leaned out and shouted something that sounded like "He stepped in front of me."

Picked up unconscious from a pool of blood, Schall had suffered a broken leg, a fractured skull, and internal injuries; his clothing had been virtually ripped from his body. He died three days later without regaining consciousness.[22]

Less than an hour before his fatal accident, Schall had dictated a six-page single-spaced letter to Cummings alleging that Governor Olson had ties with crime and asking for an investigation of Walter's murder and these criminal-political links. In the confusion that followed Schall's death, his widow did not transcribe and forward his final letter until March 12, 1936. It was barely acknowledged and never publicized. But in June 1936 a state official told the FBI that Schall had been deliberately led into the path of an oncoming car and that he "had just completed a letter... to the Attorney General... calling attention to the crime situation in the State of Minnesota and requesting that an investigation be undertaken."[23]

Schall's death provided Olson with a new political problem: whether to resign and be appointed to the Senate by his successor or to appoint someone willing to turn the seat over to him after a year. Wires flew back and forth between Washington and Minnesota, while Washington newspapers speculated about possible candidates.[24]

State offices were closed and flags flew at half-mast as an estimated ten thousand people filed past Schall's silver casket in the capitol rotunda on December 26. At the funeral, Governor Olson sat conspicuously in the second row with other state officials. During the services, politicians learned that Olson would appoint Schall's successor the next day.[25]

Edith did not attend the funeral but wrote an editorial titled "An Able Critic Lost" that concluded: "While the *Midwest American* never supported [Schall] politically, we have admired his courage.... And again and again, we, in common with the rest of the country, have found that his unpopular views were true."[26]

A month after the funeral, a coroner's jury in Washington absolved truck driver Lester Humphries of blame for Schall's death. Witnesses included Orell Leen, who had led the blind senator across the road, and Humphries, who testified that an auto had pulled in front of him and blocked his vision. Although Birkeland and Laughlin had telegraphed a demand to attend the inquest early in January, they were not present.[27]

The day after Schall's funeral, the *Minnesota Leader* announced that Olson, in response to popular pressure, would appoint Elmer Benson to the Senate seat. This appointment was one of Olson's last official acts before he went to Rochester for an operation for "stomach ulcers."[28] Some historians claim that Olson was furious at the account and appointed Benson only because he was tricked into it by the *Minnesota Leader.* Certainly Olson told several other candidates that he had not decided on Benson.[29] But Olson tended to tell people what they wanted to hear, or what he wanted them to believe. The Newspaper Committee was certainly promoting Benson for senator, and the *New York Times,* the *Chicago Tribune,* and other out-of-state papers had projected him as the likely appointee.[30]

Whether or not the *Leader* was responsible for Olson's espousal of Benson, this particular issue deserved a creative fiction award. In addition to fostering the historical quibble, it engendered two libel suits that have not yet been touched on by Farmer-Labor historians. The *Leader*'s second lead article, "Schall Death Turns Light on F-L Attacks," attempted damage control by tying together "three major 'scandal' plots aimed at Governor Olson." In one expansive sentence fragment, the article accused Walter of extortion by claiming that Walter was trying to impeach the governor to get money from Republicans while simultaneously "attempting to extort money from the Minneapolis underworld." The article also claimed, completely erroneously, that Edith had admitted that Senator Schall had helped our family financially.

The *Leader* correctly reported that Harold Birkeland—identified as the author of an "infamous, notoriously false, and maliciously libelous" book—was with Senator Schall when he was struck by a car, while denouncing as "false statements" reports that the governor had a malignant tumor.

Within the week, both Birkeland and Edith filed libel suits against the *Leader.*

The political situation in Minnesota was complicated by Olson's ultimately fatal illness and efforts to conceal it from the public. On December 30 he underwent surgery at the Mayo Clinic. Colleagues, with the cooperation of his doctors and most Minnesota newspapers, did their best to keep this information from the public. Immediately after the unsuccessful operation, Olson's physician announced that he did not believe that the governor's condition would seriously interfere with his political activities.[31]

Within eight months, Olson would be dead of cancer.

Although Olson's illness was concealed from the public, most politicians learned about it within a month of his first operation. Edith, well out of the mainstream, wrote V. F. Calverton about the effect of this news on Farmer-Labor dissidents: "It is universally believed that Olson has cancer, so the politicians, like Harry Peterson, whose sole chance was to be honest and insurgent, are now angling for the very support that Olson had—and trying to fight shy of both [Arthur] Townley and me."[32]

In a subsequent letter, Edith wrote that "the men who were all for leading a party revolt about six weeks ago become milder daily. All except old Magnus Johnson."[33] When Minnesota attorney general Harry Peterson dropped his request for funds to investigate Walter's murder, Edith wrote that it was "the last straw in my feeling towards the state and all politicians without exception."

The governor's illness inhibited dissidents in another way: it didn't look good to fight a sick man. So Hjalmar Petersen, who, like Magnus Johnson and Harry Peterson, was out of favor, limited his expressions of discontent to letters filled with references to "coteries," "manipulators," "braintrusters," and "cliques."[34]

Johnson defied the cliques by officially filing for the gubernatorial nomination on January 3, opposing Elmer Benson, the insiders' choice. "I shall use all honorable means to obtain the nomination. . . . The rank and file of our party do not want . . . a clique, or a number of cliques, plotting the selection of candidates mainly to further their own political welfare."[35]

The dissidents—Johnson, Peterson, Petersen, and Arthur Townley—had planned to air their dissatisfaction in a meeting at Fergus Falls on January 18, but both Petersen and Peterson canceled out before the meeting. ("If they are going to blow off the lid at the Fergus Falls meeting," Petersen wrote, "it . . . may hurt those who speak at the meeting more than it will benefit.")[36] Bitter weather didn't help. Only 182 people attended, driving in, as Edith described it, in old Model T cars, "with two or three neighbors chipping in for the necessary gas and with shovel and broom in the back seat to dig their way out of snowdrifts."[37]

Alf Solvold, who chaired the meeting, had been removed (illegally, he said) from his position as chairman of the Farmer-Labor Association of Clay County; the association had sent Edith a resolution regretting Walter's murder. Solvold warned the audience not to trust the *Minnesota Leader,* which had carried a three-page story on Walter's arrest for a sex offense and far less on his acquittal. Solvold understated his case: I have not been able to find a word on Walter's acquittal in the *Leader.*[38]

In his usual rousing speech, Townley advocated a primary to choose Farmer-Labor candidates. Edith wrote that "men and women who had been dues-paying members of the Nonpartisan League stamped to indicate their approval when Townley outlined the manner in which they had been thrown out of the Farmer-Labor clubs they had formed."[39]

Townley and Magnus Johnson braved the blizzard to attend a similar session at Sauk Centre. After Johnson returned to St. Paul, he was hit by an automobile on the corner of Sixth and Washington Streets. Political columnist Charles Cheney joked that he must have been struck by some All-Party man,[40] but Walter Wohlwend, the driver, blamed the icy street.[41] Treated for a cracked rib, Johnson developed pneumonia and spent more than a month in St. Luke's Hospital, mostly in an oxygen tent. His campaign was off to a slow start. After a partial recovery, he campaigned as vigorously as he could but contracted pneumonia again in August and died in September—a month after Olson's death.[42]

"Townley warned me about this being run over," Edith wrote Calverton. "He said there isn't a Chinaman's chance of my being shot—but he showed me a long list of anti-Olson Farmer-Laborites who in the past six months have strangely happened to be run over or have their cars wrecked or thrown into the ditch by state Highway department cars." She wrote that a young woman who resembled her had recently stopped at the office to get a newspaper:

> As she left a car which had been parked across the street suddenly made a U turn, crossed the street quickly—and she escaped being run over by about six inches as she jumped back on the pavement. . . .
>
> The town is in the process of being cleaned up—in moderation, and since a lot of what is going on is ascribed to the fact that I stayed on after Walter's death and demanded action, the feeling towards me is very bitter indeed. I'd probably have a month to live after the end of the trial if I watched my step—and approaching autos—damned carefully.[43]

Shortly after, Edith was almost hit by a car in front of our shop. She was unable to get the license number because the plates were covered with mud.

Watching and Waiting

I've sent the children out of this horrible city until after the trial, and you have no idea how utterly unnerving it is to be here alone, waiting for the almost certain acquittal of the man I saw kill Walter.

—Edith Liggett to V. F. Calverton

On the morning of Wednesday, January 1, 1936, the Minneapolis Municipal Court, at Edith's request, issued a warrant against Henry Teigan and the *Minnesota Leader* for "maliciously publishing" an article that exposed the memory of Walter Liggett to "hatred, contempt, ridicule, and obloquy." The St. Paul Municipal Court issued a similar warrant charging Teigan and the *Leader* with criminal libel.[44]

Later that day, Minnesota attorney general Harry Peterson disclosed that Harold Birkeland had asked him to pursue criminal libel action against C. D. (Johnny) Johnston, the *Leader*'s former managing editor, and editor Henry Teigan for this same article. Birkeland asked for immediate action, since Johnston, who had just been appointed secretary to Senator Elmer Benson, was leaving the "jurisdiction of the state of Minnesota."[45]

The January 3 issue of Edith's *Midwest American* reported that "taxpayers' money was spent for trailing [and] spying on Liggett": "When we left the office of the West Lake Press earlier than our usual time," Edith asked, "was it a state employee drawing his wages from your taxes and mine who tipped off the murderer's car to wait for us in the alley?"

That same day, Edith wrote V. F. Calverton:

> Right now, I'm fighting to keep my sanity. I can't leave Minnesota until after the trial of Kid Cann whom I saw kill Walter—the bets on the street are three to one he'll be acquitted....
>
> I wondered whether or not Walter realized the horrible danger he was in all the time.... The more I think of that wicked, needless crime, the more difficult it becomes to walk around the streets and talk to people as if it were a sane world....
>
> Send mail to the office, I've moved and am more or less in hiding.[46]

On Saturday, January 4, the final report of the Hennepin County grand jury reported that "there has been evidence before us that confirmed what the public no doubt already knows, that this community is in danger of being dominated by a lawless group that had spread fear throughout the city."[47] Although Walter's name was not mentioned, it was clear that this jury, which had returned the indictment against Kid Cann, was referring to the same lawlessness that Walter fought. The jury urged citizens to form a "united front" against racketeering and vice and recommended that applications for liquor and beer licenses be published in a daily newspaper at least one month before they were acted on.

Meanwhile, Teigan submitted to arrest in St. Paul on charges of criminal libel. He stated that his defense would be "to prove the truth of statements concerning Liggett which were inserted into the *Leader.*"[48]

That Tuesday, January 7, three hundred businessmen, complaining of crime and the Strutwear strike, held a mass meeting declaring that "law and order does not exist in this city." In Congress, Elmer Benson was seated on the Democratic side of the Senate, replacing Republican Tom Schall.

On Wednesday, January 8, the Minnesota House and Senate approved three rewards of $2,500 each for persons aiding in the conviction of Walter's killers. The Associated Press reported from Rochester that Governor Olson, convalescing in St. Mary's Hospital, was in "excellent condition."

On Thursday, January 9, my brother Wallace had a quiet twelfth birthday in Falun, Wisconsin.

A page-three box in the *Midwest American* on Friday, January 10, noted that Kid Cann was betting five to one that he would be acquitted of murdering Walter.[49]

There was an "emphatic possibility of making money with the *Midwest American*," Edith wrote Calverton. The plant was modern and in good condition and the paper had no liabilities. But she needed to move quickly:

> Since Walter's murder, the job-printing has been taken away by strong arm methods, and hence the costs have mounted. . . .
>
> It is beyond me to keep this paper going much longer without aid, but I've turned down two offers which I suspected were only for the purpose of putting the paper out of business.
>
> When you decide when you can meet me, simply wire at what hour you'll call me—and then phone Atlantic 0621, which is a friend's phone and is not tapped. . . . Your hunch is absolutely right about it being better to have any negotiations outside the state.[50]

On Monday, January 13, the state legislature approved an additional $5,000 for prosecution of the murder case. Minneapolis representative Walter Campbell proposed a bill providing for a ten-man interim commission of five senators and five representatives to investigate "crime and lawlessness in Minneapolis."[51]

On Tuesday, January 14, Olson, reported to be much better, mapped his race for the U.S. Senate and asked for a curb on the U.S. Supreme Court. The next day, Senator Schall's widow announced that she would take up his campaign. One headline read "Candidacy for Senate Complicates State Political Tango."

Trial Preliminaries

On Saturday, January 18, while the insurgent Farmer-Labor leaders were meeting in Fergus Falls, Mildred Andersch filed a divorce suit and a restraining order against her long-estranged husband, Wesley Andersch, eyewitness to Walter's murder. It was part of a series of defense actions intended to discredit him.

The suit called Wesley Andersch cruel and inhuman, and declared that he had "an extreme imaginative mind." Mildred Andersch's attorney claimed that he had "hallucinations." The couple had been separated since 1933. Wesley Andersch said he had not seen his estranged wife for two years and had never threatened her.[52]

On Sunday, January 19, the Associated Press reported that the prosecution would call twenty-five witnesses and hinted at "startling disclosures." Kid Cann's attorney, Thomas McMeekin, announced that the defense would call more than ninety witnesses. The *Chicago Tribune* reported that Edith regarded the trial as "the most terrible ordeal I ever have faced. But I will have to find the strength to stand it."[53]

Jury selection began at 9:30 A.M. on Monday, January 20. Long before that hour, curious spectators jammed the courtroom. When Kid Cann, shackled in handcuffs but dressed immaculately in a gray checked suit, entered the court, he and the deputy sheriff had to struggle through knots of fans in the corridor. The selection process went slowly. By the end of the day, only one juror, a housewife, had been chosen out of sixteen people questioned. McMeekin asked potential jurors about their views on liquor, their attitude toward Jews, their knowledge of the *Midwest American,* and their views on labor and the Farmer-Labor Party. Most jurors had disqualifying prejudices or convictions of one kind or another.

The *Chicago Tribune* repeated stories heard in the courthouse corridors; the scuttlebutt was that Cann had not killed Walter, but knew who did. If it began to look like he might be convicted, the *Tribune* wrote, his friends would not hesitate "to expose the whole mess" of political and criminal corruption in Minneapolis — a move that would reach high places in the city and state.[54]

On Tuesday, January 21, attorneys battled over names. Peter Neilson questioned the jury about their knowledge of such well-known gangsters and bootleggers as Bernie Berman, Cliff Skelly, Benny Haskell, Isadore Wolk, and Tommy Banks. McMeekin objected that "they have nothing to do with this case," but his objection was overruled.[55]

On Wednesday, January 22, the new foreman, Clive T. Naugle, announced that the grand jury would "go the limit" to clean up the liquor business.

Cann's "wife" and a group of relatives visited him in prison on January 23. Next door, the grand jury returned eight indictments against Minneapolis liquor dealers, many of them friends of Cann. These dealers were charged with falsifying affidavits in their license applications to the city council.

On Friday, January 24, reporters noted "strangers" questioning prospective jurors.

Edith wrote V. F. Calverton on January 26:

> The situation in North Dakota is better, and I'd be safe from being shot there, but I'm too disgusted and sick to care much about what happens. I've turned down two good offers for the plant and business — so the probable result will be that I'll be an involuntary bankrupt in about two weeks, and be out of business just as effectively. It's just too big a job for me to tackle without any capital at all, without

Walter, and with the promised insurgent [Farmer-Labor] support mysteriously evaporating.

There is a field here for an independent radical paper, but if your friend wants to run one, and take the name, mailing rights and legality of the *Midwest American,* he'd better let me know soon before the sheriff walks in.

Calverton replied that he and Charles Abrams had scoured New York for "a good fighting newspaperman" but had not yet found one. He enclosed his *Modern Monthly* article titled "Who Killed Walter Liggett?" and wrote: "But keep up your courage, old dear. . . . We're all with you, Edith. Goddamn it, don't let them get you, by getting on your nerves. You've got to be ever so strong now, and you will."[56]

On Monday, January 27, Olson signed the old age pension legislation for which he had convened the special legislative session.

Jury selection was completed on Tuesday, January 28. Eight men and four women had been chosen from a pool of 103. All the women were housewives, while the men included a credit manager, a grocery store manager, an insurance salesman, a real estate agent, and two Works Progress Administration workers. It was not a jury in which Edith had confidence.[57]

17. Kid Cann Beats the Rap

Somehow I must find strength to keep the *Midwest American* going since I need the purchase price to put away for the children's education. I must try to sell stuff where murder-notoriety has created a market. Somehow I must live through a trial where I'll be face to face with Kid Cann — whose grin keeps waking me up at night and interrupting my work during the day.

—**Edith Liggett to V. F. Calverton**

Prosecutor Frederick Pike opened Kid Cann's trial on January 29, 1936, by pointing out that Cann was being prosecuted jointly by the county attorney's office and the state attorney's office. "We will introduce evidence showing this was a premeditated, powerful, and brutal murder," Pike said. "We will show there was an auto occupied by at least two persons, one person driving and the other holding a machine gun. We shall offer evidence to show the defendant was the person who handled the gun that killed Liggett." The state, he said, had no knowledge of who the other person was.[1]

"Cann is the man who did it," Pike summed up. "Cann did it — and we will produce two actual eye-witnesses who will identify him as the murderer."[2] Pike meant Wesley Andersch and Edith (he was hiding Sally Baker Mairovitz), but neither was there: the prosecutors, it was said, wished to spare Edith as much as possible, while Andersch was being guarded against possible attacks.[3]

Cann listened attentively to the charge, chewing gum slowly, his chin cupped in his hand. His future wife, Lillian Lee, stylishly dressed and accompanied by her two sisters, sat in the first row of seats behind the counsel table, also chewing gum and listening attentively.

The state began the grisly process of establishing murder as the cause of death. A *Minneapolis Tribune* photographer testified about his photographs of the murder scene. Dr. Gilbert Seashore, the coroner, testified that he found five gunshot wounds at the postmortem; any of four could have caused death.[4] The morgue keeper testified that two bullets dropped from Walter's body; he pointed out five holes in Walter's overcoat that corresponded to the bullet holes in Walter's back.

William F. Hartman, the janitor at 1810 Third Avenue South, took the stand late in the day to testify about the time of the murder. He said that he and his wife were about to sit down to eat when Wesley Andersch (whom Hartman knew at that time as Isaacson) came to their door to announce that a man had been murdered. Andersch had shown them how the murderer's car had almost hit him as he went out the back door. The bulk of defense attorney Thomas McMeekin's cross-examination was intended to discredit Andersch.

Next door, the grand jury examined city records as part of its study of city council liquor license application procedures. Attempts at a cleanup under a gung ho grand jury would continue all through Cann's trial.

Predictions of ten-below cold on January 30 heralded the second day of the trial. Clara Hartman told the court that when she had accompanied Andersch and her husband to the murder scene, there were three or four persons in the alley. She knelt down and took up Walter's left hand; he was still alive. She went back to her apartment to telephone the police, then returned to the alley. By now, ten or twelve onlookers were there. Over McMeekin's objection, she testified that the police arrived seven to ten minutes later and asked Edith who did it. Edith had answered "Kid Cann."[5]

Wesley Andersch then took the stand, testifying that he had spent eight days in the Minneapolis workhouse in 1934 "for not completely paying a hotel bill" and had seen Cann there three times a day in the dining room. Pike's questioning led Andersch up to the time when he stepped out of the rear door of his fiancée's apartment building. Hurrying out, he had opened the door two or more feet when a car brushed the door. "I jerked back and swore at them," Andersch said. "The car went on down the alley. I saw two occupants in the front seat and as it moved down, I heard shots. After the car disappeared, I saw a man lying on the ground."

"How many persons were riding in the automobile?" Pike asked.

"I don't know," Andersch replied, "but I saw two men."

"Do you know who any of the occupants were?"

"Yes, one."

"Who was the occupant of the car that you know?"

"Kid Cann."

"You mean the defendant, Isadore Blumenfeld [*sic*]?"

"I don't know any Isadore Blumenfeld [*sic*]. I know Kid Cann."

"Do you see him in this courtroom?" Pike asked.

Andersch pointed at Kid Cann: "Yes, right there," he said.

Andersch testified that Cann was sitting in the right front seat, where the shooting came from. Then, Andersch said, he ran to look at the prostrate form in the alley, and then ran back to ask the caretaker in 1810 to call the police. A short while later, he came back to Dora Isaacson's apartment, then went home to his parents' house. McMeekin objected to Andersch's telling what he told his parents.

"Did you know who had been shot?" Pike asked. Andersch replied that he had heard who it was on the radio at his parents' home, where he had gone when he left the apartment building. The following day, he read about Cann's arrest in the newspapers. "Did you report to authorities your knowledge of the affair?" Pike asked.

"I did not. I left the city a few days later."

"Where did you go?"

"To my parents' farm, near Kimball."

"How long did you stay there?"

"Until the law came up and got me."

The February issue of *Liberty Magazine* carried an article titled "What Is Behind the Minneapolis Murders?" by Will Irwin, who had spent three weeks interviewing our printers and neighbors, the grocers for whom our shop printed handbills, and the stores that advertised in our weekly, as well as Farmer-Labor Party members who made vague accusations against Walter.[6]

Although Irwin had clashed angrily with Walter over President Hoover, he concluded that Walter "was roughly and generally right about one thing at least—the state of civic virtue in Minneapolis. Living he may have failed. But dead, he may go down as the man who led the way for a clean-up."[7]

According to the *Washington News,* Jacob "Dandy" Blumenfeld, who strongly resembled his half-brother Kid Cann, turned up in Paris, complaining about the plight of gangsters in America and denying that he was involved in Walter's murder. Although other gangsters had fled Minneapolis during the temporary cleanup, few had gone so far. Blumenfeld called the murder "a terrible extreme, but what the hell. Liggett persecuted the AZ Syndicate, which only wanted to live in peace with him. He was fiercely honest and he became ridiculously inconvenient."[8]

Back in Minneapolis, the predictions of cold proved more than accurate. Friday, January 31, the third day of the trial, began with the mercury at twenty below; by noon, it had warmed up to four below. It was the coldest January since 1912. Minneapolis had now had fourteen consecutive days of below-zero weather, and no letup was in sight.[9]

Outside the crowded courtroom, the corridors were packed with hundreds of persons unable to get seats, lingering in the hope that someone would leave. Inside, the tense, youthful-looking Wesley Andersch took the stand again. McMeekin grilled him for three hours about his income, his first wife, his past life, and his relationship with his fiancée — just about everything except the murder. McMeekin's cross-examination drew several sharp attacks from the judge, who warned against "an attempt to impeach the witness on insignificant matters." Under McMeekin's cross-examination, Andersch fleshed out his account of the murder.

"Was there nothing to attract your attention to the occupants of the car?" McMeekin asked.

"There was," answered Andersch.

"What was there?"

"A display in the man's hand."

"What was the display?" McMeekin asked.

"A machine gun."

"Kid Cann," Andersch continued, "was gripping the weapon, holding it at an angle toward the front of the car and with the barrel outside the open window. Both front windows were open."

Andersch could not identify the driver, who was slouched behind the wheel and wore a cap. He said he got a good view of the occupants "a split second" after the car struck his knee. Later, he had had a good view of the killer for "about a second or so — maybe two." He said it was long enough "for me to see what I did see."

He didn't tell anyone except his parents, he said. Although he realized it was his "duty as an American citizen to report the incident," he was "too damned scared." He left town, he said, because "they were coming too close to me. Everywhere I went, someone would say: 'Someone must have seen that' — even when I went into a gasoline station or a store to get a package of cigarettes." Not even what he had read in newspapers about rewards could induce him to step forward.

Edith testified in the afternoon. Dressed in black and leaning on Uncle Bob's arm, she had to enter the court through an aisle of the curious, who lined the corridors to get a glimpse of her. The courtroom was "deathly still except for a slight rustle as those in the crowd craned forward to look at her."[10] Her face clearly indicating an effort to be composed, Edith took the stand and identified Cann as the machine gunner who had shot Walter. Her effort to hold back tears was noticeable when she was asked about her husband's occupation. Her voice sank to a whisper as she began to answer Pike's questions about the events of the murder day, and the judge ordered the court corridors cleared.

"We saw an approaching car," she said. "It kept coming and it came faster than cars usually do going through an alley. I saw a man and he had a gun and flame was coming from it."[11]

Asked to identify the man, she said, "It's the man in the corner, the second one from Mr. McMeekin." Cann didn't move a muscle, but sat rigid with his face cupped in his hand.[12]

"After the shooting," Pike asked, "did you make any statement to a person who came to the scene of the murder?"

"Yes, to the first policeman who arrived."

"What did he ask?"

"He asked me who did it."

"Did you answer him?"

"Yes. I said: 'It was Kid Cann.' "

Pike then asked, "Were the lights of your car on after the shooting?" and Edith answered, "Yes, and for more than an hour afterwards."

That evening, Edith wrote a long letter to V. F. Calverton about the future of the *Midwest American:*

> I understand that it almost certainly would be necessary for me to stay with the paper for a while at least—possibly until after the election, although I hope not. However, I had promised Walter to stick it out here until after election and his murder won't make any difference if there is a means of keeping the *Midwest American* alive and accomplishing what he died for—freeing the Farmer-Labor party from the All-Party gang. But I'd be better, too, in Fargo, since a good part of my present near-collapse is due to the fact that every corner of this city is haunted by Walter. For months, since I feared his assassination if I left him, whenever he went anywhere, I was there. Now I can't enter an office building without remembering some conversation with Walter there. Every street corner in town brings visions of Walter, and the grim smile he kept on his face those last months. I stay away from the printing office for days at a time because I see him out at the stones, whistling as he and the printer make up pages. I've kept his desk rolled up, but even so it can't keep away the sight of Walter poring over figures, trying to balance the pathetic income and outgo of the business....
>
> Don't be afraid. I'm going to tell the truth in the trial. But I don't kid myself into thinking that there is a Chinaman's chance that Isidor

[*sic*] (Kid Cann) Blumenfeld will be convicted of anything in Hennepin county court house. . . .

I'll feel better after a weekend with the children. Isn't it ghastly to be so afraid of kidnappers that I daren't have them in this state?[13]

On Sunday, February 2, 1936, while a blizzard threatened to tie up traffic, liquor dealers announced that they would defy the city council — which had held up all liquor licenses — and open as usual on Monday.[14]

According to an AP dispatch, deputy sheriffs with subpoenas combed Minneapolis looking for Annette Fawcett and her secretary, Felix Doran. Their testimony on the Cann-Liggett meeting was expected to establish Cann's motives for the murder.

On Monday, February 3, Edith, "obviously refreshed and rested" from a weekend in Wisconsin, took the stand, again dressed in black; she maintained a calm demeanor through a full morning of cross-examination. She reiterated her identification of Cann and testified that an edition of the *Midwest American* in the mails on the night of the murder carried an attack on Cann and listed twelve reasons why Olson should be impeached.[15]

McMeekin questioned Edith at length on the position of the gunmen in the auto. "Did you give police a statement saying that the fire came from the back seat?" he asked.

"It is the face that is vivid, not the position of the face," Edith replied. "My little girl said the front seat. I see the thing over and over again. It is one of those horrible things you can't forget. I can see the two windows in the car, the two men, and the grinning face. The face is terrifically vivid. The position is not. I was aware of one spurt of flame. I was just vaguely aware of a gun. I was sort of petrified and I couldn't move. I watched the face disappear. He leaned out, grinning, and turned his head back for a second as the car went on."[16] Edith said she could not identify the driver, who was slumped down behind the wheel.

Late in the morning, the name of Governor Olson was brought into the testimony. "Do you remember an officer asking you who shot your husband?" McMeekin inquired.

"Yes."

"And didn't you answer 'It was either Kid Cann or Governor Olson's gang'?"

"I did not."

"Didn't you ever mention Governor Olson's name in the alley or anywhere that night?"

"When I called my mother after Walter was shot, and said 'Governor Olson's gang got Walter, mother.' She asked me, 'Do you know who did it?' I said, 'Yes, Kid Cann.' I must have associated the two together."

"Did you associate the defendant with Governor Olson's gang?" McMeekin asked.

And Edith answered, "My association is that the murder would not have been committed without Governor Olson's permission. Meaning they either ordered it or permitted it."[17]

This reply led to a host of charges and countercharges. During the mid-morning recess, Edith collapsed weeping in the county attorney's office. The court called a three-hour recess.

Later, returning to the witness stand, Edith repeated her identification of Cann as the grinning machine gunner. She described faces peering into our newspaper office prior to the assassination, and she identified Philip "Flippy" Share as one man she had seen loitering six or eight weeks before the murder. She added that "a number of criminals in Minneapolis would come there to glare at the office." She also revealed that Walter had been threatened by a member of Ed Morgan's gang.

That night, Edith wrote two long letters to V. F. Calverton. In the first she wrote:

> I did a fool thing in the trial when I let Cann's lawyer, McMeekin, egg me into saying that Olson either permitted or ordered the murder. Of course it is true, but there are at least two, and I believe three Farmer-Laborites on the jury. I was the most surprised person in the whole court room when I heard myself making that statement. . . .
>
> The remarkable thing is that, although Cann will almost certainly be acquitted, the city is terrifically aroused and cleanup is starting that will leave it as good as most American cities, instead of the wild frontier town it has become under the Olson machine. . . .
>
> My only desire now is to get out of the state as quickly as possible after the trial is over. I haven't the remotest desire right now to be an agrarian reformer. . . . After 24 successive days of below zero mercury, I can't see why the Indians weren't permitted to keep this damned state.
>
> I've done my best. I hope that I can manage to get back East within the next few weeks, find a job, and keep from going screwy — as I in-

evitably would here. In fact, the ability of McMeekin to make me blurt out what I did in court proves I'm half batty right now.

The paper I've been getting out lately is lousy for the reason that I simply haven't the faculty of impersonal righteous indignation—and it is impossible to run a crusading weekly without it. I'm so deathly sick of politicians that the need to see one nauseates me.

In a second letter to Calverton (who was often called "George" by his friends), Edith wrote that she had "found out more about that offer to buy the plant":

Funds were being collected among the All-Party politicians to see if they could make a cash offer to buy the plant and have Walter out of the state before the campaign got under way. However, the mutual friend who had been selected as a go-between had not yet contacted Walter. I knew, of course, that Walter had never heard of it, but since there actually was such a plan under way, it is more than possible that, when the Langer conversation was listened to over the phone, whoever was putting up the money decided that one way or another Walter would be fighting Olson if alive—and used the money to pay for his murder. They certainly felt it necessary to kill him at once before he could bring the impeachment charges before the Legislature—and his death decided upon, it is very easy to see how Schuldberg was enraged by being told that Walter was trying to have the permit of the Minnehaha liquor store—one of his outlets—revoked. . . .

You know, George, that what would have been one of the most interesting and bitter campaigns ever waged in America will reach election minus the three chief actors. Walter was murdered, Schall killed by an auto, Olson has a cancer of the stomach, and by election will be dead or dying.[18]

On Tuesday, February 4, Annette Fawcett wired from Illinois that she had just learned she was wanted as a witness and was willing to come back, but Pike ended the state's case without calling her. On the last day of state testimony, two radio employees, Wesley Andersch's father, supervisor of detectives John C. Hilborn, and I were called to the stand.

Wallace and I were driven in from Wisconsin, while two radio employees, two pleasant young men, came to testify as to the exact time of the *Jack Armstrong* radio broadcast when Wallace had heard the words "a palace of ice" just before he heard the shots.[19] I felt grown-up chatting with them in the anteroom about a contest that Wheaties was sponsoring. Contestants were supposed to create words from the slogan "Wheaties keeps you as warm as a cooked cereal," and I had been working on a long list of words in Wisconsin.

I was the first to testify that morning, wearing the heavy navy skirt and striped sweater Edith and I had bought the day after my birthday. Pike gave me a smile and a grandfatherly pat on my shoulder. On the stand, in a "nearly inaudible voice," I testified that I was the daughter of Edith Liggett, and that I was in our automobile on December 9. Asked the number of men in the murder car, I said, "I think it was two," and that I thought they were in the front seat.

I was disappointed by Pike's short questioning. I had wanted to tell the whole story of the evening of the murder. I wanted to be a heroine, to do something to avenge my father. McMeekin didn't ask me anything at all; he just said "No questions" with an infuriating, pseudofatherly smile. I would have liked to stick my tongue out or kick him in the shins. Instead, I walked demurely from the stand.

After the testimony of the radio men, attorneys for both sides stipulated the murder time as 5:41, making it unnecessary for Wally to testify. (This was, I believe, the first time that a radio broadcast had been used to pinpoint the time of a murder.) Wally was glad. He had not looked forward to testifying.[20]

Before the afternoon session, when Edith was expected to testify, an almost unmanageable crowd—four times as many as could fit in the courtroom— stretched in four lines from the courtroom door around the corridor outside.[21] McMeekin started off by asking Edith if she had become nervous and hysterical after the shooting.

"Naturally," Edith answered. "I was almost paralyzed. I didn't come to until my little girl started screaming."

"She was still in the car?"

"I think so."

"Did you immediately step down on the ground then?"

"Yes."

"Did you scream?"

"I don't think so. Some people came and I begged them to get an ambulance. I thought Mr. Liggett was still alive."

She said that she had named Cann before seeing his picture, and that the picture in the newspaper was not a good likeness. She reiterated that our car lights were not turned off until long after the murder.

Next Louis Andersch, Wesley Andersch's father, took the stand. Despite McMeekin's objection, he was able to state that Wesley had come home around 6:30 on the evening of the killing and said, "Pa, I've seen something—I've been witness to something—if I had a million dollars, I would give it up if I hadn't."

McMeekin objected, but Pike was finally able to get a simple statement from Louis Andersch that Wesley had said he had just seen a man killed.

"Did he follow that up with a statement that he knew the man who did it?"

"He mentioned a name."

"What name did he mention?" Pike asked.

In a loud voice, Louis Andersch blurted out "Kid Cann."

The radio announcement had not come on until ten to fifteen minutes later, Andersch said.

In the defense's opening statement, McMeekin announced that Cann would take the stand in his own defense and that between seventy-five and one hundred witnesses would sustain his alibi.[22] "We will prove that the defendant arrived at the barber shop between 5:30 and 5:35 and remained there until after 6 o'clock," he told the jury.

By this time, the media-driven fracas between Edith and Governor Olson had begun to overshadow the trial. From his sickbed in Rochester, Olson issued a statement denying that he had ever harbored enmity for Walter. "For Mrs. Liggett," he said, "I have only sympathy. In her bereavement, she is entitled to and has the sympathy of everyone. But that does not give her the right to make false and unfair statements such as her charge that I was connected with the murder of her husband."

"Mrs. Liggett has been incited by some crafty, politically minded men to make various statements reflecting upon me," he asserted. "I can name the men if I am challenged."

Edith replied that it was "the duty of any governor to see that the safety of every citizen is protected" and that "by a curious coincidence in Minnesota, the men who are opposing the governor are in danger."[23]

On Wednesday, February 5, the sensation of the day was the testimony of four policemen called as defense witnesses. Patrolmen Richard Miller and Ralph Jacobson and detectives Art Olson and Charles Wetherille all described the alley as dark and Edith as hysterical. Miller claimed that he had heard Edith say in our apartment that the murder car was a coupe. He also testified that Edith had said, "It must have been Kid Cann or one of Olson's gang."

Jacobson testified that the lights of our apartment were out and that Edith had told him that the car was a light coupe, and that, when he asked her if she recognized anyone in the car, she said, "Kid Cann. Schuldberg was sitting right next to him."

As the Associated Press noted, the trial testimony of these policemen contradicted their own official police reports.[24]

Thursday, February 6, was the twentieth successive day of subzero temperatures, shattering a record set in 1899. The attack on Edith's and Wesley Andersch's eyewitness accounts of the shooting continued. A defense witness claimed that at the death scene she had heard someone ask Edith who shot her husband, and that Edith had replied, "How should I know? I was looking out of the window at the time."

City jailer Milton E. Winslow testified that he was in charge of the police lineup at which Edith identified Kid Cann. Three men in the lineup had worn overalls, he said; one had worn overall pants with an overcoat, and one wore a sweater. In response to a question, he agreed that the defendant had probably worn an overcoat and hat.

On cross-examination, Pike reminded Winslow that he had been instructed to pick out persons as near the defendant's general type as possible. Had he followed these instructions? Winslow first replied that he had not had enough men in jail, and then answered that he had done so "to the best of my ability." He did not recall how prisoners had been dressed in three other lineups that week.[25]

Weatherman Martin R. Hovde took the stand next, testifying that a slight fog (which I do not recall) had lifted at 5:40 on the day of the murder. Hovde said that the temperature was 22 degrees at 5:40, and that when the fog lifted at 5:40, there was moonlight from a full moon.[26]

William Hartman, the janitor at 1810 Third Avenue South, now a defense witness, described the alley as between dark and light, a change from his original statement. McMeekin brought in a twenty-five-watt bulb to demonstrate the only light in the alley—a light over the rear entrance to our building. On cross-examination, Hartman recalled that lights had been on in our apartment window and in the apartment across the alley.

Meyer Schuldberg took the stand late in the afternoon. He said that he had met Walter in either July or August 1935, and that he had heard from him again on December 9, when Walter called him about 3:30 P.M. He denied that he threatened to sue or that he yelled over the telephone. On the day of the murder, Schuldberg said, he had first seen Cann at 9:30, and saw him again at noon, when they had gone to lunch at the East Side Cafe. Cann was using his—Schuldberg's—green Dodge all day; Cann returned to the plant between 4:30 and 4:45, and left again at six minutes after five.[27]

In Rochester, Governor Olson named A. B. Gilbert as one of the men who had incited Edith to attack him: "Gilbert is one of them, but he doesn't count. He's a Non-Partisan League renegade." He never did name any others.

State Representative Marius Waldal of Plummer, however, declared that only Olson's illness and the expense of a long investigation had prevented a probe on impeachment charges in the recent special legislative session. Several leaders of the antiadministration faction contradicted this statement, but none was willing to be quoted.[28]

A janitor at the *Midwest American* called the police four times on February 6 and twice on February 7 to report prowlers.[29]

A new cold wave was forecast for February 7, while Kid Cann refused to testify because it was Friday. His attorney remarked that Cann was "extremely superstitious" but still made full use of the day, bringing in Schuldberg, an alcohol tax investigator (who testified that he was sitting in Schuldberg's office when Walter called Schuldberg, and that Schuldberg did not yell or make any threats), and more than a dozen witnesses who affirmed Cann's alibi. When Pike asked Schuldberg about his cars on cross-examination, Schuldberg had alibis for both the green Dodge and the Chevrolet coupe. He said he had driven the Dodge home and that the sales manager took the coupe around 5:30.

Three bankers (some of whom knew Cann as Bloom) testified that Cann was in their bank at two in the afternoon. Sam Shink, Cann's brother-in-law and a bartender at the Keystone, testified that Cann came to the Keystone at 2:15 and stayed twenty-five or thirty minutes. A policeman who happened to be in the Keystone at 2:15 and 2:45 agreed that he had seen Cann there.[30] Max Levine testified that Cann was in his produce market between 2:30 and 3:00, while his partner, Robert Lindgren, remembered that Cann was there from approximately 2:00 or 2:30 until approximately 3:45. The switchboard operator at the Colonial Warehouse testified that Cann arrived there at 3:00. A. T. Fleming from next door said that Cann was there at 3:15 and was still there at 4:15 and 4:30. Cann's alibi had similar redundancies throughout.

While the defense paraded witnesses through the court, forty Minneapolis civic and religious organizations declared the week of February 22 Good Government Week; a thorough study of the inner workings of Minneapolis government would determine how to clean up the city.[31] Meanwhile, the grand jury indicted nine more liquor dealers on perjury charges for failing to list their prior convictions on their liquor license applications. The total was now sixteen.[32]

In the February 7 issue of the *Midwest American*—the last—Edith in her lead story headlined "Why Do Mill City Police Keep Protecting Cann?" commented on "the amazing spectacle of four police officers of Minneapolis deliberately committing perjury in the attempt to win the release of Kid Cann":

> That their statements [at the trial] were intentionally false instead of mistaken is beyond dispute. They quoted me as saying that Meyer Schuldberg drove the death car, whereas I have never seen Mr. Schuldberg, do not know what he looks like, and have repeatedly told questioners that whereas I believe I have seen the driver before, I could not recognize him. Innumerable pictures were shown me in the attempt to make me name the driver but I repeated the truth—that I could not identify him—that the sole face I recognized was the grinning murderer—Isadore Blumenfield. . . .
>
> With a boldness explained only by the fact that life-long immunity to punishment for any crime had made the murderers bold to the point of recklessness, the killers wore no masks, did their shooting in an alley where there might have been a dozen eye-witnesses—killed my husband while I was . . . no more than two or three feet away—and the grinning killer passed so close to me that I could have touched him.
>
> Possibly he did not know that I had had him pointed out to me and would be able to identify him. . . . For once, there was a witness that could not be either bought or intimidated.

On Saturday, February 8, Clive T. Naugle, foreman of the active new grand jury, pledged to continue investigating. "There's enough stuff here to keep us busy until next December," he said.[33]

On February 9, as a blizzard surpassing the famous storm of 1888 blocked highways, halted rail services, and closed stores in Minnesota, the *Chicago Tribune*'s second full-page article on murder in Minneapolis came out in the Sunday edition. A smaller section with a large picture of Olson, captioned "How Floyd B. Olson Treated Gunmen and Boodlers," described the Syndicate and charged that Olson, as Hennepin County attorney, had failed to prosecute certain criminals. The article ended with a long discussion of aldermanic graft cases of 1928 and 1929 that the author claimed Olson had used to build himself up politically.[34]

Court opened on Monday, February 10, with the testimony of two employees of Chesapeake Brands—B. W. Beidelman, the sales manager, and Louis Malkin, the shipping clerk. Beidelman's testimony was nearly the same as the account he had given the county attorney's office on December 16, when he had said that Cann came in at 10:30 and that he himself had left at 5:45; on the stand, he testified that Cann came in around 9:30 and that he himself had worked until 6:00, at which time he drove the coupe home. This car was in front of the plant when he came out, he said, but he had no personal knowledge of where it was between 5:30, when Malkin gave him the keys, and 6:00.

Malkin gave a detailed account of driving Cann to a nearby garage shortly before the murder. Malkin punched out at 5:06 and drove Cann in Beidelman's Chevrolet coupe to St. Anthony Motor Company, where Cann got out with an auto heater. Cann returned around 5:20 or 5:25, and then Malkin dropped Cann off at the Liquor Mart. Malkin returned to Chesapeake Brands between 5:30 and 5:35; he went in and gave the car keys to Beidelman.[35]

Cann, dressed in a natty green suit, a white shirt, and a dark red tie, and making an obvious effort to steady himself, arrived in court through a line of spectators. As they craned forward to get a better look at him, he looked the court clerk in the eye; taking the oath, he blurted out a loud "I do" that startled the courtroom. Attempting nonchalance, he stumped to the chair and cupped his chin in his hand, resting his elbow on the rail until McMeekin directed him to sit up straight.

Questioned about his background, Cann testified that he had been working for Chesapeake Brands since March 1934, when he got out of the workhouse. He admitted to having been arrested three times during Prohibition. Asked if he had had anything to do with the murder, he replied, "Not a thing in the world." He gave a full account of his activities the day of Walter's murder, although some of the times he gave differed slightly from those of his witnesses and those in his first alibi.[36]

When Cann was questioned the next day, it came out that his name was really Blumenfield, not Blumenfeld, as it was spelled on the indictment and in most newspapers. Under cross-examination, Cann explained that he often called himself Bloom because "Blumenfield is sort of a complicated name."

Cann withstood Pike's assault on his alibi and questions about his bootlegging background. Cann claimed that he had been in the bootlegging business "by myself." He denied any knowledge of firearms, although the police had found a pistol in his drawer. (Indeed, this pistol and its cartridges were Exhibits O and P.) Asked if he had ever used them, he said, "Never in my life," and he maintained that he had no idea who had killed Walter.[37]

Cann gave a plausible account of his arrest: He had dropped into Curley's Restaurant next door to the Liquor Mart sometime before 7:00. He had just ordered a steak when a friend came in to tell him that two detectives were waiting for him in the Liquor Mart. He canceled his steak order and called his lawyer, who agreed to meet him downtown in half an hour. Then he reordered — this time a sandwich, soup, and a cup of coffee — and ate. Stepping outside, he heard newsboys shouting out extras announcing Walter's murder. Cann and a friend read the paper before Cann strolled over to Detectives Kramer and Eisenkramer.

"We'll have to take you down," Kramer told Cann. "Mr. Liggett got killed and Mrs. Liggett mentioned your and Schuldberg's name."

The two officers apparently had left the station without knowing where Schuldberg lived, and they asked Cann for his address. Together, Cann said, he and the police looked in the telephone book. Then they allowed him to telephone Schuldberg. When Schuldberg did not come out in response to the police honking outside his house, one of the policemen gave Cann a flashlight to check the address. The detectives, Cann, and Schuldberg then went back down to the Liquor Mart, where Cann was allowed to get out of the car to talk to his attorney alone. As Pike pointed out, the police were far more courteous to Cann than to Edith.

Cross-examined on his dealings with Annette Fawcett, Cann admitted meeting her on October 23 but denied that he had arranged with her to meet Walter in her apartment at the Radisson. He contended that when he met Walter in her apartment, Walter was "drunk and intoxicated" and had "made a pass" at him. Still, Cann claimed the meeting ended in a "friendly way." They had not fought in the café, and he had remained in the café for twenty-five minutes after Walter left.[38]

While Cann was on the stand, the *Minneapolis Journal* published an exclusive story: Meyer Schuldberg had reported that two police officers had approached him on Christmas Day, offering to fix the case for $10,000. Both Peter Neilson and the grand jury were looking into Schuldberg's charges; one of the officers was supposed to be of high rank.[39]

Meanwhile, Minneapolis police, stirred by reports of a sweeping grand jury investigation that would "tear the lid off the town," raided liquor and gambling resorts and arrested twenty-five people as just about every group from the Better Business Bureau to the YMCA and the Women's Welfare League mobilized for Good Government Week.[40]

On Wednesday, February 12, when the court was recessed for Lincoln's birthday, missing witness Felix Doran called the county attorney's office from New York, declaring that he had left Minneapolis on January 1 "without the aid of false whiskers" and was ready "to be of service." The prosecution had, however, completed its case.[41]

On Thursday, February 13, the defense announced that it would rest its case. Most of Cann's witnesses were unshaken, even though it was pointed out that they had given different times during the investigation and on the stand. The state did manage to confuse the barber who had shaved and steamed Cann. Ultimately he said that Cann had entered the Artistic Barber Shop at 5:24.[42]

The defense now came up with a new alibi witness — fifteen-year-old newsboy Isidore Brodsky, who testified that he sold Cann a newspaper on a downtown street between 5:30 and 5:35 (six minutes before the murder). Brodsky recalled the time because both Cann and the man he was talking to stood almost in front of a large clock in a nearby store window. "I can still picture that clock," he said. He could not name any other customers he had served that day.[43]

As the court opened on Friday, February 14, McMeekin requested that the jury visit the scene of the murder and see the door from which Wesley Andersch had emerged. The judge said that he would instruct bailiffs to take the jury there on Saturday. The defense rested.

Pike started his rebuttal with stenographers who read from defense witnesses' original statements that differed from their testimony on the stand.

Marguerite Van Wold reiterated her description of the murder car as a sedan or coach that slowed down beneath her window as she looked out. Edward Kriege testified that he saw Edith right after the shooting, that the alley was fairly well lit, and that he had stayed until after the officers arrived and had never heard Edith say "How should I know?" when she was asked who shot her husband.

Alice Delaney testified that she was with Edith constantly from after the murder until late at night, and that Edith had said that Kid Cann killed Walter and had never described the killer's car as a coupe.

"How did you happen to notice the headlights in the Liggett car were on?" McMeekin asked.

"You could see Mr. Liggett's body in the lights," Alice replied.[44]

Patrolman Fred Higgins, called to the stand as a rebuttal witness, testified that he had heard Edith testify that the killer's car was a coach or sedan.

"Did you hear her mention Kid Cann and Schuldberg as the slayers?"

"No."

On cross-examination, Higgins was asked if he had heard Edith mention Schuldberg's name, and he said he overheard it while she was engaged in a telephone conversation. Higgins's testimony on the stand — unlike that of other Minneapolis policemen — was consistent with his written report.[45]

Returning to the stand to be questioned by Pike, Edith said that two uniformed policemen and two plainclothesmen had questioned her the night of the murder.

"Did you at any time state Schuldberg killed your husband?"

"I did not. I have never seen Schuldberg in my life." The last portion was stricken by McMeekin's objection.

Edith repeated her identification of Cann and denied that she ever gave any other name.[46]

Testimony concluded on February 17. Both sides rested after rebuttal evidence showed that Cann had indeed used a gun before. A detective showed the .38 Colt revolver and cartridges that he had confiscated from Cann's home on December 15, and a patrolman testified that he had seen Cann in the Cotton Club in Minneapolis early in the morning in February 1928 running between the tables with a gun in his hand.

Pike made his final attack on Cann's alibi; notably, on a twenty-minute gap between the times—5:30 and 5:50—when reputable witnesses saw Cann in the barber chair. Pike claimed Cann would have had time to shoot Walter and return to the barbershop, since the distance between our alley and the barbershop was only about a mile and a half. He launched a sharp attack on the Minneapolis police force, noting that after Walter's murder officers had attempted to confuse Edith rather than sending men at once to pick up Cann. Pike also cited the sympathetic treatment given Cann.[47]

Additional armed guards were ordered on duty on February 18 after Sheriff John Wall reported that six Chicago criminals were in the courtroom.[48] As court opened, Pike rose to conclude his argument. He called Cann's alibi "spurious" and noted that witnesses placed Cann at two or three different places at noon, and several places at three o'clock.

McMeekin made a vigorous summation: "We are not here to try Governor Olson's administration, to foster the political ambitions of the attorney general's office, to discredit the Minneapolis police force nor uphold the Hennepin county attorney's office...."

"And what do we find?" McMeekin asked dramatically. "The very officers of the law who were at the scene first and should have known the truth were not called. And the defense was criticized for calling them."

McMeekin asserted that Schuldberg and Cann had no motive for the crime; Schuldberg was running a legitimate plant under government supervision, while Cann had a job in a legitimate business after he came out of the workhouse. He attacked Edith's credibility, although, he said, his heart went out to her. It was natural for her to have made mistakes about Schuldberg and Cann "during this terrible kind of shock and trial." Touching on Edith's testimony, he observed that "she would ask the jury to believe that the highest executive officer in the state was involved in the murder." Throughout his argument, Edith sat in the courtroom, wan and pale and dressed in black, within six feet of Cann, who at times appeared bored by what was going on.[49]

In his charge to the jury, the judge pointed out that the rule of reasonable doubt was not intended to protect the guilty or to shield the jury from a difficult duty: "It is a defense which is easy to fabricate and hard to disprove, and you are cautioned to scrutinize it with care."

The jury began its deliberation at 4:15. Although the jurors reached a verdict on the first ballot, they took time out for dinner after notifying the judge that they were ready to report. Edith was not present when the jury returned its verdict at 8:22 before a small group of reporters and Cann's friends.

Cann was led into the courtroom, handcuffed to a deputy and guarded by four other deputies. The verdict was obvious, as each of the jurors turned toward Cann and smiled. When the judge read, "We, the jury, find the defendant not guilty," spectators, mostly friends of Cann, cheered wildly. Cann broke through a circle of friends and rushed to the jury box to kiss the hands of the four women jurors and shake the hands of the men.[50]

A big party at the Radisson Hotel followed. The hundred or more celebrants included Farmer-Labor officeholders, McMeekin, a score of local and out-of-town reporters, and a "workable majority of the Loop's most prominent figures."[51] Bennie Meshbesher, brother of Mildred Andersch's attorney, was the maître d'.

"I'm back in the crowd and I'm going to stay there," Cann vowed. He reported that he had lost thirty pounds during his stay in the county jail and asked, "How in the world could Mrs. Liggett ever pick me out for a person that would kill her husband? I didn't have any reason to harm him like that. And I would not be a party to any such terrible act that would rob a wife and two little kiddies of the protection of a husband and a father."[52]

Meanwhile, county attorney Ed Goff demanded that Harry Bloom, Cann's brother, appear before the grand jury to testify about offers to Cann's friends for "fixing" the Cann trial jury. The grand jury also wanted to ask Bloom about his connection with the Syndicate's Lake Street Liquor Store. The inquiry was supposed to be balked by Bloom's failure to appear. Although Andrew Crummy had a subpoena ordering Bloom to appear, he could not locate either Bloom or the lawyer's investigator who was wanted for questioning in the extortion plot. It shouldn't have been too hard to find Bloom since newspaper accounts put him in the courthouse awaiting the verdict.[53]

It was an expensive victory: Cann's defense reputedly cost about $25,000. He was said to have paid McMeekin $12,500, while his defense investigator, William Dannenberg, was said to have received $6,000.

Cann still had a four-year-old indictment hanging over him for liquor conspiracy in New Orleans, where he had been indicted in December 1932 but never tried. The United Press quoted Rene Viosca, the federal district attorney for New Orleans, as saying that Cann might still be prosecuted; the decision would have to be made by the Department of Justice in Washington.[54]

18. Loose Ends

One in a family is enough to sacrifice.

—**Edith Liggett, interview, March 5, 1936**

Leaving Town

Edith, not surprised by the verdict, had prepared a statement:

> The amazing part of the trial, to one unaccustomed to the close tie-up between a large part of the police force and the liquor syndicate to which Kid Cann belonged, was the spectacle of four police officers calmly perjuring themselves in the successful effort to win his freedom.
>
> This, of course, is an old Minnesota custom. . . .
>
> No attempt has been made by the police force to discover who drove the car, who provided the machine gun, if there was any mistake in the identification, or to produce the killers.

The chief declared that his department was checking all the angles: "There are six detectives assigned to the investigation. . . . Every possible lead has been and will be followed. We have . . . spent more money in this investigation than in any other in my experience. Never has there been a more thorough search for clues."

While the state attorney general promised "appropriate action" if any new evidence came to light, Governor Olson announced that every available state agency would "concentrate on the effort to detect and apprehend Liggett's slayers." The attorney general announced that he was ready to call the state Bureau of Criminal Apprehension to investigate rumors of a machine gun, and bureau head Melvin Passolt said his operatives were "tracing every possible clue."[1]

Edith reported to the attorney general that after she had taken the stand in Cann's trial, a car parked up the street from the *Midwest American* office swerved sharply at her when she stepped off the curb. "It wasn't just a skidding car," she said. "It was a deliberate attempt at murder."[2]

The county attorney's stenographic staff had to work overtime to get charges prepared for the grand jury meeting on February 21. The grand jurors voted indictments charging seven more Minneapolis liquor dealers with perjury in making out license applications, bringing the total to twenty-one.

Good Government Week opened with sensational charges that the four women and eight men who had acquitted Cann had been warned to "vote for acquittal or else — ." Efforts to tamper with the grand jury were also reported.[3]

Meanwhile, Edith, who had located three prospective purchasers, went to probate court to prepare to sell the *Midwest American*. "As soon as the sale is completed," she declared, "I expect to leave Minneapolis."[4]

In New York City, where our family was headed, the Communist *Daily Worker* ran the first of a series of articles "explaining the causes and significances of Walter Liggett's death" on February 24, 1936. The articles were signed by Martin Young, a comrade who had recently come to Minnesota to assist with implementation of the Communist Party's Popular Front policy of unity with the Farmer-Labor Party, but were instigated and perhaps written by *Daily Worker* editor Clarence Hathaway, a native Minnesotan who had returned to help guide the Minnesota Communist Party into the Farmer-Labor Association. Hathaway had been hanging out in Minnesota after Walter's murder, frequently conversing, he later said, with Governor Olson, Henry Teigan, Howard Williams, and other Farmer-Labor officials and third-party advocates.[5]

The first article was a lengthy front-page story headlined "Liggett Was Murdered by the Underworld for His Scavenging." Like those that followed, it employed the vituperative rhetoric of Communist Party polemicists and was wildly inaccurate. The date of Walter's death, for example, was given as December 29 (twenty days off), and although he was killed two weeks before Schall died, the *Worker* denounced Walter for writing an overfriendly obituary of Schall. This article called Walter a traitor to the Farmer-Labor Party, a blackmailer who demanded loans from underworld characters, and a cheap tool of the Republicans.

"Liggett's guilt is clear," the *Worker* declared: "Liggett had a 'habit' before printing stories of the workings of certain liquor interests to ask these very people for a loan. How well he succeeded is of little interest to us." This information came from "newspaper reports which no one has as yet disproved"—almost certainly from the *Minnesota Leader.*

The *Worker* accused Edith of "trying to capitalize, politically and financially, on [Walter's] death" and went on to say that "it is especially disgusting to see the widow of the slain publisher selling the corpse limb by limb to the highest bidder of the Minnesota Republican party."

"Liggett's Anti-Labor Bias Aided Scabs in Strutwear Strike" and "Liggett Undermined Farmer-Labor Party" were the *Daily Worker*'s February 25 and 27 stories. The paper called Walter "an unprincipled character" who "degenerated into a tool of the most reactionary Republican and labor-hating interests."

Throughout February 1936 and beyond, Farmer-Labor officials continued to denounce Edith in hit-and-run attacks by word of mouth and private letters. Since Edith was suing Teigan and the *Minnesota Leader* for libel, the *Leader* itself was more circumspect.

V. F. Calverton must have mailed Edith a copy of the February 24 issue of the *Daily Worker*, for Edith wrote him just before we left Minnesota:

> The article in the *Daily Worker* is along the lines of the stuff Olson's press agents have been putting out. . . .
>
> There's no use repeating again how ridiculous the accusation that Walter "attempted to get money from the underworld." . . . Anyone who knows as I do the repeated efforts to bribe both of us can only laugh at the story. . . . It is a matter of credibility — and of knowledge of underworld psychology. The underworld is always willing and anxious to pay. That is their language. What they cannot understand is a man like Walter who refused to take bribes.[6]

By this time, we were free to leave. The probate court had settled Walter's estate — a total of $1,324. The *Midwest American*, which had launched all this brouhaha, became history as its equipment was sold and the Cedar Lake Ice Company took possession of the building. Edith kept the title to the *Midwest American*, mainly for sentimental reasons.[7]

In an interview on the morning of our departure, Edith told reporters, "I am leaving Minneapolis because I fear for my life and for my children. Already, an attempt has been made to kill me." The next week, C. D. Johnston, Elmer Benson's secretary, wrote Teigan that he and Senator Benson "both had a good laugh" over Edith's expressed fear for her life.[8]

"No Stone Unturned"

Despite the promises and proclamations of state and city officials, the search for Walter's killer ended when Fred Witters, the state's sole investigator, withdrew from Case 5226 at 8:30 P.M. on the evening of Cann's acquittal. In his final report, Witters, an honest if not sparkling investigator, wrote:

> It was apparent to me that efforts were made constantly to block my progress in following my investigation.... The case was, in my opinion, very poorly handled. The County Attorney's office is probably to blame for most of the inefficiency shown as well as the deliberate distribution of advance information. This point is generally admitted by even attaches of the County Attorney's office.[9]

Some newspapers and reporters made sporadic efforts to keep the case alive. John Harvey, who had risen from cub reporter to city editor of the *Minneapolis Star* in three years, had quit his job to investigate the case. He threw a lot of ingenuity into the pursuit, but to no avail: no official agencies—local, state, or national—were interested.[10]

Harvey, it appears, had first been hired by Ed Goff to investigate the murder (or to get him out of the way). In February, Harvey sent Goff "complete information on the Liggett case and the so-called Alcohol Syndicate from 1928 through Feb. 7th, 1936" to present to the Hennepin County grand jury.

To check on ties between the Syndicate and Cann's defense attorneys, Harvey had rented a room next to that of the defense counsel, and had learned that defense witnesses met with the Syndicate in Shakopee, Minnesota. Felix Doran had shown up at the hotel on the very day he was supposed to be a state witness in Minneapolis. Harvey had even managed to glean information on some of the Syndicate's future plans. It had taken him more than a hundred hours to gather this data, although he had not charged for his time. So far as I can ascertain, Goff neither paid for nor made any use of this information.[11]

From Chicago, Harvey sent deputy attorney general Roy Frank a special delivery, registered letter claiming that the Syndicate and the Liggett case were "so closely connected I have placed them together in my report and my enclosed detailed expense account."[12] Harvey then took off for New York City and Washington, D.C., where he attempted to interest the FBI and the Alcohol Tax Unit in his briefcase full of documents. The FBI scolded him for his efforts.[13]

When Harvey wired Frank to ask for the state's share of investigation expenses, Frank told Harvey to collect from Goff: "Neither Mr. Pike nor myself had the authority to retain anyone or incur any expense without the express approval of the Attorney General." But in fact the legislature had allocated extra funds for an investigation, and both Pike and Peterson publicly claimed they were pursuing the case.[14]

Harvey replied that Pike had approved "expenses in the neighborhood of $200."[15]

Harvey wanted Pike and Frank to meet him in Chicago. He even offered to pay their airfare. It was, he wrote, "extremely important regarding the Kid Cann case, and will give you the great pleasure of having a second crack at him." Roy Frank replied:

> Both Mr. Pike and myself have read your letter very carefully and have discussed the matter at some length. We should be personally very much interested in knowing the information to which you refer; but we are now met with the fact that so far as our office duties are concerned there is nothing assigned to either of us for present consideration in regard to the subject of your letter. . . . Neither Mr. Pike nor myself is at liberty at this time to make any official engagements in regard to this subject.

Where were the funds allocated by the legislature for the investigation? And all the pledges to track down Walter's killer? Unfortunately, Harvey's $350.15 expense account is all that remains of the only thorough investigation of my father's murder. It seems a bargain even at Depression prices.[16]

For all practical purposes, this ended the investigation. Over the years, city, county, and state police and the FBI noted down information that was offered them; when they happened to stumble across something of interest, they usually let it drop. John Hilborn mailed out inquiries for the Minneapolis police, but, judging from the files, drew few responses.[17]

There was a flurry of interest in the case in August 1936 after Walter Wendt, a private investigator who sometimes worked for the *Chicago Tribune,* impersonated a federal agent to get a copy of an anonymous letter mailed from California a few days after the murder; this letter named two Kansas City men as the hit men and Jack Davenport as the payoff man. Minneapolis police had denied the existence of this letter, and later claimed it was lost.[18]

In October, after Wendt received a suspended sentence for impersonation, the *Minneapolis Star* got hold of the letter. Within an hour, a reporter identified the two criminals by phoning Kansas City. The paper gave the names to the Minneapolis police, who again dropped the inquiry.[19]

But if the *Tribune* was involved in 1936, it apparently dropped its investigation. Much later, in 1958, A. B. Gilbert told a reporter that he was with investigator Alexander Jamie when Colonel McCormick of the *Chicago Tribune* wired Jamie to end his probe of Walter's murder. According to Gilbert, "Jamie thought he had the case about solved, and was bowled over by McCormick's order." Gilbert thought that someone must have pressured McCormick.[20]

In February 1937, state senator A. J. Rockne headed a Senate Finance Committee inquiry into the Bureau of Criminal Apprehension's handling of the investigations of the Guilford and Liggett murders. The committee, in fact, withheld state funds from the bureau for a while, but had little effect overall.[21]

19. Home to Brooklyn

On the first day of March 1936, we fled Minneapolis in our Ford V-8, the blue sedan that newspaper stories had called "the murder car." A young friend drove the car, for ever since my father's death, Edith had been troubled by a racing heart and bouts of nervous exhaustion.[1]

Great drifts of grimy snow four to eight feet high were piled by the roadways as we drove through Minnesota, Wisconsin, and Illinois. They dwindled and eventually disappeared as we drove farther east, and by the time we reached my grandmother's house in Brooklyn, it was sunny and the streets were clear.

We traveled light. My mother badly needed a respite. But she took with her the title to the *Midwest American* and left behind, postponed until May, her libel suit against the *Minnesota Leader*. She told friends that she might return then to resume publication of the *Midwest American* until the general election in November. Learning this, Vince Day wrote: "She is doubtless on the payroll of the Republican party."[2]

In reality, we, like many poor families in the Depression, had to move in with relatives until we could get back on our feet. Edith and I shared her girlhood room on the second story of my grandmother's Flatbush home. At night, I slept with a pillow over my head while Edith tried to type her way out of poverty. At the age of ten, I became her confidante and manuscript reader.[3]

For my mother, the city was a refuge — a place where nobody stared at her and pointed her out, where she could walk down the street without hearing the whispers that had tormented her in Minneapolis: "That's her, that's Mrs. Liggett. They'll get her, too!" But it was hard for her, despite her skills and experience, to get a full-time job on a New York paper — even though all the New York papers had supported my father editorially. She worked as a specialty reporter on journalistic piecework, covering the Union Party campaign of 1936 for the *Herald Tribune* and a few political and criminal trials for the *New York Journal-American*. It was, in retrospect, a good period in New York City. Fiorello LaGuardia was mayor, and Thomas Dewey was beginning the racketeering prosecutions that were to lead him so close to the presidency.

For bread with a modicum of butter, Edith relied on the Sunday supplements of the *Times,* the *Herald Tribune,* and the *Brooklyn Eagle.* Until the *Eagle* discontinued its Sunday supplement, she wrote most of its articles under a variety of pseudonyms: everything from fashion to political profiles. After that, she had to move to pulp magazines, initially factual detective stories, to support the three of us.[4] One *Crime Detective* article described the murders of two editors and two labor leaders and Minneapolis's well-deserved reputation as a haven for criminals and hoodlums. Just like old times, county attorney Ed Goff banned this issue in Minneapolis, warning the magazine that if it attempted to distribute it, he would proceed against them for defaming the memory of Governor Olson.[5]

Whenever news was scanty in Brooklyn, a reporter would drop by my grandmother's house for a human-interest story. Edith told the *World-Telegram:*

> If there is any solace at all from the tragedy, it's in the knowledge that Walter died fighting, and that he had crippled the corrupt machinery of government so badly before his death that they had to kill him to insure themselves a little longer life. . . . But there's no point in carrying on alone. One in a family is enough to sacrifice. . . . [One] glorious and terrible [memory was] the picture I have of Walter, shot in the back, and swinging around almost instinctively, the six foot four of him, his arms thrown up, his fists clenched to fight his assassin, before he fell forward. He died fighting. That's something for me, for his children, to remember.[6]

When Governor Olson was dying of cancer in August 1936, the *New York Mirror* looked for the local angle in Flatbush, marveling that my grandmother's "attractive house on a shady street in Brooklyn" could shelter "the gentle little family of a man slain in gang fashion." The reporter wrote:

> More than any other person she [Edith] might feel she had reason to be glad and to gloat because the governor . . . was dying a slow, hideously painful death. Yet, with quiet dignity, she sits composed. "I don't hate him. I can't hate him. It is impossible to hate a man who is dying so horribly.
>
> "Had they discovered his condition three weeks sooner, my husband would still be alive. He [Olson] would have known his career was

over and my husband's crusade could have made no difference. But I don't hate him."[7]

Edith met editor Marlen Pew of *Editor & Publisher* for the first time the day after we came back to New York. Pew understood that it was not only the murder of her husband and Cann's farcical trial that made Edith heartsick, but also the radicals who had slandered Walter after his death. Many she had once considered idealists had joined in the character assassination, and she had read and heard lies that sickened her. Edith credited the sheer force of Pew's personality with rescuing her from her "fog of horror" and restoring her will to live. She especially appreciated his continued efforts to help end the slanders against Walter's memory.[8]

I, too, remember Pew as warm and kindly. Edith took me once or twice to *Editor & Publisher*'s Times Square headquarters, where Pew, a busy man in a busy office, seemed delighted to see me and went out of his way to make me feel welcome.

In his "Shop Talk at Thirty" column, Pew called the "whispering campaign" conducted by Minnesota and New York radicals "the most indecent exhibition of political viciousness known to this writer. . . . The situation has interested me because of the amazing callousness of the persons involved and because it indicates that radicals can abuse power as viciously as the soulless public exploiters they denounce." Before Pew died in October, he wrote many letters to the American Civil Liberties Union seeking a meeting between Edith and the full board. He suggested an open roundtable with board members to explore why they had failed to help Walter, but the meeting never took place.[9]

In fact, the radical whispering campaign and the hostility of some Newspaper Guild members may have been partly responsible for Edith's unreasonable difficulty in finding full-time employment. I remember that she had to quit the WPA Writers' Project because of abuse from Communists.

The fiftieth annual convention of the American Newspaper Publishers Association met in New York shortly after our return. The theme of the four-day convention was worldwide freedom of the press, with firsthand accounts of press persecution in Germany and speeches by Walter Lippmann and H. L. Mencken, among others. On the last day, the full convention of approximately six hundred publishers adopted four resolutions. One of them read:

> Whereas, officials of the state of Minnesota have long sought to restrain
> the press in the performance of its functions, as evidenced not only by

the newspapers injunction law later declared unconstitutional but by other acts, and

Whereas, these oppressions of the press have been characterized by a campaign of violence against editors criticizing improper political gangster alliances, culminating in the murder of Walter Liggett; therefore

Be it Resolved, that the press of this country should resist the attempts of such alliances in Minnesota or in any other state to abridge the freedom of the press, whether the abridgement be attempted by lawlessness, legislation or by any other means.[10]

In a December 5, 1936, article in *Editor & Publisher,* Edith called Floyd Olson an "American Stalin" and compared, by implication, Walter's murder and the attempt to blacken his reputation with the treason trials then taking place in Moscow.

Fighting Words: The *Daily Worker* Libel Cases

If Comrade Hathaway writes an article, it is not Comrade Hathaway's personal article, it is an article expressing the opinion of the PolBuro, and giving the leadership of the PolBuro to the Party.

—*Party Organizer,* **February 1934**

Poverty prevented Edith from going back to Minneapolis in May to press her libel suit against the *Minnesota Leader,* but within a few days after our arrival in New York City, she initiated a similar suit against Clarence Hathaway and the *Daily Worker.* Lacking a lawyer, she researched the law and filed under Section 1349 of the Penal Code, which made it a misdemeanor to libel the dead.[11]

Too poor to pay a process server, she camped out at the *Daily Worker* for two weeks while Hathaway entered and left through a door in the mechanical department. She was never able to serve legal notice because, as the *Worker* noted, he left for Minneapolis to guide Communist delegates at the Farmer-Labor Party convention.[12]

Soon she attracted a lawyer. Fortunately for us, Morris Forkosch took the case pro bono, or I would probably still be paying the costs.[13] The *Worker*'s basic strategy was delay rather than any attempt to prove the accuracy of its statements.[14] Forkosch's strategy was to pursue the case for criminal libel in Manhattan and then to sue for civil libel in Brooklyn. The cases dragged on into 1942, through magistrate's court, a grand jury, two jury trials, and several appeals.[15]

The *Worker*'s major attempt at factual defense was its claim that the *Minnesota Leader* had printed the same material and that it was "generally believed." When a magistrate suggested a retraction, the *Worker* offered to publish a statement saying no personal attack was intended in the declaration that Edith was "selling the corpse of the slain publisher limb by limb to the highest bidder in the Minnesota Republican party," claiming it was libelous only if it implied a literal dismemberment. Personal or not, such comments caused Edith "the distinct sensation of a sharp, narrow knife twisting" in her heart.[16]

When Edith filed her civil case in Brooklyn as a poor person, defense lawyer Edward Kuntz protested that the case was political and that she evidently had funds to travel to Mexico to visit Trotsky for her "very sympathetic" profile in the *Brooklyn Eagle*. This was not the case. All her political profiles for the *Eagle* — including those of Irish prime minister Eamon De Valera and Czech president Tomás Masaryk — were written without benefit of foreign travel. At the *Eagle*'s rate of pay, she could barely afford typing paper and the nickel subway fare to Manhattan to do research in newspaper morgues and the New York Public Library.[17]

Hathaway testified in the criminal trial that he had commissioned the articles on which Edith's suit was based after discussing Walter's murder and its relation to Minnesota politics with Farmer-Labor leaders, third-party advocate Howard Williams, and Governor Olson. He had, he said, conferred with Olson half a dozen times.

Edith testified that she had not pursued the impeachment of Olson because of his fatal illness; Hathaway denied that Edith could have known in February 1936 that Olson was dying of cancer.

The *Worker*'s coverage of the case ignored the issue of libel, insisting that the trial was a politically inspired conspiracy "spawned by the Trotskyites and utilized by [prosecutor Thomas] Dewey to further his Presidential ambitions." Morris Forkosch told me in 1987 that the Manhattan district attorney's office had been reluctant to pursue a criminal libel case but was persuaded after the civil case was won in Brooklyn.[18]

Before it undertook the criminal libel trial, Dewey's office, well known for its ruthless investigations, sent a representative to Minnesota to check Edith's credibility. Dewey's investigators came up with a lot of dirt, especially from the state attorney general's office, where "responsible people" described Edith and Walter as bigamists and said that Edith had egged Walter on to attack Minnesota politicians. These informants said Edith had "a violently poisonous and vicious tongue [and] a desperate character" and was "entirely untrustworthy." According to these sources, Edith was a publicity seeker who had brought newspapermen to photograph my brother and me during Kid Cann's trial. Deputy attorney general Roy Frank claimed that he could produce a hundred reputable businessmen who would swear that Edith and Walter attempted to shake them down for advertisements. Kid Cann's defense attorney Thomas McMeekin opined that, had he chosen, he could have attacked Edith's credibility with a hundred witnesses.[19]

Still, Dewey's chief investigator also received a letter from a friend in the Minneapolis Police Department "in whose knowledge and reliability I have the greatest confidence." This letter stated: "There was no evidence, whatever, of any blackmail," and "as to Mrs. Liggett, I am very sure that nothing in the community does in the slightest degree reflect upon her character or reputation."[20]

Similarly, Robert "Tommy" Thompson, a reporter for the *St. Paul Pioneer Press,* told Dewey's investigator that he had made an exhaustive — and futile — search to locate anyone who would state that either Walter or Edith had ever blackmailed them or falsely accused them. The reporter considered my parents crusaders, with perhaps a touch of revenge in their writings.[21]

The Manhattan criminal cases lasted from 1936 to 1942, the civil cases in Brooklyn from 1937 through 1940. In May 1938, Edith was awarded $25,000 when Hathaway failed to show up for a trial set for May 2; Hathaway convinced a Supreme Court judge to set aside the award.[22] After another year of delays, a Brooklyn jury awarded Edith $2,672.11, which the judge declared was "inadequate" for an "outrageous, vile, and cowardly libel."[23]

By June 1, 1939, the Comprodaily Company, which published the *Daily Worker,* had, with capitalistic acumen, transferred its assets to a maze of holding companies to avoid paying the judgment. The maze was so intricate and confusing that in the criminal trial the *Worker*'s city editor testified that he was paid in cash and did not know the name of the corporation for which he worked.[24] Clarence Hathaway was detained briefly in the civil section of Brooklyn city prison and then posted bond to cover the judgment.[25]

Daily Worker investigators eventually looked for something in Edith's life with which to discredit her; in 1940, when I was in high school, I became aware that we were intermittently being spied on.[26] Investigators who went to Minnesota to search returned with one witness, one deposition, and copies of the *Minnesota Leader.* On Edith's third day on the witness stand, the defense tried to introduce as evidence the issue of the *Minnesota Leader* that denounced Walter as a traitor in gaudy headlines.[27]

Edith testified that there was a united front between the Communists and the Olson machine.[28] In her four days on the stand, she asserted convincingly that Walter's crusade against a political machine linked to the underworld and the Communist Party had brought him only privation and death. After Edith stated that Minneapolis police perjured themselves at Kid Cann's trial, *Daily Worker* lawyer Edward Kuntz asked, "Did you state at the trial that Governor Olson either ordered or permitted your husband's murder?"

Edith replied, "I did, and Governor Olson was alive then."

"Do you repeat that charge now?"

"I repeat it now. He was certainly an accessory to the murder."

To show that Edith was a political polemicist who herself indulged in unseemly language, Kuntz questioned Edith's use of the terms *pimp, muscleman,* and *gunman* to describe Kid Cann.[29] These terms, however, were not political invective, but accurate job descriptions.

When Hathaway took the stand, he testified that he had written the articles and still believed they were true. He stated that he had advised the Communist Party to take a stand against attempts of the reactionary forces in Minnesota to use Walter's murder to the detriment of the Farmer-Labor Party.[30]

The *Worker*'s other defense witness was Frank Ellis, whom Edith had tried so hard to get the ACLU to help after Walter's murder. Ellis, then in the CIO and supported by Communists, testified that he had gone to see Olson in August 1934 and at that same meeting Walter had attempted to get some state printing from Governor Olson; he said that Olson had ordered Walter to leave the office.[31]

The criminal libel trial had its oddities. Although the *Worker* had accused Edith of profiting by Walter's murder, Hathaway's attorney objected when the prosecutor asked Edith about her financial condition when she returned from Minnesota and how much money she had made from the articles she wrote after Walter's death. She was able to state for the record that she had never received a penny from the Minnesota Republican Party.[32]

Ironically, the ACLU, which had refused to help Walter when he was framed and whose board had refused to meet with Edith in 1936, took an interest in the criminal libel case against the *Worker.* Osmond Frankel of the ACLU was the main drafter of Hathaway's appeal, an appeal largely based on the use of a blue ribbon jury in the criminal trial, as well as the claim of the Defense Committee for Civil Rights for Communists that the case fitted in with "a certain general drive towards getting our country into the European war." Part of the costs of this appeal were paid, Edith heard, by Charles Ward.[33]

During the course of the trials, the Communist Party moved from antifascism to pacifism after the signing of the Hitler-Stalin pact, then on to interventionism when Hitler invaded Russia. When Hathaway was convicted of criminal libel in May 1940, the *Worker* was publishing Dalton Trumbo's powerful antiwar work "When Johnny Got His Gun" and leading peace parades for May Day. Hathaway's drinking—always heavy—increased when he was assigned the task of popularizing and justifying the Nazi-Soviet nonaggression pact that had been signed in August 1939. In October 1940, shortly after Hathaway's conviction, he was kicked out of the party, ostensibly for alcoholism. In 1941, still out of the party, he asked not to be sentenced because he was working as a machinist for the war effort. Eventually, he served thirty days, and both he and the *Worker* paid the $500 fines assessed against them in the criminal case.[34] Edith settled the civil case with the *Worker* and the Comprodaily Company for $2,100, which she split with Morris Forkosch.[35]

The money—though we certainly could have used more—didn't really matter to Edith. What counted was the vindication of Walter's reputation. I have a picture of her smiling after the criminal conviction, looking relaxed and relieved. With this verdict, I believe, she was finally able to put the murder behind her and go on with her life.[36]

After the last appeals had been filed in 1942, after Hathaway had served his thirty-day sentence and paid his $500 fine, Edith retrieved from the district attorney's office the papers, newspapers, and magazines that she had submitted and donated them to the New York Public Library, that most public of public libraries, for the benefit of scholars and historians.[37] The papers are still there, now yellowed, dusty, and disintegrating.

Edith had married my father for love and happiness—for his looks, intelligence, ideals, warmth, humor, and joie de vivre. In my childhood cosmogony, our family was a self-sufficient unit. My father was our sun, warm and benevolent if somewhat distant, and family life revolved around him. We lost our core when he died.

Left to pick up the pieces and to support our family during the Depression in an exceedingly hostile environment, Edith was courageous and graceful under pressure. But, although she was a crackerjack journalist and a conscientious and capable mother, she was somehow at loose ends without my father. She threw her energy into providing for my brother and me.

Wally and I, growing up without a father, retreated into reading and independent scholarship, both family traits exacerbated by years of starting a new school each fall. After we graduated from college, Edith followed us to California, where, far from the editors who knew her, she found it difficult to get freelance writing assignments. She ended up working at a series of clerical jobs. Fortunately, she lived to see and enjoy her three grandchildren before she died of heart failure in 1972.

Appendix. Who Done It? And What Happened to Kid Cann?

Who ordered Walter Liggett's death? Who paid for it and how much? Who drove the death car? Who supplied the machine gun? Who was the lookout? . . . While these questions go unanswered, has Minneapolis any right to call itself a law abiding city? Murder and slander of the dead may be convenient weapons. To America at large no city which permits these crimes with impunity seems even civilized.

—**Edith Liggett, letter to the *Minneapolis Journal* from Brooklyn**

My goal in researching this book was not to find out who organized my father's murder or who pulled the trigger of the machine gun in the alley behind our apartment house. Rather, I hoped to gain an adult perspective on my parents' characters and motivations by exploring their sojourn and agony in Minnesota. I also wanted to understand the sources and orchestration of the attacks on my parents' reputations.

Still, I believe the attempts to stifle the investigation and to destroy my father's reputation after his death were not unrelated to his murder. I also believe that Walter was correct in tying the proliferation of crime in Minneapolis and Minnesota to the power structure.[1]

Who done it?

Hennepin County attorney Ed Goff presented a host of plausible scenarios to the grand jury that indicted Cann: that Walter's attacks on the Syndicate aroused enmity; that his attacks on gambling and vice resorts inspired the killing; that a political fanatic plotted the murder because of Walter's denunciations; that those who brought false charges could have been involved; and that the killers could have been the same as those who killed Howard Guilford. But the grand jury indicted Cann on the basis of the testimony of two witnesses: Edith Liggett and Wesley Andersch.[2]

The trial jury, faced with choosing between two convincing eyewitness accounts and Cann's many alibi witnesses, chose to go with the latter, even though some of Cann's witnesses lacked credibility and contradicted themselves. The defense attorney's unceasing attacks on Wesley Andersch, along with the testimony of the Minneapolis police, may have carried the day. Andersch seems to have led a blameless life after the trial, while Kid Cann's key witness, known subsequently to the Minnesota press as the "alibi barber," had a long series of minor collisions with the law, including charges of assault, gambling, nonpayment of taxes, and the like.[3] In 1988, an anonymous caller told me that the barber, Dave Garfinkle, had been given a fishing boat in return for his testimony.

When I phoned Wesley Andersch's brother, he told me that he never was completely certain that his brother was correct in naming Cann, that Wesley truly had a strong imagination. Still, Andersch's account is entirely congruent with my memory and my mother's testimony; the visual details of the alley and the car ring completely true. Both Andersch and Edith vividly recalled the gunman's grinning face. And Andersch certainly had strong motives for *not* testifying. Because I trust my mother's veracity and Andersch's visual recall, I believe that the murderer was probably Cann or a Cann lookalike.

There is some evidence for a lookalike. After the Minneapolis *Star-Tribune* published the story of my research in 1988, I received a letter from George E. MacKinnon, a judge on the U.S. Circuit Court of Appeals who had been a young Minnesota legislator at the time Walter was killed. He wrote that some time after Walter's murder, Senator A. J. Rockne from Zumbrota, who chaired the Senate Appropriations Committee, showed him a small picture — "practically an exact likeness of Kid Cann" — and asked MacKinnon what he thought. MacKinnon replied that it looked like Kid Cann, but Rockne told him that it was the Chicago hoodlum who had killed Walter.[4]

Earlier, in June 1936, an informant told an FBI special agent in St. Paul that "Olson's clique had brought in a man from Chicago who looked like Kid Cann and who did the machine gunning." Although the informant had supplied the gunner's name, the FBI blacked it out in the copy they sent to me.[5]

If Rockne and the FBI informant were right, the Chicago hoodlum might have been Frank Nitti, Al Capone's enforcer, who headed the remnants of the gang after Capone went to jail. Nitti, who had a strong facial resemblance to Cann, was seen several times in Minneapolis shortly after Walter was acquitted, while the phone lines between Meyer Schuldberg, Chesapeake Brands, and Chicago had had heavy use immediately before he was killed. In fact, the state attorney general's file contained an allegation that Schuldberg called someone at one o'clock on the day of the murder to make the arrangements.[6]

Nitti could even have had his own motives for killing Walter. Walter had explored the connection between crime and politics in Chicago at a time when Chicago's "Secret Six" offered a $1,000 reward for Nitti's capture. Nitti may have thought that Walter played some role in this. Nitti, who later killed himself rather than be arrested, was well aware of the value of an out-of-town hit man: he explained to radical organizer Saul Alinsky that when the killer didn't know the victim, it was only a job, but when the killer knew the victim, it became more like murder.[7]

The Chicago connection is certainly intriguing from a historical perspective. At the turn of the century, Minneapolis criminals had turned to a Chicago "slugger" to eliminate a persistent prosecutor. In 1927 journalist Howard Guilford was shot by Chicago hoodlums who resembled local hoods, and in 1934 he was killed by someone driving an out-of-state car.

Early on, Chicago deputy coroner William Schlaeger proposed that Walter might have been killed by hired killers from Chicago. The mother of Leo Vincent Brothers, a contract killer accused of killing Jake Lingle, even claimed that Walter was shot because of his investigation of the Lingle murder. But when the police queried Edith about this, she told them that Walter had no more to do with the Lingle case than other newsmen. Still, she said that Charles Ward, whom she believed was part of the same crime ring, might know who killed Walter.[8]

A lookalike also could have been local, or could have been a double for the alibi. The files of the state Bureau of Criminal Apprehension contain a handwritten document implicating local criminals: "Frank Bannon and a fellow named Howard (first name) hit Liggett and received $2,500 for it." This may or may not be true. FBI files contain an allegation that Philip Share (Flippy Shere) was widely believed to have killed Walter,[9] as well as an allegation that Thomas Gannon, an inmate in the Minnesota state prison in 1944, had admitted to another inmate that he had been hired by Charles Ward to murder my father.[10] And machine gunner Arthur Wickey Hansen, employed by Charles Ward, was also associated with Jack Davenport, who was mentioned as payoff man.[11]

Who drove the death car, and who was the lookout?

The first question has a likely answer. Sally Baker Mairovitz identified Ray Appeal as the driver of the murder car;[12] certainly this man, if Mairovitz's account is not fantasy, drove one of the two cars in the alley. He could have been the driver of the lookout car. Another account identified the murder car as Schuldberg's and the driver as a Chicago gangster named Davis.[13]

Despite the supposed efforts to find the driver of the murder car, prosecutor Frederick Pike failed to call Mairovitz, the only witness who could have identified Appeal.

Since Appeal was in the alley for three days in a row fishing for information on our apartment and Walter, and was a friend or acquaintance of Cann's, it seems plausible that he was the lookout man, and might have driven the blue car that pointed my father out in the alley.

Who paid—and how much?

Someone bankrolled an expensive murder involving at least two cars and five hoodlums—three in one car, two or three in another. Quite possibly more cars and more hoodlums were used, if even some of the accounts of stalking cars are true. It was not an ad hoc attempt, although the timing could have been triggered by one of Walter's telephone calls on his last afternoon, or by one of Schuldberg's calls to Chicago, or, as Edith thought, by the December 6 issue of the *Midwest American* demanding the impeachment of Governor Olson.

Edith believed that Charles Ward, the millionaire former convict who had inherited the firm of Brown and Bigelow after Bigelow drowned, probably bankrolled the murder. Ward, an ardent supporter and personal friend of Olson's, had both money and motives—as well as contacts with criminals.

Edith was not the only person who thought of Ward after Walter's death. On December 13, 1935, Howard Williams wrote: "Liggett had been attacking the gambling syndicate of Minneapolis and it is most likely that he was shot down by one of their number. There is the additional possibility that Charlie Ward, now head of Brown and Bigelow, may also have had something to do with it. . . . He has been a strong supporter of Governor Olson's, undoubtedly contributing considerable sums, etc., and then trying to control political action and legislation."[14] Williams recalled that Walter had repeatedly reprinted the story of Ward's former life. "It was pretty bad medicine for Ward to take and he might possibly have cooperated with the gambling racketeers," Williams concluded.

When the police interviewed Annette Fawcett on December 24, 1935, she declared that it appeared to be a professional job, and she mentioned Charles Ward. While she didn't think Ward had anything to do with having Walter killed, he had been kind to so many ex-convicts that some of those he had befriended might have taken it upon themselves to do the job. In the same interview, she mentioned that Cann had called her around two o'clock on the day of the murder—a time at which trial testimony later placed him at two other locations.[15]

Because of his openhandedness, Ward had great influence in Minnesota politics even though his estate was just over the border in Hudson, Wisconsin. Ward was one of Olson's pallbearers, and subsequently a financial angel to Progressives. Nationally and in Minnesota, Ward received a great deal of favorable publicity for his work in rehabilitating convicts and for his gifts to charity. *Look* magazine wrote him up as "the world's most generous man," and he was known as "Uncle Charlie" for his Christmas party for St. Paul orphans.[16] Due to his rehabilitation efforts, he had a host of former convicts on his payroll (at least forty-five in 1938, when someone counted), including machine gunner Wickey Hansen.

The general belief was that Ward was completely reformed. Still, Brooklyn prosecutor William O'Dwyer accused Ward of having ties with Murder, Incorporated, a cold-blooded murder-for-hire operation. And, after Los Angeles police arrested Bugsy Siegel in 1940, they found papers showing that Ward had lent Siegel at least $105,000. Bugsy was certainly part of Murder, Incorporated, as well as a frequent visitor to St. Paul.[17]

In 1939, two men, Mathew W. Stegbauer and Harold McAvoy, attempted to extort $15,000 from Ward by accusing him of arranging Walter's murder "in behalf of your political constituents." They said that he contacted a Johnnie Lane, who then hired Wickey Hansen and Frankie Richards to do the actual killing. Stegbauer and McAvoy denied in a plea bargain that there was any factual basis to their charges, claiming that they got the idea from an article by Edith. However, she had not supplied the other names. Wickey Hansen, on Ward's payroll, seems a plausible candidate for the gunner.[18]

Stegbauer also knew Jack Davenport, who had been mentioned as a payoff man in an earlier anonymous letter that the Minneapolis police did not explore. But the confession in the Bureau of Criminal Apprehension files named a "Charlie" as the payoff man.[19]

Who ordered Walter Liggett's death?

It is hard to say now who ordered Walter's murder, although it is clear that many people were relieved by it. Many of them were involved in obfuscating a comprehensive investigation, either through omission or commission. Both Pike and Minneapolis police chief Frank Forestal spoke vaguely of "forces" or "circumstances" beyond their control that prevented a competent investigation. My assumption is that these forces came from above.

A disgruntled officeholder told the St. Paul FBI office in November 1937 that members of the Olson administration had had Walter followed by out-of-town individuals who were responsible for his murder. It would seem, from Walter's recognition of the Purple Gang and Edith's recognition of Flippy Share, that out-of-state and local criminals, as well as state employees or volunteers, all spied on our family and visitors, while Farmer-Laborites chided their friends and acquaintances for visiting us. Similarly, the effort to frame Walter and Frank Ellis had involved cooperation between the county attorney's office, Farmer-Laborites, state officials, and union officials, while Ed Goff at least attempted to discuss the case with Olson.

Although Edith twice stated in court that Governor Olson either ordered the murder or permitted it, I think it is doubtful that he was directly involved. My belief is that Olson would have preferred not to know the details. I also assume that he — unlike some Minneapolis hoodlums — was astute enough to realize that my father's murder could prove to be more troublesome than my father alive.

Robert Wilson, an elderly bootlegger I interviewed in 1988, told me that he didn't think that Olson ordered the murder, but "he might have known about it." This seems plausible. Certainly some of his less savory companions might have undertaken the task as a favor. I believe that the atmosphere was sufficiently poisonous and that criminals had sufficient clout to know they would not be convicted.

If the murder had not caught widespread interest, the chief beneficiaries probably would have been the Farmer-Labor clique in power. And, although I don't think Walter's efforts to impeach Olson would have succeeded, they might have hurt Olson nationally with third-party advocates.

Still, I think that the Syndicate helped plan and execute the murder, quite likely abetted by Ed Morgan's gang; both probably knew that the police were not likely to investigate carefully. Edith's information that Ed Goff's brother Art was at the murder scene could well have been correct. The Syndicate certainly had a motive. As Kid Cann's brother Jacob noted from Paris, the Syndicate had wanted to live in peace with Walter, but he was intransigently honest and became "ridiculously inconvenient."

This brings up the question of why Cann's brother was in Paris. Edith told me that one of Kid Cann's brothers resembled him strongly. Could a brother have been in the car or the barbershop?

This is not the only theory of the murder. Others range far afield. Joe Murphy, an elderly Wobbly and San Francisco AFL organizer, told me in 1986 that Communists were responsible for the murder of three journalists, namely, Walter, Louis Adamic, and Carlo Tresca. He recited a long, circumstantial, detailed account of how word had circulated among San Francisco Communists that there was a $1,000 contract on Walter. When Joe was in a San Francisco restaurant, someone queried loudly, "Anyone want a trip to Minneapolis?" Joe didn't know how to get hold of Walter, he said, and two or three weeks later read that he had been killed.

But even though the Minnesota Communists were newly teamed up with the Farmer-Labor Party in December 1935, and even though the local party lit into Walter in December and the *Daily Worker* trashed him two months after his death, it is hard for me to believe that anyone issued such a blatant public offer, or that the new alignment was sufficient motivation for Communists to kill him. Walter, with his aversion to Red-baiting, had written little about the new Communist role change, which had occurred just before his death.

Joe's background circumstances were off as well; he told me, correctly, that the Communists had taken over Tom Mooney's defense by 1935, but I couldn't verify any other part of his story. Joe admitted that, in his eighties, he did not remember dates too well.

Still, this theory showed up, minus any supporting evidence, in a 1940 article by D. H. Dubrovsky in *Collier's* magazine. Dubrovsky, one-time head of the Russian Red Cross, averred that Walter was murdered in Minneapolis by Communist agents. Dubrovsky indicated that he could provide further details, but never did. At the time he wrote the article, Edith was suing the *Daily Worker* for libel; this could have been the source of his confusion. Or maybe there was a persistent rumor in Communist (or anti-Communist?) circles. I don't know.[20]

There is also the contrarian theory postulated by Jack Quinlan, a jaunty Minneapolis columnist, who suggested that a group of local gamblers, irked by Cann's intrusion in the rackets, had "brought a couple of 'marksmen' into the city to melt down Liggett, gambling on the chance that the rap would be pinned on Mr. Blumenfield."[21]

Who covered up the murder or failed to pursue likely leads?

Although individual investigators tried to get to the bottom of the crime, all the agencies flubbed the case and missed valuable leads. Even today, I, who never even read detective stories, can see glaring acts of omission and commission. Since public opinion wanted the murder explored, it is difficult to believe that the investigation would have been so sloppy unless the word was given, actively or tacitly, from above.

Certainly, Walter was out of favor with the power structure: with county attorney Ed Goff, who had tried to frame him and whose brother headed gambling in Minneapolis; with the crooked elements of the Minneapolis Police Department who benefitted from the spread of vice; with crooked elements of the Farmer-Labor Association who benefitted from connections they did not want investigated; with All-Partyites whom Walter denounced as crooked opportunists. And Walter certainly attacked Governor Olson unceasingly for betraying Farmer-Labor Party ideals.

Who tried to destroy Walter's reputation after his murder?

Governor Olson's press agents—soon joined by the editors of the *Minnesota Leader*—called Walter a yellow journalist and a blackmailer. These were the same allegations made about Guilford after his assassination. Olson, in his interview with Forrest Davis, implied that Walter was killed for violating some underworld code. George Leonard used his personal clout with the ACLU to blacken Walter's reputation among radicals in New York City. Some third-party advocates and the Communist Party members who were advocating a Popular Front joined the denunciations, following the lead of Olson, Teigan, Leonard, and the *Leader*. Although out-of-state reporters and firsthand investigators did not find these charges credible, they have been picked up and repeated, without any supporting evidence, by some Minnesota historians.

What happened to Kid Cann?

It is amazing that a large, intelligent community like Minneapolis could be visited so long by such an unhealthy influence.

—Judge Edward Devitt, sentencing Kid Cann in 1961

Kid Cann rather enjoyed his status as an underworld celebrity and political fixer; it helped his career as an entrepreneur in Minneapolis, Miami, and Cuba. Throughout his life, government agencies collected vast—though not very informative—quantities of data on him, but mostly left him alone.

FBI files described Cann in 1942 as the "recognized leader of graft and racketeering in Minneapolis"; he was "known to have corrupted City and County officials . . . and has been known to harbor criminals of various types." They reported his boast that he had the city council in the palm of his hand.[22]

In Miami and Cuba, Cann worked closely with Mob leader Meyer Lansky. The *Miami Herald* reported in 1967 that Cann and Lansky had leases on or financial stakes in at least ten of Miami's best hotels and had set up a labyrinth of corporations, deeds, mortgages, leases, and subleases to conceal ownership and confuse the IRS. From 1939 on, the FBI's Miami field office frequently listed Cann in its yearly General Survey of Crime, though no one acted either federally or locally. In Las Vegas, Cann was associated with Bugsy Siegel in the El Cortez Hotel. The Chicago Crime Commission implicated him in the jukebox racket in 1954.[23]

From time to time, FBI reports mentioned the names of "various liquor establishments" under Cann's control—basically the same connections that Walter had exposed in 1935 and that the Hennepin County grand jury had explored in 1936.

In Minneapolis in 1945, yet another newspaperman, Arthur Kasherman, was shot to death; his fellow journalists took little note of his violent end. That same year, another grand jury investigated gangster ownership of saloons and liquor stores; again, no one acted.[24]

Leonard E. Lindquist of Minnesota's Railroad and Warehouse Commission finally took Cann on in 1951, charging before the state legislature that ex-bootleggers and people known to and wanted by the police had taken over the Twin Cities Rapid Transit Company. In fact, Cann and Fred Ossanna—once a Farmer-Labor heavy in Minneapolis—were major stockholders in the company, and had received kickbacks from sales of scrap metal when it converted from streetcars to buses. An article in *Collier's* revealed how mobsters and Ossanna, working together, had gained control of the transit company.[25] In 1958, George MacKinnon—both as a U.S. attorney and as a gubernatorial candidate—attacked Cann for his actions in disposing of the transit company's iron and steel, and for illegally holding multiple liquor licenses in Minneapolis.

A federal grand jury in Minneapolis indicted Cann in 1959 for violating the White Slave Traffic Act; in 1960 a jury found him guilty of enticing a Chicago prostitute to Minneapolis for purposes of debauchery.[26] While his lawyer appealed, another Minneapolis federal grand jury indicted Cann, Ossanna, and six other officers of the Twin Cities Rapid Transit Company for mail fraud, wire fraud, and taking fraudulently obtained property across state lines. Two cases were dropped, but the jury found the remaining defendants guilty—except for Cann, who was acquitted of all thirteen counts against him.[27]

In yet another federal trial in 1960, the IRS used its ownership forms to show how Cann and his relatives and other Syndicate members illegally controlled the Minneapolis liquor trade. Cann attempted to bribe a juror with $10,000 but was found out within hours. He was convicted and sentenced to two years for white slavery and five for jury tampering.[28]

After Cann was released from Leavenworth in 1964—it was his second and last jail sentence—he resumed his manicured and expensive lifestyle in Miami and Minneapolis. He supposedly was responsible for manipulating the Magic Marker stock prices in 1978. Although he was a felon and had never become a citizen, efforts to deport him never got far.[29]

Kid Cann died in Minneapolis in 1981, at the age of eighty, leaving an estate conservatively valued at $10 million.[30]

Notes and Sources

Abbreviations

ACLU	American Civil Liberties Union and its archives at Princeton University Library, Princeton, New Jersey
AP	Associated Press
BCA	Minnesota Bureau of Criminal Apprehension files
Bingham	Alfred M. Bingham, correspondence and papers on *Common Sense* at Yale University Library, New Haven, Connecticut
BPL	Brooklyn Public Library, *Brooklyn Eagle* clipping file
BSC	Brooklyn Supreme Court repository of documents on Edith Liggett's civil libel suit against the *Daily Worker*
Burnquist	Joseph A. A. Burnquist Papers, Minnesota Historical Society
Day	Vincent A. Day papers, Minnesota Historical Society
DW	*Daily Worker*
E&P	*Editor & Publisher*
EFL	Edith Fleischer Liggett
EWC	Jay Robert Nash, *Encyclopedia of World Crime* (Paragon, 1989)
FBI	Federal Bureau of Investigation and its files
HCDC	Hennepin County District Court case files
HH-NYPL	Walter W. Liggett's files on Herbert Hoover, New York Public Library Manuscript Collection
MAG	Minnesota attorney general's file on Liggett murder
MHS	Minnesota Historical Society (library and archives)
MJ	*Minneapolis Journal*
MPD	Minneapolis Police Department and its homicide records
MPL	Minneapolis Public Library (Special Collections or clipping file)
MS	*Minneapolis Star*
MT	*Minneapolis Tribune*
MWA	*Midwest American*
NA	National Archives, Washington, D.C.
NYDA	New York City District Attorney's Office files on *Daily Worker* libel case, Indictments 211288–90, at Room 103, 31 Chambers Street, New York City
NYPL	New York Public Library
NYT	*New York Times*
Sinclair	Upton Sinclair papers, Manuscripts Department, Lilly Library, Indiana University, Bloomington, Indiana

SPD	*St. Paul Dispatch*
SPPL	St. Paul Public Library and its clipping collection
SPPP	*St. Paul Pioneer Press*
Teigan	Henry G. Teigan papers, Minnesota Historical Society
TJM	Thomas Jeremiah Mooney Collection, Bancroft Library, University of California, Berkeley
UP	United Press
VFC	Victor Francis Calverton (George Goetz)
VFC-NYPL	Victor Francis Calverton Manuscript Collection at the New York Public Library
WF	Walter Fletcher, younger brother of Edith Liggett
Williams	Howard Y. Williams papers, Minnesota Historical Society
WWL	Walter W. Liggett
WWL-NYPL	Papers on the murder of WWL, New York Public Library

A Note on Newspaper Citations

I used many newspaper accounts for contemporaneous and background information for this book, taking advantage of locatable clipping files. The clipping files at the Brooklyn Public Library (BPL) and the Minneapolis Public Library (MPL) are derived from old newspaper morgues, while the St. Paul Public Library (SPPL) clipping file may be in part the work of library staff. In such clipping files, dates on the crumbling or photocopied newspapers are not always clear, while the names of the newspapers are not easily identified, even if someone scrawled or rubber-stamped the date or the newspaper name or abbreviation on a clipping sometime in the past (*T*s look like *J*s, twos look like threes, threes look like eights.) Often the names or dates are faded into illegibility. Other organizations, such as the FBI and the ACLU, and people also collected clippings, not always clearly marked as to source or date. The FBI, for example, while it dated most clippings, sometimes omitted sources. And datelined news service reports — from the Associated Press, United Press, Universal Service, and others — often, but not always, appear in newspapers the following day.

The situation is complicated by the profusion of newspaper editions; articles clipped and filed by subject may not be retained in whatever edition was eventually microfilmed for the record. Dates that are hard to read in microfilm readers can become illegible in blurry photocopies. And even sources that provide readable, dated newspaper clippings omit editions and page numbers.

Notes

Introduction

1. WWL-NYPL.

2. *EWC,* Kasherman entry; MPL clipping file; MPD Kasherman murder investigation.

3. George H. Mayer, in *Political Career of Floyd B. Olson* (University of Minnesota Press, 1951), called WWL a "blackmailing newspaperman." Millard Gieske, in *Minnesota Farmer-Laborites: The Third Party Alternative* (University of Minnesota Press, 1979), characterized WWL's accounts of specific political-criminal tieups as "poison pen" attacks. John Beecher's *Tomorrow Is a Day: The Story of the People in Politics* (Vanguard, 1980), pp. 299–302, called WWL "indubitably damned" and accused him of "generally believed" blackmail and "obscurely dickering" with the Minneapolis mobster who was later acquitted of murdering him.

1. Prairie Activist

1. For the Cincinnati Riot, see *NYT,* Mar. 28–Apr. 1, 1884. See also *EWC;* Richard Wade, "Violence in the Cities: A Historical Review," in *Riot, Rout, and Tumult,* Roger Lane and John J. Turner, eds. (Greenwood, 1978); and M. H. Reynolds, "Our Retiring Dean and Director," *Farm Students Review,* Sept. 1907, University of Minnesota Archives.

2. University of Minnesota Archives; MHS Scrapbook, vols. 53, 59; Robert F. Bartlett, *Roster of the Ninety-Sixth Regiment, Ohio Volunteer Infantry, 1862 to 1865* Souvenir Edition (Hann & Adair, 1895); J. T. Woods, *Service of the Ninety-Sixth Ohio Volunteers* (Blade Printing and Paper Co., 1874); *History of Union County* (W. H. Beers, 1883).

3. MHS Scrapbook, vol. 59; University of Minnesota Archives, *Farm Students Review;* Ralph E. Miller, *The History of the School of Agriculture, 1851–1960* (self-published, 198?).

4. SPPL clipping file; MPL Special Collections clipping file.

5. SPPL clipping file; *MJ,* Apr. 17, 1905.

6. My personal collection; SPPL and MPL clipping files.

7. Robert I. Vexler, *Chronology and Documentary Handbook of the State of Minnesota* (Oceana, 1978).

8. *Encyclopedia of the Left* (Garland, 1990), including article on Agrarian Radicalism.

9. Ibid.; Charles B. Cheney, *The Story of Minnesota Politics* (reprint from the *Minneapolis Morning Tribune,* 1947).

10. *MJ,* June 13, 1905.

11. Herman H. Chapman papers, Yale University.

12. *SPD,* Dec. 13, 1935.

13. *McClure's* 20, no. 3 (Jan. 1903): 227–40.

14. Theodore Petersen, *Magazines in the Twentieth Century* (University of Illinois Press, 1956); Harold L. Wilson, *McClure's Magazine and the Muckrakers* (Princeton Uni-

versity Press, 1970); Frank Luther Mott, *History of American Magazines,* vol. 4 (R. R. Bowker, c. 1930), pp. 596–603; vol. 5, pp. 66–71.

15. *E&P,* Aug. 22, 1936, in Marlen Pew's Shop Talk at Thirty column.

16. Ibid.; Cornelius C. Regier, *Era of the Muckrakers* (P. Smith, 1932).

17. Regier, *Era of the Muckrakers.*

18. Pew, Shop Talk, Aug. 22, 1936. (Boodle: ill-gotten gains.)

19. Will Irwin, *Propaganda and the News* (McGraw-Hill, 1936).

20. Jon W. Perry, "Facts Win Crusade, Older Says," *E&P,* Nov. 26, 1932, p. 9.

21. DeForest Odell, *Fighting Editor: A Biography of Marlen Edward Pew* (unpublished; given to *E&P* Jan. 25, 1959).

22. Wilson, *McClure's Magazine and the Muckrakers.*

23. Edward Wagenknecht, *American Profile, 1900–1909* (University of Massachusetts Press, 1982), especially pp. 195–208.

24. MHS, biography file.

25. *Skagway Alaskan,* Jan. 22, 1909.

26. Background sources include a personal visit and talks with Irma Ask, Charles Ask, Joan Ask, and other former residents. Print sources include Pierre Berton, *The Klondike Fever* (Carroo & Graff, 1958), James B. Stanton, *Ho for the Klondike* (Hancock House, 1974), and *Skagway Alaskan,* 1909–12.

27. Al Pine's "Get Your Man," a feature article on WWL in the *Brooklyn Eagle,* Apr. 25, 1926, contrasted Alaskan and Canadian law enforcement.

28. *MWA,* Apr. 3, 1935.

29. *Skagway Alaskan,* Nov. 26, 27, 1909.

30. Pine, "Get Your Man."

31. *Skagway Alaskan,* Oct. 29, 1910.

32. Marjorie Hales, "The History of Pasco, Washington, to 1915," M.A. thesis, Washington State University, 1964.

33. Two basic sources on the League are Robert L. Morlan, *Political Prairie Fire: The Nonpartisan League, 1915–1922* (MHS, 1985), and Stanley Philip Wasson, "The Nonpartisan League in Minnesota: 1916–1924," thesis, University of Pennsylvania, 1955. Wasson is particularly informative on Minnesota. Other general sources for this chapter include contemporary reports uncovered by the *Readers' Guide;* pamphlets in the papers of Henry G. Teigan at MHS; and books by participants, especially Charles Edward Russell's *The Story of the Nonpartisan League* (Harper Brothers, 1920) and his memoirs, *Bare Hands and Stone Walls* (Scribner's, 1933).

34. Andrew A. Bruce, *Nonpartisan League* (Macmillan, 1921), provides a good account of the League's antecedents. Scott Ellsworth's thesis "Origins of the Nonpartisan League" (Duke University, 1982) is a good academic overview of the Nonpartisan League's origins.

35. Herbert E. Gaston, *The Nonpartisan League* (Harcourt, Brace, and Howe, 1920), pp. 83–91.

36. Frederick M. Davenport, "The Farmer's Revolution in North Dakota," *Outlook,* Oct. 11, 1916, pp. 325–27.

37. Wasson, "Nonpartisan League," pp. 189–93; O. A. Hilton, *The Minnesota Commission of Public Safety in World War I, 1917–1919* (1951); National Civil Liberties Bureau, *War-Time Prosecutions and Mob Violence* (1919).

38. H. C. Peterson and Gilbert C. Fite, *Opponents of War, 1917–1918* (University of Wisconsin Press, 1957), provides a thorough discussion of La Follette's speech on pp. 69–72.

39. Frank O'Hara, "The Grievances of the Spring Wheat Growers," *Catholic Century,* Dec. 1917, pp. 380–87, provides good background on the convention; the papers of Governor J. A. A. Burnquist at MHS include a clipping that says Burnquist had threatened to have La Follette arrested if his speech before the conference was seditious.

40. See Peterson and Fite, *Opponents of War,* for La Follette's speech.

41. Although La Follette forced the Associated Press to retract the misquote, the Senate kept the accusations bottled up until January 1919, when it finally dismissed the charges.

42. Morlan, *Political Prairie Fire,* p. 152; Teigan, letters, WWL to O. J. Rischoff, Dec. 7, 11, 1917; replies Dec. 10, 12, 1917.

43. Dispatch-Pioneer Press St. Paul Papers, MHS, contains a scrapbook of clippings, mostly of Minnesota newspapers, with clippings on WWL, Nonpartisan League politics, and political persecution.

44. That same year, he had written *Banking and Currency and the Money Trust* as a companion to Louis Brandeis's articles on "Other People's Money" in *Harper's Weekly.*

45. Wasson, "Nonpartisan League," p. 262.

46. WWL, "The Lindbergh Who Was Almost Lynched," *Common Sense,* Mar. 30, 1933.

47. Wasson, "Nonpartisan League," pp. 305–7.

48. Robert L. Morlan, "The Nonpartisan League and the Minnesota Campaign of 1918," *Minnesota History,* Summer 1955, pp. 221–26.

49. Morlan, *Political Prairie Fire,* pp. 200–201.

50. WWL, "The Lindbergh Who Was Almost Lynched."

51. Morlan, *Political Prairie Fire,* pp. 200–201.

52. The most extensive account of WWL's role is in Joseph H. Mader, *The Political Influence of the Nonpartisan League on the Press of North Dakota,* thesis, University of Minnesota, 1937; a briefer version is in *Journalism Quarterly,* Dec. 1937.

53. Job Wells Brinton papers, Nebraska Historical Society, letter from WWL to editor H. A. Knappen of the *Burleigh County Farmers Press,* May 26, 1919.

54. Brinton papers, letters from WWL to H. A. Knappen, May 26, June 13, July 31, Aug. 13, 25, Sept. 10, 22, 23, Oct. 13, 1919.

55. Sinclair, letters dated Sept. 23 and Oct. 4, 1919.

56. William Langer, *The Nonpartisan League: Its Birth, Activities, and Leaders* (Morton County [N.D.] Farmers Press, 1920), identifies WWL as manager of the Publishers

National Service Bureau in Oct. 1919, and says he was on the payroll of the Immigration Commission in 1920.

2. The Roaring Twenties

1. ACLU, miscellaneous clippings on Debs, 1920; a letter from EFL to Lucille Milner, dated Oct. 14, 1935, in the ACLU archives refers to WWL's role.

2. Committee of 48 papers, MHS.

3. Stanley Shapiro, "Hand and Brain: The Farmer-Labor Party of 1920," *Labor History,* Summer 1985, pp. 410–21.

4. Amos Pinchot papers, Library of Congress, Committee of 48 (Box 40), Minutes of the Executive Committee, Aug. 30, Oct. 4, 18, 1920.

5. U.S. Congress. Senate. Committee on Immigration, *Hearing before Committee on Immigration, United States Senate on H.R. 14461. Emergency Immigration Legislation,* Jan. 3, 1921.

6. An informative contemporaneous account of these senators appeared in "Sons of the Wild Jackass," chapter 8 in Robert S. Allen, *Washington Merry-Go-Round* (Liveright, 1931).

7. WWL, "Mystery Murders of Washington," *Real Detective Tales,* Mar. 1931.

8. WWL's files on Herbert Hoover (HH-NYPL) provide substantial background on the American Committee for Russian Famine Relief, including correspondence, a contract, an audit, and news releases. Other sources include the Harding Papers of the Russian Relief Purchasing Commission in the Herbert Hoover Presidential Library, and the FBI report on WWL. Specific cites in FBI Liggett file include reports dated Jan. 17 and 24, 1922, and an unheaded, undated thirty-five-page report, pages numbered 14755–89, mostly statements by WWL.

9. Family anecdote.

10. EFL's undated, anecdotal résumé, probably from the 1950s, provides details of her work on the *Call.*

11. Joan Ask Nelson, Norma Ask's niece, kindly supplied information on Norma's career in Washington, D.C., after she and WWL separated.

12. Background on EFL from childhood into her twenties is largely from family accounts and the records of my cousin Hilda Pearlman.

13. NYDA, letter from EFL to Herman Stichman dated Nov. 10, 1938.

14. Background on the *Call* and its demise came in part from VFC-NYPL, letters from David Karsner to VFC, Jan. 23, 1936, and EFL to VFC, Feb. 3, 1936.

15. Charles W. Ervin, *Homespun Liberal: The Autobiography of Charles W. Ervin* (Dodd, Mead, 1954), pp. 64–101, provides an interesting account; the *Call,* especially Dec. 13, 1922, covers Ervin's resignation. The papers of the Garland Fund, American Fund for Public Services, 1922–41, Archives, in the NYPL also contain information on the *Call.*

16. Family anecdote from EFL and my uncle Walter Fletcher.

3. Freelance Writer, Freelance Radical

1. Letter to me from EFL, May 18, 1950.

2. Charles Angoff, *Tone of the Twenties* (A. S. Barnes, 1966), suggests the flavor of publishing in the 1920s.

3. *N. W. Ayer and Son's American Newspaper Annual and Directory,* 1880–1929.

4. Most information on *Plain Talk* comes from the publication itself; the H. L. Mencken papers at NYPL contain letters to and from G. D. Eaton, Burton Rascoe, and WWL that shed additional light on Eaton and *Plain Talk.*

5. Walter Fletcher (WF).

6. Family members, including WF and my second cousin Ernest Gross, told me of staying with the Liggetts in Manomet and Provincetown. EFL and WF told me that WWL wrote three books at Cape Cod.

7. Most background on Frank Kellogg stems from WWL's Senate testimony: U.S. Congress. Senate (69th Congress, Second Session) *Hearing before a Subcommittee of the Committee on Foreign Relations on S. Res. 329. Relations with Mexico,* Feb. 21, 1927 (U.S. Government Printing Office, 1927), pp. 20–32.

8. Ibid.

9. Sinclair papers, letter from WWL to Upton Sinclair, Jan. 16, 1920.

10. *EWC* succinctly discusses the Morelli angle in the Sacco-Vanzetti case; it is mentioned in several other sources as well.

11. Background on the Citizens National Committee (sometimes called the National Citizens Committee) is in ACLU, including a telegram from O'Connor to Morris L. Ernst, Aug. 15, 1927. Sacco and Vanzetti Archives, Harvard Law Library, also contains relevant letters: one dated Aug. 16, 1927, to Arthur D. Hill from HBE:K, and another on Citizens National Committee letterhead, dated Nov. 15, 1927, from Robert Morss Lovett to Ehrman. *NYT* articles dated Aug. 23 and Oct. 19, 1927, also report on this committee.

12. MPL clippings dated Aug. 17 and 19, 1927; Sinclair, letter from WWL to Upton Sinclair, Jan. 16, 1929.

13. WF told me of waiting (by the phone and the radio) with EFL in Provincetown for word on the execution of Sacco and Vanzetti.

14. Walter collected the facts and figures that affirm my childhood memories. They ended up in a government report: U.S. Congress. Senate (72nd Congress, First Session) *Hearings before a Subcommittee of the Committee of Indian Affairs, Survey of Conditions of Indians in the United States, Part 23, Montana* (U.S. Government Printing Office, 1932).

15. ACLU, letters from WWL to Roger Baldwin, April and May 1929; copies in TJM.

16. Bismarck, North Dakota, *Leader,* Dec. 12, 1935.

17. TJM, letters from WWL to Tom Mooney and Mary Gallagher, Jan. 15, 1929, through June 1929, with return correspondence; TJM also contains relevant letters from WWL to Roger Baldwin, dated Mar. 10, 19, 20, and a return letter from Baldwin, dated Sept. 7, 1929.

18. Good books on the Mooney case include Curt Gentry, *Frame-up: The Incredible Case of Tom Mooney and Warren Billings* (Norton, 1967), and Ernest Jerome Hopkins, *What Happened in the Mooney Case* (Brewer, Warren, & Putnam, 1932).

19. Gentry, *Frame-up,* and Hopkins, *What Happened in the Mooney Case.*

20. TJM, WWL to Mooney, Jan. 15, 1929.

21. TJM, WWL to Mooney, June 20, 1929; WWL to Mary Gallagher, June 20, 1929; telegram from WWL to Lena Morrow Lewis, June 19, 1929.

22. *Plain Talk,* Sept. 1929, pp. 257–69; Dec. 1929, pp. 641–56.

23. From *Herald Tribune* Washington Bureau, Nov. 9, 1929.

24. *E&P,* Nov. 16, 1929.

25. My mother told me this story.

26. *E&P,* Dec. 14, 1929.

27. WWL, "Holy Hypocritical Kansas," *Plain Talk,* Feb. 1930, pp. 129–42.

28. *New York American,* Feb. 13, 1930.

29. U.S. Congress. House of Representatives, *The Prohibition Amendment: Hearings before the Committee on the Judiciary, House of Representatives, 71st Congress, 2nd Session, on H.J. Res. 11, 38, 99, 114, 219, and 246* Serial 5, Feb. 12, 13, 19, 20, 26, 27, Mar. 4, 1930 (U.S. Government Printing Office, 1930); *NYT* reports appeared on Feb. 13, 15, 16, and Mar. 3, 1930.

30. EFL and WF—a family account that was told to me by my parents.

31. *E&P* accounts of jailings and beatings of journalists appeared Mar. 8, 15, May 24, 1930; Dec. 5, 1931; and Jan. 9, 16, 23, Feb. 13, 20, 1932, among other dates.

32. "Jungle Days in Journalism," *World's Work,* Dec. 1926, pp. 213–22; Marlen Pew, "Local Government and the Press," in *Dynamic Journalism,* H. B. Rathbone, ed. (New York University, Department of Journalism, 1941).

33. Editorial, *Plain Talk,* May 1930, p. 547.

34. G. D. Eaton's editorial comments on the Prohibition series appeared in *Plain Talk,* Feb. 1930, pp. 152–53; Mar. 1930; Apr. 1930, pp. 410–14; May 1930, pp. 544–48; June 1930, pp. 684–87. (Page numbers for Mar. 1930 not available.)

35. *Plain Talk,* Apr. 1930, pp. 385–400.

36. *Plain Talk,* May 1930, pp. 513–28; June 1930, pp. 641–58; July 1930, pp. 1–22; Aug. 1930, pp. 129–52.

37. WWL, editorial, *Plain Talk,* Aug. 1930, p. 165.

38. Two letters that shed light on *Plain Talk*'s demise are in VFC-NYPL, letter from Delbert Clark to VFC, Aug. 13, 1930, and in H. L. Mencken papers, Manuscript Division, NYPL, letter from Burton Rascoe to Mencken, June 22, 1930.

39. A few items in NA file 234743 (Department of Justice, Mail and Files Division) bear on WWL's Chicago investigation: a letter to G. A. Youngquist from George E. Q. Johnson, "Re Chicago Gang Situation," dated Oct. 1, 1930; a letter from Frank Knox to Attorney General William D. Mitchell dated Oct. 22, 1930; a memorandum for Johnson

dated Oct. 27, 1930; and a reply to Frank Knox from the assistant attorney general dated Oct. 27, 1930. Both EFL and WF told me that WWL took Frank Knox a thick sheaf of papers about Chicago's political-criminal connections.

40. Background on Jake Lingle's murder and reporting appears in *E&P,* June 14, 21, 28, July 5, 12, 19, 26, Aug. 2, 9, 23, 30, Sept. 20, Nov. 8, 1930; *EWC* discusses the case in an entry on Leo Vincent Brothers, Lingle's murderer.

41. TJM, including telegrams from WWL to Barnsdall, Jan. 2, 5, 13, 1931; Barnsdall to Tom Mooney, Jan. 11, 1931.

42. *Oakland Tribune,* Jan. 29, 1931; other brief reports are in *Oakland Tribune,* Dec. 24, 1930, and *San Francisco Chronicle* and *San Francisco Examiner* of the same date.

43. Memories of the apartment, our illnesses, and my visit to Mooney are mine.

44. TJM, WWL to Clara Lee, Feb. 6, 1931; Lee to WWL, Apr. 30, 1931.

45. TJM, Feb. 1931, including WWL to "Dear Editor," Feb. 25.

46. TJM, WWL to Broun, Mar. 23, 1931; Broun to WWL, Apr. 21, 1931; Siegfried Ameringer to Anna Mooney, July 9, 1931.

47. Teigan, WWL to Teigan, Mar. 3, 23, 1931; Teigan to WWL, Mar. 9, 1931.

48. Teigan, WWL to Teigan, Mar. 23, 1931.

49. TJM, WWL to Baldwin, Mar. 10, 1931.

50. TJM, WWL to Thomas R. Lynch, Feb. 6, 16, 24, 27, Mar. 4, 1931; Lynch to WWL, Feb. 13, 25, Mar. 2, 7, 1931.

51. TJM, WWL to Barnsdall, Feb. 16, 19, 1931; Barnsdall to Anna Mooney, Feb. 16, 1931.

52. Symes was the wife of Travers Clements, who worked with Walter.

53. HH-NYPL, WWL to Baird, Feb. 2, 1931.

54. HH-NYPL, telegrams from Albert Boni to WWL, Apr. 25, May 5, 1931.

55. HH-NYPL, correspondence with Murray King, Harry Elmer Barnes, Senator Joseph France, Henry A. Wallace, et al.

56. Herbert Hoover Presidential Library, Misrepresentations file.

57. HH-NYPL, WWL to H. E. Barnes, Dec. 22, 1931.

58. HH-NYPL, Dec. 7, 1931; WWL to H. E. Barnes, Jan. 1, 1932.

59. *Plain English,* June 1932; also available in HH-NYPL.

60. Rosanne Sizer, "Herbert Hoover and the Smear Books, 1930–1932," *Annals of Iowa,* Spring 1984, pp. 343–61, contains an interesting, if not completely accurate, account of efforts to contain unfavorable books about Hoover; my comments on the article appear in a letter in Winter/Spring 1988, pp. 323–25.

61. Hoover Library, Misrepresentations file.

62. Sizer, "Herbert Hoover and the Smear Books."

63. *Nation,* Mar. 30, 1932.

64. *E&P,* Apr. 2, 1932.

65. Sinclair, WWL to Upton Sinclair, Apr. 4, 1932.

66. Sinclair.

67. Information on *Common Sense* comes from its pages and from Bingham; WWL, "Mr. Mellon's Pittsburgh," *Common Sense,* Dec. 5, 1932.

68. Sinclair, July 9, 1933.

69. Sinclair.

4. Meanwhile, in Minnesota

1. EFL, *Prairie Caesar* outline (1936?).

2. Wayne Thomis, *Chicago Tribune,* Feb. 2, 9, 16, 1936.

3. Steve D. Jansen, "Floyd B. Olson: The Years prior to His Governorship, 1898–1930," Ph.D. dissertation, University of Kansas, 1984.

4. Personal interviews with Judge George E. MacKinnon and bootlegger Robert Wilson.

5. Burnquist; *E&P,* Sept. 15, 1934 (article on Guilford's death).

6. Jansen, "Floyd B. Olson"; Stanley Philip Wasson, "The Nonpartisan League in Minnesota," thesis, University of Pennsylvania, 1955.

7. WWL, *Radical or Racketeer: The Truth about Floyd B. Olson* (*MWA,* 1934).

8. "An Analysis of Floyd B. Olson's Record as County Attorney, Hennepin County," *Owatonna Journal,* Oct. 24, 1930; reprinted by the Voters Information Club of that city. *Proceedings of the Attorney-General's Conference on Crime* (Dec. 10–13, 1934, in Washington, D.C.) also noted on p. 60 the extreme number of nol-prossed cases in Minneapolis.

9. According to columnist Westbrook Pegler, in a column dated Feb. 19, 1934 (newspaper not provided), from an FBI report on murder of WWL.

10. WWL, *Radical or Racketeer.*

11. ACLU, letter from EFL dated Oct. 30, 1935; similar information is in FBI file 62-69850, and in MPD file on WWL murder investigation; a similar list of Cann's arrests appeared in *MT,* Jan. 27, 1952.

12. FBI, MPL clipping file, and MPD.

13. Jansen, "Floyd B. Olson"; Harrison E. Salisbury, *A Journey for Our Times* (Harper & Row, 1983).

14. Howard Guilford, *A Tale of Two Cities: Memories of Sixteen Years behind a Pencil* (1932?); 1988 interview with Warren Guilford; MPL clipping file.

15. Guilford, *A Tale of Two Cities,* and MPL clipping file.

16. *Saturday Press,* Sept. 14, 24, 1927.

17. Guilford, *A Tale of Two Cities,* and MPL clipping file.

18. *Saturday Press,* Oct. 1, 1927.

19. *Saturday Press,* Sept. 24 through Nov. 19, 1937.

20. Guilford, *A Tale of Two Cities.*

21. *Saturday Press,* Nov. 19, 1927.

22. ACLU files; American Newspaper Publishers Association file on press censorship in WWL-NYPL.

23. ACLU files, mostly between June and Sept. 1928; the files contain letters between Near and Forrest Bailey as well as Carol Weiss King's letters on the case, and letters between George Leonard and Bailey, Near and King, and Bailey and King.

24. ACLU, King to Bailey, June 22, 1928.

25. ACLU, Near to Bailey, July 2, 1928.

26. ACLU, Bailey to King, Nov. 23, 1928.

27. *E&P*, Dec. 7, 1929.

28. *E&P* covered the gag-law case in depth and detail from early on (1927) through the Supreme Court verdict (June 6, 1931, with full text of the decision) and beyond; a tribute to Justice Brandeis appeared Nov. 14, 1931, articles on the backing of the American Society of Newspaper Editors Apr. 20, 27, 1929, ANPA referendum Apr. 5, 1930, among other dates.

29. *NYT,* Jan. 31, 1931.

30. *E&P,* June 20, 1931.

31. FBI file on Clarence Hathaway, 100-9138-x, documents his simultaneous involvement with Farmer-Labor politics and the Communist Party; John Earl Haynes, "Liberals, Communists, and the Popular Front in Minnesota," thesis, University of Minnesota, 1978, especially pp. 19–22.

32. Teigan.

33. Wasson, "Nonpartisan League," pp. 570–86 and 595–97 cover the end of the League; see pp. 588–90 on the ill-fated third-party convention in St. Paul. This is also covered extensively in contemporaneous left-wing literature, such as William Hard, "Bolshevism and Populism," *Nation,* July 2, 1924, and R. M. Lovett, "The Farmer-Labor Communist Party," *New Republic,* July 2, 1924.

34. Wasson, "Nonpartisan League," pp. 588–90; Jansen, "Floyd B. Olson."

35. George H. Mayer, *The Political Career of Floyd B. Olson* (University of Minnesota Press, 1951); Millard H. Gieske, *Minnesota Farmer-Laborism* (University of Minnesota Press, 1979).

36. *NYT,* Dec. 8, 1929.

37. Mayer, *Political Career of Floyd B. Olson,* p. 55.

5. Return to Minnesota

1. *Bemidji Daily Pioneer,* June through Oct. 1933, and *Bemidji Sentinel,* Aug. through Oct. 1933.

2. *Bemidji Daily Pioneer,* Aug. 24, 1933.

3. *Bemidji Daily Pioneer,* Sept. 20, 1933.

4. *SPD,* Sept. 27, 1938.

5. Ward biography file, MHS.

6. *Bemidji Daily Pioneer,* June 19, 22, July 14, 24, 25, Aug. 1, 1933, among other dates; *EWC,* entries on kidnapping and specific criminals.

7. *SPD,* Sept. 18, 27, 1933; *SPPP,* Sept. 21, 1933.

8. *SPD,* Sept. 18, 27, 1933; *SPPP,* Sept. 21, 1933; *Bemidji Daily Pioneer,* Sept. 28, 1933.

9. *Bemidji Daily Pioneer,* Sept. 28, 29, 1933.

10. Summons dated Aug. 2, 1934, in Vincent A. Day papers, MHS, Box 11; EFL, first of a series of syndicated articles, published in *New York World-Telegram,* Dec. 20, 1935.

11. N. W. *Ayer & Son's Directory,* 1932 and 1933.

12. *MWA,* Nov. 24, Dec. 28, 1933.

13. *Union Advocate* (St. Paul), Jan. 11, 1934.

14. Date on *Milaca Times* article is not clear.

15. Frank W. Schultz, "Historical Sketches of the Growth of the Packinghouse Union in Austin, Minnesota, 1933–1949" (typescript, 1949?).

16. My phone interview with Svend Godfredsen (former union member) on Oct. 25, 1986; State Historical Society of Wisconsin *United Packinghouse Workers of America Oral History Project Interviews, 1985–86,* Godfredsen interview, May 18–20, 1986.

17. NYDA, undated notes by EFL.

18. Day papers at MHS contain a file titled "Walter Liggett and the *Austin-American*" that includes WWL's pamphlet "Why I resigned as editor of the *Austin-American*" (1934) and a typed, union-oriented but unattributed "Brief History of the Relations of the Union with the *Austin-American.*"

19. NYDA, undated notes by EFL.

20. Day, "Liggett and the *Austin-American*"; machine gun allegation is in a memo to the governor dated Jan. 24, 1934.

21. BCA file (on Frank Ellis) 2808, entry dated Feb. 8, 1934.

22. WWL, "Why I resigned."

23. Ibid.

24. Day, letter from Fosso to Olson, June 21, 1934.

25. *MWA,* June 15, 1934.

26. Ibid.

27. EFL in NYDA.

28. Day, Goldie's letter dated July 19, 1934.

29. Day, "Liggett and the *Austin-American.*"

30. EFL, syndicated article in *New York World-Telegram,* Dec. 20, 1935.

31. *MWA,* May 4, 11, June 8, July 18, 1934, among other dates.

32. 1934 *Platform of Minnesota FLP* (Farmer-Labor Party) is available in *MWA,* Apr. 20, 1934, and in Dan C. McCurry, *The Farmer-Labor Party History, Platform and Programs* (Arno Press, 1975), among other sources; *MJ* reprinted the platform Apr. 15, 1934, with comments from Minnesota editors.

33. WWL comments, dated Nov. 28, 1934, are in Howard Y. Williams papers, MHS; *MWA* newspaper commentary on the platform includes May 25, June 8, Aug. 24, 1934, among other dates.

34. *MWA,* Aug. 31, 1934.

35. *MWA,* July 20, 1934.

36. *MWA,* July 13, 1934.

37. *MWA,* July 27, Aug. 10, Sept. 7, 28, 1934; *Saturday Press,* June 16, 1934.

38. NYDA; *New York Sun,* Apr. 24, 1940.

39. MPL; *NYT,* June 6–9, 1934; *E&P,* June 2, 9, 16, 1934 (text of Olson speech June 9); FBI file 61-7554-Serial 93 provides a typed summary of newspaper reports of the 1934 Newspaper Guild Convention.

40. Broun's account in *Nation,* June 19, 1934; his appraisal of Olson as presidential timber in *Union Advocate,* June 28, 1934.

41. While there are many accounts of this strike, I have relied largely on primary documents and accounts of participants, including Steven Brill, *The Teamsters* (Simon and Schuster, 1978), James P. Cannon, *The History of American Trotskyism* (Pathfinder Press, 1972), Farrell Dobbs, *Teamster Politics* (Monad, 1975), and *Teamster Rebellion* (Monad, 1972). Secondary interpretations of the strike appear in George H. Mayer, *The Political Career of Floyd B. Olson* (University of Minnesota Press, 1951); Richard Valelly, *Radicalism in the States* (University of Chicago Press, 1989); Meridel Le Sueur, "What Happens in a Strike," *American Mercury,* Nov. 1934, pp. 329–35. These agree on little more than dates; the *Organizer* is also available at MHS.

42. *E&P,* Aug. 4, 1934.

43. Twin Cities daily newspapers covering the events include *MS, MJ, MT,* and *SPD.*

44. *E&P,* Aug. 4, 1934, includes text; *MJ,* July 26, 27, 1934; *NYT,* July 18, 25, 26, 27, 28, 31, 1934; additional accounts in *SPD, MS,* and *MT.*

45. Cannon, *History of American Trotskyism; MJ,* July 27, 1934; *MT,* July 28, 1934.

46. Cannon, *History of American Trotskyism.*

47. *E&P,* Aug. 4, 1934; contains partial text of the telegrams.

48. *E&P,* Aug. 11, 1934.

49. *MWA,* Aug. 3, 1934.

50. Day, memos to the governor, Jan. 24, Aug. 10, 24, 1934, among other dates.

51. Day, memos to the governor, Aug. 20, Nov. 22, 1934.

52. Day, memos to the governor, Jan. 24, Aug. 10, 24, 1934.

53. Fred Friendly, *Minnesota Rag* (Random House, 1981), p. 165; American Newspaper Publishers Association account in WWL-NYPL; *MWA,* June 29, Aug. 27, Nov. 15, 1935; *E&P,* Sept. 15, 1934.

6. Break with Olson

1. *MWA,* Sept. 7, 1934; *MJ,* Sept. 4, 17, 1934; *Swift County Monitor,* Sept. 7, 1934.

2. *MWA,* Sept. 7, 1934.

3. *MWA*, Sept. 7, 1934; "I'll see about you later" in EFL syndicated article in *Buffalo Times* (and other publications), Dec. 20, 1935.

4. *E&P*, Sept. 15, 1934; American Newspaper Publishers Association account in WWL-NYPL; *MWA*, Aug. 27, Nov. 15, 1935.

5. MPL, clippings dated Sept. 7 and Sept. 9, 1934; MPD, Guilford homicide file; *EWC* entry on Guilford.

6. *MWA*, Aug. 27, 1935.

7. MPD, Guilford homicide file; MPL clipping file, especially "Men Here Describe Guilford Killers," Sept. 7, 1934, and "Witness Describes Guilford Killing," Sept. 9, 1934.

8. MPL clipping file; MPD, Guilford homicide file.

9. *SPPP*, Sept. 7, 1934.

10. MPD, Colestock interview, filed under Liggett; I refiled it under Guilford.

11. MPD, Colestock interview.

12. My interview with Warren Guilford, May 25, 1988.

13. My interview with Robert Wilson, Sept. 23, 1988.

14. *SPD*, Sept. 7, 1934.

15. WWL editorial, "Why Do They Justify Murder?" *MWA*, Sept. 28, 1934.

16. *News-Week*, Sept. 15, 1934.

17. MPD contains copies of Guilford's two final clip sheets; last is dated for release Oct. 1, 1934.

18. My Guilford interview.

19. *MWA*, Oct. 24, 1934; Day, memo, Sept. 13, 1934.

20. *MWA*, Oct. 24, 1934.

21. Minutes, Newspaper Committee, Apr. 30, 1934, in MHS.

22. Hjalmar Petersen papers, letter to A. N. Jacobs, Sept. 14, 1934.

23. Williams, Bingham letter dated Oct. 2, 1934.

24. WWL editorial, "Why Do They Justify Murder?" *MWA*, Sept. 28, 1934, p. 5.

25. *MWA*, Oct. 12, 1934.

26. EFL, United Features Syndicate article in *SPD*, Dec. 21, 1935.

27. VFC-NYPL, letter from WWL to VFC, Sept. 24, 1934.

28. *MWA*, Nov. 23, 1934.

29. Almost certainly *MWA*, Oct. 24, 1934. Information on printers came from Hertha Schwisow; she also told me that printers slept at the shop to prevent sabotage.

30. MPL, clipping dated Sept. 10, 1936.

31. Gus Wollan, "State Capitol Chatter," *MWA*, Nov. 16, 1934.

32. *MWA* editorial, "More of Olson's Hypocrisy," Nov. 23, 1934, p. 7.

33. Reprinted on editorial page, *MWA*, Dec. 7, 1934.

34. Reprinted on editorial page, *MWA*, Nov. 16, 1934.

35. VFC-NYPL, letter dated Nov. 12, 1934.

36. *MWA*, Nov. 30, 1934.

37. Williams, WWL letter dated Nov. 26, 1934.

38. Williams.

39. VFC-NYPL, Dec. 3, 1934.

40. Day, Nov. 22, 1934.

41. Ibid.

42. Day, Nov. 23, 1934.

43. Day, including undated letter ascribed to Dec. 1934; Sherwood Anderson papers in Newberry Library, Chicago, include a letter to Olson dated Dec. 5, 1934, and a reply from Day dated Dec. 27, 1934.

44. Fred C. Kelly's rather inaccurate two-part series on Olson, "You Bet Your Life I'm a Radical," appeared in *Today,* Dec. 22, 29, 1934; Sherwood Anderson's "Northwest Unafraid" appeared Jan. 12, 1935.

7. Move to Danger

1. Howard Kahn, editor of the *St. Paul News,* conducted a rather successful anticrime crusade that is covered retrospectively in *E&P,* Feb. 22, 1936, among other dates, and in *SPD,* Mar. 11, 1936, and *St. Paul News,* Apr. 3, 1936. Also see WWL, "Minneapolis and Vice in Volsteadland," *Plain Talk,* Apr. 1930. Accounts of corruption are based on general knowledge backed by letters in the National Archives: Federal Archives File 95-39-3 (U.S. Attorney General's Office), including Enclosure 681947 from FBI; underworld conditions in Minneapolis in 1934 are also discussed in FBI 62-30730 and 30731.

2. VFC-NYPL, WWL to VFC, Jan. 23, 1935.

3. Williams, Kirchwey to Williams, Jan. 10, 1935.

4. Williams, letter dated Jan. 18, 1935.

5. Details of our departure from Rochester, our new home, and the newspaper plant are based on my memories, with addresses confirmed through school records and the Minneapolis city directory.

6. *MWA,* Mar. 27, 1935; VFC-NYPL, letter dated Mar. 25, 1935.

7. Olson's FBI file 62-?9278-43 (the third digit could be 0, 2, or 3); the informant claimed to have read some of these reports but told the FBI that at least two of the copies had been destroyed.

8. *MWA,* Mar. 27, Apr. 3, 1935.

9. *MWA,* Mar. 10 through Apr. 17, 1935.

10. *MWA,* Mar. 20, 1935.

11. VFC-NYPL, letter May 11, 1935; *MWA,* Dec. 13, 1935.

12. *MWA,* Dec. 13, 1935.

13. Sinclair, undated letter from WWL, ascribed to Apr. 20, 1935.

14. Sinclair, reply dated Apr. 23, 1935.

15. Day; *Reader's Guide.*

16. Rodman's reply, with WWL's rebuttal, appeared in *Modern Monthly,* Apr. 1935, as "Third Party Free-for-All."

17. Day, Rodman letter dated Apr. 13, 1935.

18. *Modern Monthly,* Apr. 1935.

19. Ibid.

20. *Minnesota Leader,* May 4, 1935.

21. Bingham and VFC-NYPL, WWL letter to Bingham, Mar. 28, 1935.

22. Job offer noted in VFC-NYPL, letter dated Mar. 25, 1935.

23. Day, in memos of Jan. 21, 1935, and Nov. 25, 1934; Rome Roberts's (pseudonym) partisan KSTP radio commentary on the Minnesota Legislature from January through Apr. 10, 1935, is compiled in Sylvester Hubert McGovern, *The Minnesota Merry-Go-Round, or A Diary of the Legislature of the Day: The Best That Money Could Buy* (n.p., 1935).

24. McGovern, *Minnesota Merry-Go-Round;* typical statements appear on pp. 11, 43, 60, 79, 146, 192, 200.

25. Day, letter to Selden Rodman, Feb. 2, 1934.

26. McGovern, *Minnesota Merry-Go-Round.*

27. "Invisible Government Blocks Olson Probe," *MWA,* Apr. 17, 1935; "Senate Probers Discover Many Signs of Graft," *MWA,* May 1, 1935; Day; *Minnesota Leader,* May 4, 1935. Carley final report to members of the State Senate of the 1935 Legislature is cited as *Report of the Senate Investigating Committee under Resolution No. 2,* Apr. 22, 1935.

28. VFC-NYPL, letter, Mar. 25, 1935.

29. Day.

30. Olson's FBI file 62-9278-43.

31. VFC-NYPL, Mar. 30, 1935.

32. *MWA,* Dec. 6, 1935.

33. Day, memo, June 13, 1936.

34. EFL, "Frank Ellis Is Convicted on Frame-Up Plot," *MWA,* Dec. 6, 1935.

35. EFL, United Features syndicated article, published in *New York World-Telegram,* Dec. 20, 1935.

36. VFC-NYPL, May 11, 1935.

8. Framed and Beaten Up

1. VFC-NYPL, letter from EFL to VFC, Feb. 27, 1936, describes the circumstances of our move; other memories are mine.

2. *Minnesota Leader,* June 1, 1935; aside from scandal sheets and the conservative press, the *Leader* attributed dissent within the Farmer-Labor party to "sinister 'agents provocateur,' [*sic*] whose baseness is to bore from within Farmer-Labor ranks stirring up local rows . . . inspiring tales of favoritism and unfair patronage distribution."

3. EFL, United Features syndicated article, *New York World-Telegram,* Dec. 20, 1935, and *SPD,* Dec. 27, 1935. Other background comes from WWL's "Why I Am Being Framed by the Olson Gang," *MWA,* Aug. 27, 1935; "Why Liggett Is Being 'Framed' by Olson Gang," *MWA,* Nov. 9, 1935; and trial testimony reported in *MWA,* Nov. 15, 1935.

4. EFL, "Frank Ellis Is Convicted on Frame-Up Plot," *MWA,* Dec. 6, 1935.

5. Ibid.

6. Ibid. and HCDC.

7. *MT,* June 25, 1935; *MWA,* June 29, 1935.

8. *MT,* June 25, 1935; *MWA,* June 29, 1935.

9. Day, memo, June 24, 1935; *MT,* June 25, 1935.

10. EFL, syndicated article.

11. Ibid.

12. MPL clipping file.

13. VFC-NYPL, EFL letter dated "Friday night," probably Jan. 24 or 31, 1936.

14. EFL, syndicated article; one EFL letter is quoted in Pew, Shop Talk at Thirty column, *E&P,* Feb. 15, 1936; an EFL article praising Pew's role appeared in *E&P,* Dec. 5, 1936.

15. Pew, Shop Talk at Thirty, *E&P,* June 29, 1935.

16. *E&P,* June 29, 1935.

17. MPL clipping file.

18. *Minnesota Leader,* June 29, 1935.

19. HCDC, "Exhibit E: Request for Change of Venue," Sept. 6, 1935.

20. Ibid.

21. "Minutes of the Farmer-Labor Newspaper Committee," MHS.

22. Teigan.

23. *Minnesota Leader,* July 27, 1935; *MWA,* Aug. 27, 1935.

24. Summer memories of Wisconsin are mine; EFL's reaction of terror is in VFC-NYPL, letter dated "Friday night," probably Jan. 24 or 31, 1936.

25. *MWA,* June 29, 1935.

26. Ibid.

27. *MWA,* July 12, 1935.

28. *MWA,* July 19, 1935.

29. *MWA,* Sept. 4, 1935.

30. *MWA,* Sept. 4, 11, 18, 25, 1935, among other dates.

31. *MWA,* Oct. 2, 1935.

32. *MWA,* Aug. 7, 1935.

33. EFL, *MWA,* Oct. 30, 1935.

34. *MWA,* Oct. 30, 1935; telegram is in NYDA.

35. *MWA,* Sept. 4, 11, 18, 1935.

36. *MWA,* Oct. 30, 1935.

37. *MWA,* Oct. 2, 1935.

38. *Modern Monthly,* Sept. 1935.

39. VFC-NYPL; *Encyclopedia of the American Left* (Garland, 1990), entry on *Modern Quarterly/Modern Monthly;* V. F. Calverton Memorial Issue, *Modern Quarterly,* Fall 1940.

40. Sinclair and ACLU, letter from Sinclair to Baldwin, Aug. 8, 1935.

41. Day, memo, Aug. 8, 1935.

42. MPL clipping file; *Chicago Tribune,* Dec. 15, 1935, an overview; *NYT,* Aug. 25, 1935, with prior dateline, includes balanced summary and history of the indictment.

43. MPL clipping file; *MS,* Aug. 2, 1935, pleads not guilty; *E&P,* Aug. 3, 1935, new charges.

44. ACLU, EFL to Baldwin, Aug. 12, 1935.

45. Ibid.

46. ACLU, communications Aug. 15, 17, 19, 1935.

47. ACLU, EFL to Baldwin, Aug. 19, 1935.

48. ACLU.

49. *Chicago Tribune* (date not clear) in MPL.

50. *E&P* editorial, "A Weird Case," Aug. 24, 1935.

51. ACLU; VFC-NYPL.

52. HCDC, "Official Request for Change of Venue," apparently prepared on Sept. 6, 1935, and filed with District Court, Fourth Judicial District, Sept. 7, 1935; *NYT,* Sept. 8, 1935.

53. HCDC, "Official Request."

54. *NYT,* Sept. 8, 1935; MPL clipping file; *E&P,* Sept. 14, 1935.

55. ACLU.

56. ACLU.

57. *E&P,* Sept. 21, 1935.

58. *E&P,* Sept. 14, 1935; ACLU, EFL to Baldwin, Nov. 12, 1935.

59. ACLU, Baldwin to Leonard, Oct. 9, 1935.

60. EFL, "Taxpayers' Money Was Spent for Trailing, Spying on Liggett," *MWA,* Jan. 3, 1936.

61. Ibid.

62. *E&P,* Oct. 19, 1935 (datelined Oct. 14).

63. ACLU, EFL to Milner, Aug. 28, 1935.

64. Ibid.

65. ACLU, Leonard to Baldwin, Oct. 19, 1935; *E&P,* Oct. 19, 1935.

66. Wayne Thomis, "Officials Pass Buck in Liggett Slaying Inquiry," *Chicago Tribune,* Dec. 15, 1936, p. 4.

67. Minutes of the Newspaper Committee, MHS; Day.

68. Day.

69. ACLU, EFL to Baldwin, Oct. 21, 1935.

70. HCDC.

71. ACLU, Baldwin to Leonard, Oct. 22, 1935.

72. VFC-NYPL, EFL to VFC, Oct. 22, 24, 1935.

73. ACLU; HCDC.

74. MPL and MHS clipping files have substantial information on Wilford H. (Captain Billy) and Annette Fawcett; Theodore Peterson, in *Magazines in the Twentieth Cen-*

tury (University of Illinois Press, 1936), discusses Fawcett's pulp magazine empire on pp. 265–69; Harrison E. Salisbury, in *A Journey for Our Times* (Harper & Row, 1983), provides details of the Fawcett resort at Breezy Point.

75. "Twin Cities," *Fortune,* Apr. 1936, comments on Annette Fawcett's salon; EFL in *MWA,* Oct. 30, 1935.

76. *MWA,* Oct. 30, 1935.

77. My reconstruction of the events that took place in Fawcett's suite is from Edith's account: *MWA,* Oct. 30, 1935.

78. Ibid.

79. Ibid.

80. MPD, Liggett homicide file.

81. *Chicago Tribune,* Oct. 26, 1935; MPD, Fawcett interview, Dec. 24, 1935.

82. This was not the first or last time that Cann was accused of assault or that the Minneapolis police and power structure were accused of covering up for him. A minor but well-documented incident occurred eleven years later, when Hubert H. Humphrey was mayor.

According to Allen H. Ryskind's *Hubert: An Unauthorized Biography* (Arlington House, 1968) and *MT* (Jan. 13, 14, 15, 17, 1947), Cann and three friends decided to beat up Rudolph "Rudy" Parapovich, a bouncer at the Dome at the Nicollet Hotel. They attacked him in the hotel lobby on New Year's Eve 1946, but Parapovich, a skilled bouncer, could more than hold his own. Two uniformed police squads were called in; they arrested only Parapovich. The police took Cann to the hospital, where he was carried on hospital records as "Mr. J. B. Davis." The police omitted Cann's name from the police report, even though Chief Glenn MacLean and Detective Inspector Eugene Bernath admitted knowing that "Davis" was Cann. The Happy Hour Cafe, which the police had just cleared for license renewal, paid Cann's hospital bills. Cann himself claimed that he was in Florida during the fracas. This, like Walter's beating, was called a "drunken brawl." Then, on January 15, apparently as a favor to Cann, the Minneapolis police arrested Parapovich.

Farmer-Labor historian Arthur Naftalin, then secretary to Mayor Humphrey, telephoned Humphrey in Washington and took down Humphrey's message that Humphrey had "complete confidence" in the police chief. Bernath, speaking before the Commonwealth Club, recommended that citizens "go after those dirty newspapers who are digging up skeletons."

83. *NYT,* Oct. 26, 1935.

84. *MS,* Oct. 25, 26, Dec. 10, 1935.

85. *MT,* Oct. 26, 27, 1935. Other accounts are in *SPD,* Oct. 25, 1935; *MJ,* Oct. 25, 1935; *E&P,* Nov. 2, 1935. AP accounts with details on Walter's injuries are in *New York Post,* Oct. 25, 1935, and *New York Herald Tribune,* Oct. 26, 1935.

86. *Minnesota Leader,* Nov. 2, 1935.

87. *E&P,* Nov. 2, 1935.

88. *NYT,* Oct. 26, 1935.

89. *Cleveland Plain Dealer,* Dec. 16, 1935, p. 9.

90. ACLU, EFL to Baldwin, Oct. 30, 1935.

91. ACLU, Baldwin to EFL, Oct. 26, 1935.

9. On Trial

1. Dr. Joseph Prim's statements are in Ramsey County Criminal Case Files 1930–36, #14999; EFL, "Jury Vindicates Liggett As Olson's Frame-Up Fails," *MWA*, Nov. 15, 1935.

2. Ramsey County records; ACLU.

3. ACLU; Day.

4. HCDC, District Court Second Judicial District, Affidavit; Ramsey County records; ACLU.

5. *MWA*, Nov. 15, 1935; MPL clipping file.

6. Ramsey County records; ACLU, EFL to Baldwin, Nov. 15, 1935.

7. *MWA*, Nov. 15, 1935.

8. *SPD*, Nov. 5, 1935.

9. *MWA*, Nov. 15, 1935.

10. MPL clipping file.

11. Since transcripts of the trial have disappeared, *MWA*, Nov. 15, 1935, provides the most detailed account; information not attributed to other sources is from that issue of *MWA*.

12. *Chicago Tribune*, Nov. 7, 1935.

13. *MWA*, Nov. 15, 1935.

14. My account of Francine's and Jenny's testimony is based on *MWA*, Nov. 15, 1935.

15. *SPD*, Nov. 6, 1935; *MWA*, Nov. 15, 1935.

16. *SPD*, Nov. 6, 1935; *Chicago Tribune*, Nov. 7, 1935.

17. Day, memo, June 13, 1935.

18. *Chicago Tribune*, Nov. 7, 1935; *MWA*, Nov. 15, 1935.

19. *MWA*, Nov. 15, 1935.

20. *E&P*, Nov. 9, 1935.

21. *Chicago Tribune*, Nov. 8, 1935.

22. *MWA*, Nov. 15, 1935.

23. *E&P*, Nov. 9, 1935.

24. *SPD*, Nov. 7, 1935.

25. *SPD*, Nov. 7, 1935; *MWA*, Nov. 15, 1935.

26. *MWA*, Nov. 15, 1935.

27. My account of Ellis's testimony is based on *MWA*, Nov. 15, 1935, supplemented by the *Chicago Tribune*, Nov. 8, 1935.

28. *MWA*, Nov. 15, 1935.

29. *Chicago Tribune*, Nov. 8, 1935.

30. *MWA*, Nov. 15, 1935.

31. *MWA*, Nov. 15, 1935; *Chicago Tribune*, Nov. 9, 1935.

32. *MWA*, Nov. 15, 1935.

33. ACLU.

34. *MWA,* Nov. 15, 1935.

35. Ibid.

36. *SPD,* Nov. 8, 1935.

37. Ibid.; Ramsey County records; *MWA,* Nov. 15, 1935.

38. *MWA,* Nov. 15, 1935.

39. Ibid.

40. *Chicago Tribune,* Nov. 9, 1935.

41. *MWA,* Nov. 15, 1935.

42. *Chicago Tribune,* Nov. 9, 10, 1935.

43. Edith noted in *MWA,* Nov. 15, 1935, that court attachés could not remember any other occasion in Ramsey County when a defendant was not kept in custody until the verdict was reached.

44. *SPD,* Nov. 9, 1935.

45. Ibid.

46. *Chicago Tribune,* Nov. 10, 1935.

47. *E&P,* Nov. 16, 1935.

48. Sinclair Lewis, *It Can't Happen Here* (Doubleday, Doran, 1935).

49. VFC-NYPL, letter from EFL to VFC, Oct. 30, 1935.

50. Bingham, telegrams dated Sept. 30 and Oct. 9, 1935.

51. Bingham, includes telegrams from Day to Bingham dated Oct. 9 and 21, 1935.

52. Bingham, Floyd Olson Mass Meeting Committee Minutes, letters from Marie MacDonald to Bingham, Oct. 17, 25, 1935 (and other dates).

53. *NYT,* Nov. 15, 16, 17, 1935; *MWA,* Oct. 30, 1935.

54. I spoke with Winkles on Feb. 7 and 21, 1988.

55. I spoke with Jenny on Apr. 12, 1988.

10. Crescendo of Horror

1. ACLU, EFL to Baldwin, Nov. 11, 1935.

2. ACLU, EFL to Baldwin, Nov. 21, 1935.

3. ACLU, EFL to Baldwin, Nov. 12, 1935.

4. ACLU, EFL to Baldwin, Nov. 15, 18, 1935.

5. ACLU, Baldwin to Pettijohn, Nov. 14, 1935; Baldwin to EFL, Nov. 19, 20, 1935.

6. ACLU, EFL to Baldwin, Nov. 8, 1935.

7. *MWA,* Nov. 27, 1935.

8. *MWA,* Nov. 22, 1935.

9. Specific accounts of Ed Morgan appeared in *MWA,* Aug. 14 and Nov. 15, 1935, among other dates; an editorial on Morgan appeared on Nov. 22, 1935; attacks on Olson and corruption appeared in most *MWA* issues.

10. *MWA,* Nov. 22, 1935.

11. VFC-NYPL, WWL to VFC, misdated Oct. 28, 1935, probably Nov. 28, 1935.

12. HCDC, WWL trial records.

13. *American Press,* Jan. 1936.

14. Ibid.

15. The Syndicate, part of a national crime organization, cooperated with Murder, Incorporated, and Al Capone over the years, as well as with the Combination.

16. *MWA,* Oct. 30 and Nov. 15, 1935.

17. VFC-NYPL, EFL to VFC, Jan. 10, 1936.

18. *NYT,* Dec. 13, 1935; MAG file 695 on WWL murder.

19. Minutes, Newspaper Committee Meeting, June 10, 1935; *MWA,* Nov. 22, 1935; BCA file 5226.

20. *MWA,* Nov. 27, 1935.

21. HCDC, *State of Minnesota vs. Frank Ellis,* trial transcript 32845; *MWA,* Nov. 27 and Dec. 6, 1935.

22. *MWA,* Dec. 6, 1935.

23. Ibid.; HCDC.

24. VFC-NYPL, WWL to VFC, misdated Oct. 28, 1935, probably Nov. 28, 1935.

25. *Northwest Organizer,* Apr. 16, 1935.

26. *United Action,* Oct. 1, 1935.

27. Both *United Action* and *DW* place Browder in Minneapolis in Oct. 1935: his picture is in *United Action,* Oct. 1; Oct. 18 reports a speech, as does *DW,* Oct. 22, 1935. His secret visit to Olson was mentioned in John Earl Haynes, *Dubious Alliance: The Making of Minnesota's DFL Party* (University of Minnesota, 1984), and Harvey Klehr, *The Heyday of American Communism: The Depression Decade* (Basic Books, 1984). Day contains an Oct. 18, 1935, letter written by Robert Happ that details Browder's speech on Oct. 18, 1935.

28. "Clarence Hathaway, Here Nov. 7" (with picture), *United Action,* Oct. 18, 1935.

29. HCDC trial transcript 32845.

30. Ibid.

31. VFC-NYPL, WWL letter misdated Oct. 28, 1935, probably Nov. 28, 1935.

32. HCDC trial transcript 32845.

33. HCDC trial transcript 32845; *MWA,* Dec. 6, 1935.

34. HCDC trial transcript 32845.

35. *MWA,* Dec. 6, 1935.

36. *MWA,* Dec. 13, 1935.

37. *MWA,* Dec. 6, 1935.

38. Ibid.

39. *MWA,* Nov. 27, 1935; *DW,* Dec. 3, 1935.

40. Hjalmar Petersen, "Weekly Review of the Minnesota Legislature," Dec. 2–7, 1935, in Knut Wefald papers, MHS.

41. *SPD,* Dec. 11, 1935.

42. "Build the Farmer Labor Party," *United Action,* Dec. 13, 1935; *DW,* Dec. 28, 1935, provides a detailed report of Minnesota Communist Party's District Committee meetings of Dec. 7 and 8, 1935; earlier, *DW,* Dec. 3, 1935, covered legislation. A third or farmer-labor party was a *DW* obsession in 1935; articles included "Farmer-Labor Party Urgent Need of Masses," Dec. 9, 1935, and "American People Begin to See Growing Danger of Fascism," Dec. 12, 1935.

43. MPD, statement by Catherine Doherty, Dec. 21, 1935.

44. MAG file 695, interview with Sally Baker Mairovitz, Jan. 24, 1936; to the best of my knowledge, this file has never been cited or published.

11. Last Day: Family Recollections

1. Details of WWL working at home on the day of his murder and the phone calls are from EFL's deposition, Dec. 9, 1935, MPD, reprinted in several newspapers the following day.

2. According to North Dakota newspapers: *Mandan Pioneer* and *Fargo Forum,* Dec. 10, 1935; *Grand Forks Herald,* Dec. 11, 1935; *Bismarck Leader,* Dec. 12, 1935. Also an AP account datelined Dec. 10, 1935, in the *New York World-Telegram,* Dec. 11, 1935, and *San Francisco Chronicle,* Dec. 12, 1935; *New York World-Telegram,* Dec. 23, 1935.

3. I picked up information on Gilbert while I was researching the Nonpartisan League; a file of his papers is now available at MHS.

4. Recollections of the final drive are mine, except that I reviewed EFL's deposition for street names.

5. Accounts of children's voices came from police interviews, MPD.

12. The Cops Arrive, a Little Late, with Their Notebooks

1. This chapter is based largely on MPD homicide investigation files on WWL, including transcripts of notebooks, and the depositions of EFL and Kid Cann.

2. MAG criminal file 695.

3. MPD.

4. MPD.

5. MPD.

6. John Hilborn, the supervisor of detectives, finally questioned Alice Delaney with a police stenographer at police headquarters on Feb. 11, 1936.

7. MPD, Delaney interview, Feb. 16, 1936.

8. MPD, Delaney interview.

9. MPD, Delaney interview.

10. MPD, EFL deposition dated Dec. 9, 1935; also available in MPL clipping file and *MT,* Dec. 10, 1935.

11. MPD, Delaney interview.

12. *MS,* Dec. 10, 1935.

13. MPD; *MT,* Dec. 10, 1935.

14. NYDA.

15. MPD, deposition dated Dec. 9, 1935; *MT,* Dec. 10, 1935.

16. MPD; *MS,* Dec. 10, 1935.

13. The Word Goes Out

1. *MS, MT,* and *NYT,* Dec. 10, 1935.

2. *E&P,* Dec. 14, 1935.

3. *St. Louis Post-Dispatch,* Dec. 12, 1935.

4. *NYT,* Dec. 15, 1935.

5. *New York Daily Mirror,* Dec. 10, 1935.

6. *San Francisco Chronicle,* Dec. 10, 1935, among other sources.

7. *New York American,* Dec. 10, 1935.

8. AP accounts appeared Dec. 10, 1935, in many papers, including the *Washington Post, New York Herald Tribune,* and *Cleveland Plain Dealer.*

9. *Cleveland Plain Dealer,* Dec. 16, 1935.

10. *SPD,* Dec. 10, 1935.

11. *Bismarck Tribune,* Dec. 11, 1935.

12. *Fargo Forum,* Dec. 12, 1935.

13. *Times* (London), Dec. 12, 1935.

14. *NYT,* Dec. 11, 1935.

15. *Christian Century,* Dec. 25, 1935.

16. *New Republic,* Dec. 18, 1935.

17. *MT,* Dec. 10, 1935.

18. *SPD,* Dec. 10, 1935.

19. *SPD,* Dec. 11, 1935.

20. *Union Advocate,* Dec. 12, 1935.

21. MPL clipping file, Dec. 10, 1935; AP dispatches dated Dec. 10, 1935, in *Wisconsin News* and *New York Sun.*

22. MPL clipping file, Dec. 10 and 11, 1935.

23. *MS,* Dec. 11, 1935; *St. Paul News,* Dec. 12, 1935.

24. *Boston Globe,* Dec. 11, 1935; ACLU clippings.

25. ACLU.

26. BCA file 5226.

14. No Time to Mourn

1. Memories of my aunt Caroline's visit are mine; BCA mentions her presence.

2. *SPD,* Dec. 10, 1935; MPD.

3. *SPD,* Dec. 11, 1935.

4. Charlie Granger, *MS,* Dec. 12, 1935; Louis Gollop, *St. Paul News,* Dec. 11, 1935.

5. *MS,* Dec. 12, 1935.

6. *St. Paul News,* Dec. 11, 1935.

7. *MS,* Dec. 11, 1935.

8. Account of the lineup stems largely from MAG criminal file 695, which contains handwritten notes on John Hilborn's observations, a typed interview with Hilborn (probably his testimony from Cann's trial), and a discussion in a transcribed report of a police conference dated Dec. 12, 1935; *SPD,* Dec. 11, 1935, reported fully on the event.

9. *MT,* Dec. 11, 1935; this also has a full account of the lineup.

10. MAG file 695; AP reports in *Chicago American* and *Fargo Forum,* Dec. 11, 1935, also quote Hilborn's comment that EFL was "very cool" in her identification.

11. MAG file 695; *SPD,* Dec. 11, 1935; *MT,* Dec. 11, 1935.

15. Aftermath of Murder

1. ACLU, EFL to Baldwin, Dec. 16, 1935, Baldwin to EFL, Dec. 18, 1935. ACLU files of 1935 and early 1936 also contain letters and telegrams between Baldwin and Leonard, and Baldwin and Olson as well as letters to the ACLU urging action on the Liggett case.

2. Minneapolis city council reward in ACLU, EFL to Baldwin, Dec. 16, 1935, and *MS,* Dec. 13, 1934. Schuldberg's offer is in *SPPP,* Dec. 12, 1935; *St. Paul News,* Dec. 11, 1935; and *MS,* Dec. 13, 1935. *MT,* Dec. 12, 1935, notes suggested state and county rewards, as does *Chicago Herald & Examiner,* Dec. 14, 1935.

3. EFL told me that WWL had borrowed on his insurance policy to meet the *MWA* payroll, and the policy had lapsed before his death.

4. *E&P,* Dec. 28, 1935, and Jan. 4 and 11, 1936, provide background information on the fund; Monte Bourjaily quotes are in *American Press,* Jan. 1936, and *E&P,* Dec. 21, 1935.

5. The interpretation of political events in Minnesota is mine.

6. *Chicago Tribune,* Dec. 13, 1935; other accounts of police guards appeared in *MT,* Dec. 12, 1935, and in *MS* and *SPPP,* Dec. 13, 1935.

7. Accounts of the funeral are in *MS* and *SPD,* Dec. 13, 1935, and in a UP account in the *Washington Herald.*

8. Dr. Parish's tribute is in *MWA,* Dec. 20, 1935; Mecklenburg's comments were reported in *New York World-Telegram,* bylined Dec. 15, 1935, *Chicago Herald & Examiner,* Dec. 15, 1935, and *Washington Post,* Dec. 16, 1935.

9. *SPD,* Dec. 17, 1935; *Chicago Tribune,* Dec. 19, 1935; *St. Paul News,* Dec. 19, 1935; *MS,* Dec. 20, 1935.

10. EFL's wire to Cummings was reported in *MWA* and *Washington Star,* Dec. 13, 1935, and in *Willmar Daily Tribune* and *NYT,* Dec. 12, 1935; *SPD,* Dec. 13 and 14, 1935, provides a full account; documentation is available in FBI file 62-39278-A and NA Justice Department files on WWL.

11. NA Justice Department files on WWL.

12. AP, Dec. 12, 1935, in *Washington Times,* same date.

13. MPD; FBI file 62-39278-A.

14. Copies of telegrams exchanged between Olson and the Justice Department are in MAG file 695.

15. FBI file 62-39278-A.

16. *MS,* Dec. 11, 1935; *SPPP,* Dec. 12, 1935; *MT* and *St. Paul News,* Dec. 13, 1935.

17. *SPD,* Dec. 13, 1935, and other newspapers; MAG.

18. *SPD,* Dec. 11, 1935.

19. *MWA,* Dec. 13, 1935.

20. VFC-NYPL, EFL to VFC, Jan. 3, 1936; other letters in Jan. and Feb. 1936 discuss efforts to sell *MWA.*

21. VFC-NYPL, letters between EFL and VFC, Dec. 1935 through Feb. 1936.

22. *Chicago Herald & Examiner* and *MS* reported on Dec. 15, 1935, that Nitti had been in Minneapolis shortly before WWL's murder; *St. Paul News* reported this Dec. 12 and 15, 1935; a UP story appeared in the *Washington Herald* and the *New York Enquirer* the same day.

23. *MS* and *SPD,* Dec. 15, 1935; *MT,* Dec. 16, 1935; AP story datelined Dec. 16, 1935, appeared in *Chicago American* that day and in the *Washington Post* Dec. 17, 1935.

24. *Union Advocate,* Dec. 12, 1935.

25. AP, datelined Dec. 11, 1935, in *Washington Times,* Dec. 12, 1935; barbershop alibi interviews are in MAG.

26. MPD; *St. Paul News,* Dec. 18, 1935.

27. MAG contains an undated letter (dictated over the phone) from the workhouse superintendent, confirming Andersch's account.

28. MAG contains two typed transcripts of Andersch's statements of Dec. 16, 1935.

29. *NYT, Chicago Tribune,* and *Washington Post,* Dec. 20, 1935.

30. State legislative action and rhetoric can be followed through the *Journal of the Senate* and the *Journal of the House* for the 1935–36 special legislative session; the Senate journal of Dec. 12, 1935, contains Olson's request for special funds; the House's mentions bills and resolutions on Dec. 12, 1935, and Jan. 25, 1936, among other dates. Newspaper accounts of legislative action and proposals appeared in *MT* and *SPPP,* Dec. 12, 1935; *Washington Star,* Dec. 13 and 17, 1935; *Boston Globe* and *Washington Herald,* Dec. 14, 1935; *St. Paul News,* Jan. 7, 1936; *Washington Post,* Jan. 8, 1936; and *Chicago Tribune,* Dec. 13, 19, 20, 22, 23, 1935. Accounts of Waldal are in *SPD* and *Washington Star,* Dec. 13, 1935, and *Chicago Tribune,* Feb. 6, 1936, as well as in legislative journals. Galvin's demand for an investigation is in *SPD* and *Washington Star,* Dec. 17, 1935, and *New York American,* Dec. 18, 1935.

31. Davis's accounts appear in *New York World-Telegram* Dec. 18, 19, 20, 21, 23, 24, and 27, 1935.

32. *New York World-Telegram,* Dec. 19, 1935.

33. Day.

34. Williams.

35. ACLU file, letters between Baldwin and Leonard, Dec. 1935–Jan. 1936.

36. ACLU, correspondence between Baldwin, McCormick, and Le Sueur, Dec. 1935– Jan. 1936.

37. *MWA*, Dec. 20, 1935.

38. *New York World-Telegram*, Dec. 24, 1935; it was mentioned on the air on Christmas Eve by Boake Carter.

39. *MWA*, Jan. 3, 1936.

16. Hard Times

1. *MWA*, Oct. 30, 1935; MAG file 695, "Conference in the County Attorney's Office, Dec. 12, 1935."

2. The interpretation in this chapter is my own, based largely on official records: Minneapolis Police Department records, cited as MPD, are in the basement of City Hall, arranged by year and case. State Bureau of Criminal Apprehension records for Case 5226 are cited as BCA. The remains of Pike's records are in MHS as Attorney-General Criminal Case File 695, cited as MAG. Relevant Justice Department files are available in the National Archives as LE 234743 Correspondence Re: Walter Liggett, Dec. 1935–Aug. 1936, cited as NA. Pages of the FBI report on WWL, cited here as FBI, are stamped 2-39278- plus various numbers.

3. MPD; *MT*, Dec. 13, 1935.

4. MPD.

5. MPD, police interview, Dec. 18, 1935 (Crummy and Engel); *MS*, Dec. 17, 1935; *Washington Herald*, Dec. 18, 1935; MAG, one interview dated both Dec. 17 and Dec. 18, 1935.

6. MPD, police interview, Dec. 13, 1935 (Kramer and Eisenkramer); *MJ*, Dec. 14, 1935.

7. MPD.

8. *St. Paul News*, Dec. 18, 1935; *Chicago Tribune*, Dec. 28, 1935.

9. MPD, "St. Paul Police Miscellaneous Report," undated.

10. MAG.

11. MAG.

12. BCA.

13. Ibid. According to a detailed article in *United Action*, Oct. 18, 1935, Walter Quigley, at times a Farmer-Laborite, headed Schall's 1930 campaign.

14. MAG.

15. BCA.

16. FBI; NA.

17. Interestingly, this information was not in the FBI files I received, only in the Justice Department archives (NA).

18. *MS*, Dec. 10, 1935; *SPPP*, Dec. 10, 1935; *MT*, Dec. 10, 1935; *St. Paul News*, Dec. 11 and 14, 1935; *Washington Star*, Dec. 12, 1935.

19. *United Action,* Oct. 1 and 18, 1935; George H. Mayer, *The Political Career of Floyd B. Olson* (University of Minnesota Press, 1951), pp. 48–49. As late as 1930, a political alliance of sorts between Schall and Olson continued through Tom Davis, while Walter Quigley, who had worked for Olson's election in 1924, ran the 1930 Schall campaign.

20. *St. Paul News,* Dec. 14, 1935; *Chicago Tribune,* Dec. 15, 18, 1935; *NYT,* Dec. 18, 1935.

21. NA contains Schall's letters of Dec. 16 and 19, 1935, with enclosed petition.

22. *SPPP,* Dec. 20, 21, 22, 23, 1935; *SPD,* Dec. 20, 21, 1935; *Chicago Tribune,* Dec. 23, 1935; *Washington Times,* Dec. 20, 21, 1935. *Washington Post,* Dec. 23, 1935, and *Washington Herald,* Dec. 20, 1935, provide the detail about Lux.

23. FBI file (on Olson) 31-43913, Serial 16, p. 16.

24. "Death of Schall Provides Olson with Problem," *Washington Post,* Dec. 23, 1935. *MJ,* Dec. 23, 1935, summarizes Schall's political career; *MS,* Dec. 23, 1935, reviews his life. Other obituaries are in *News-Week,* Dec. 23, 1935, and *Time,* Dec. 30, 1935.

25. *MJ* and *Washington Times,* Dec. 23, 1935, provide details of the prospective funeral; *Chicago Tribune,* Dec. 27, 1935, provides an account.

26. *MWA,* Dec. 27, 1935.

27. *Chicago Tribune,* Jan. 28, 1936; MPL clipping dated Jan. 1, 1936.

28. *Minnesota Leader,* Dec. 28, 1935, but issued earlier.

29. Mayer, *Political Career of Floyd B. Olson,* pp. 284–87; MHS, transcript of interview with Francis A. Johnson, July 24, 1973, pp. 21–22.

30. *NYT,* Dec. 23, 28, 1935; *Buffalo News,* Dec. 27, 1935.

31. *MS,* Jan. 3, 1936; AP dispatch, *New York Herald Tribune,* Jan. 1, 1936. Other AP reports are in MPL clipping file, although the dates are not clear. Such suppression was not unusual at the time; most newspapers concealed President Roosevelt's physical condition.

32. VFC-NYPL, EFL letter dated only "Friday night"; next letter was dated Feb. 3, 1936.

33. VFC-NYPL, EFL letter dated Feb. 3, 1936.

34. Hjalmar Petersen papers, MHS, provide comments on Olson's illness, Petersen's ambivalence, and his opinion of the clique.

35. *MJ,* Jan. 3, 1936, contains quotes; *SPD?,* Jan. 3, 1936 (clipping, dimly stamped).

36. *MWA,* Jan. 10, 1936.

37. *MWA,* Jan. 24, 1936.

38. *Fergus Falls Daily Journal,* Jan. 20, 1936; *MWA,* Jan. 24, 1936.

39. *MWA,* Jan. 24, 1936.

40. *MJ,* Jan. 23, 1936, p. 14.

41. *MT,* Jan. 21, 1936.

42. *Brown County Journal,* Sept. 18, 1936; *SPPP,* Sept. 14, 1936.

43. VFC-NYPL, EFL letter dated Feb. 3, 1936.

44. *MS,* Jan. 1, 1936; *E&P,* Jan. 4, 1936. *MS* through January is a good source on the grand jury investigations and liquor store ownership, as well as for the trial preliminaries. Unascribed items for the balance of this chapter are from *MS* and MPL clipping file.

45. *MS,* Jan. 1, 1936; *MWA* editorial, Jan. 3, 1936.

46. VFC-NYPL, EFL letter dated Jan. 3, 1936.

47. *MS,* Jan. 11, 1936, contains a full account; *Chicago Tribune,* Jan. 5, 7, 1936; *New York Sun,* Jan. 11, 1936; *E&P,* Jan. 11, 1936.

48. *Minnesota Leader,* Jan. 11, 1936, contains its interpretation of libel charges against Teigan.

49. *MWA,* Jan. 10, 1936.

50. VFC-NYPL, EFL letter dated Jan. 10, 1936.

51. *Chicago Tribune,* Jan. 15, 1936.

52. *MS,* Jan. 18, 1936; *Chicago Tribune,* Jan. 19, 1936.

53. *New York Herald Tribune,* Jan. 19, 1936; *Chicago Tribune,* Jan. 19, 1936.

54. *Chicago Tribune,* Jan. 22, 1936.

55. *Chicago Tribune,* Jan. 21, 22, 23, 1936; MPL clipping dated Jan. 27, 1936. MAG file 695 contains a memo to Neilson with a series of questions and names of attorneys, gangsters, and police officers supposedly friendly with Cann. An anonymous caller told me in 1988 that Neilson's questions to the jury panel were intended to establish a basis for a mistrial in case of a conviction.

56. VFC-NYPL, VFC to EFL, undated.

57. *Chicago Tribune,* Jan. 29, 1936.

17. Kid Cann Beats the Rap

1. Most of this chapter was adapted from Twin Cities newspaper reporting, especially *MJ* (evening edition) and *SPD,* and dated but unascribed clippings in SPPL. Unascribed quotes come from these sources. FBI file 62-39278-A also contains clippings, not all identified as to source, that provide a good chronological overview of the trial. HCDC criminal case file 33179, "State of Minnesota vs. Kid Cann," contains only the indictment, judgment, jury list, lists of exhibits, and Harry H. Peterson's "Certificate of Authorization" for Fred Pike and Roy J. Frank. MAG file 695 contains preliminaries to the trial and excerpts of some testimony, including that of police officers.

2. Reporting of Jan. 29, 1936, is largely from AP, *MJ,* and *SPD;* Pike quotes are from *MJ* and *SPD.*

3. *MJ.*

4. Photographer's exhibits A, B, C, F, and G are in HCDC; his testimony is in MAG.

5. Unascribed reporting of Jan. 30, 1936, is from *MJ* and AP.

6. *Liberty Magazine,* Feb. 1936; VFC-NYPL.

7. *Liberty Magazine,* Feb. 1936.

8. UP dispatch on Cann's brother appeared in *Washington News,* Jan. 30, 1936, and in FBI. So far as I can find out, this account did not appear in any New York City or Minnesota newspaper, although *MJ* reported that "Paris papers quote Cann's half-brother."

9. Andersch's testimony and weather report are from *MJ.*

10. *MJ.*

11. AP in *New York Herald Tribune.*

12. *MJ.*

13. VFC-NYPL.

14. City council action was reported in *MJ* Feb. 1, 1936; weather report also is from *MJ.*

15. *E&P,* Feb. 10, 1936.

16. AP in *New York Herald Tribune* and *SPD,* Feb. 3, 1936; *MJ,* Feb. 4, 1936; MAG contains part of her testimony.

17. *SPD* and *MJ,* Feb. 3, 1936; MAG and AP.

18. VFC-NYPL, EFL letters dated Feb. 3, 1936.

19. A partial copy of the radio script is in MAG.

20. *MJ,* Feb. 4, 1936, described my voice and testimony; recollections of my clothes, and of my feelings and my brother's, are mine.

21. Appearance of courtroom and afternoon testimony are from AP and *NYT,* Feb. 5, 1936.

22. McMeekin's statements are in *MJ,* Feb. 5, 1936.

23. The exchange between EFL and Olson is reported in *NYT,* Feb. 4, 5, 1936, and *Chicago Tribune,* Feb. 4, 5, 1936.

24. Police testimony is in AP, *MJ, NYT,* and MAG. Original police reports, written and typed, are in MPD.

25. Winslow's testimony is from *MJ* and *Chicago Tribune,* Feb. 7, 1936.

26. Hovde's report is from MAG and *MJ.*

27. Schuldberg's and Hartman's testimony is in *MJ,* Feb. 7, 1936; Schuldberg's also is in *Chicago Tribune,* Feb. 7, 1936.

28. Olson and Waldal statements are from *MJ,* Feb. 7, 1936.

29. *MJ,* Feb. 7, 1936.

30. Lawrence Leonard, the Keystone's owner, had just been indicted by the grand jury.

31. *Chicago Tribune,* Feb. 7, 1936; *MJ,* Feb. 8, 1936. According to a UP dispatch datelined Feb. 8, 1936, this initiative grew out of an investigation by J. M. Simmons, a special investigator hired by a citizens' group. Simmons told the Real Estate Board that the underworld had divided the city into four districts, each with a captain, lieutenant, and fixer, and that all kinds of gambling devices operated, with wire connections to Chicago to place bets. He reported that two brothers had concessions for permanent brothels and brought in young girls of fifteen and sixteen on the pretext of getting legitimate jobs. He declared that the current grand jury investigation had hindered underworld activities, but had not stamped

them out. "These conditions could not exist unless they were backed by someone in authority," Simmons charged. "This may be at the top or some place in the middle, with those at the top of the political structure kept in ignorance of real conditions."

32. *MJ, Chicago Tribune,* and *NYT,* Feb. 9, 1936.

33. AP dispatch in *Los Angeles Examiner,* Feb. 9, 1936.

34. *Chicago Tribune,* Feb. 9, 1936.

35. Beidelman's and Malkin's testimony is in *MJ,* Feb. 10, 1936.

36. Cann's arrival and testimony are from *MJ,* Feb. 11, 1936.

37. *MJ,* Feb. 11, 1936; MPL clipping file.

38. Cann's cross-examination is from *SPD,* Feb. 13, 1936.

39. AP dispatch dated Feb. 11, 1936, in *New York Herald Tribune,* Feb. 12, 1936.

40. *MJ,* Feb. 11, 1936.

41. *MJ,* Feb. 13, 1936.

42. *SPD,* Feb. 12, 1936.

43. *SPD,* Feb. 13, 1936.

44. Delaney's testimony is in MAG and *MJ,* Feb. 14, 1936.

45. SPPL clipping file.

46. EFL's rebuttal testimony is in *MJ,* Feb. 15, 1936.

47. Trial details of Feb. 17, 1936, are from *MJ.*

48. AP dispatch dated Feb. 18, 1936, in *Washington Star;* most details of Feb. 18, 1936, are from *MJ,* Feb. 18, 1936.

49. *E&P,* Feb. 22, 1936.

50. Acquittal account is based on UP dispatch in *New York Sun,* Feb. 18?, 1936, and *Literary Digest,* Feb. 29, 1936.

51. Jack Quinlan, *MJ,* Feb. 19, 1936.

52. *SPD,* Feb. 18, 1936.

53. *SPD,* Feb. 18, 1936.

54. *MJ,* Feb. 20, 1936; federal indictment is discussed in a UP dispatch.

18. Loose Ends

1. Alleged action by city police and state agencies is in MPL and AP dispatches dated Feb. 20, 1936, and in *MJ,* Feb. 20, 1936; a UP dispatch providing EFL's viewpoint is in *New York World-Telegram,* Feb. 20, 1936.

2. SPPL clipping file.

3. International News Service dispatch dated Feb. 24, 1936, in *Washington Times,* Feb. 25, 1936; editorial comment in *SPD,* Feb. 19, 1936. John Thayer wrote me in July 1996 about an attempt to bribe his mother, who served on that grand jury; he confirmed in 1997 that Cann *had* attempted to bribe his mother.

4. EFL's preparations for leaving and sale of the *MWA* are in *MJ,* Feb. 19, 1936; *MT,* Feb. 20, 1936; *SPD,* Feb. 23, 25, 1936; and *Milwaukee Journal,* Feb. 26, 1936. The last two provide the amount of the sale.

5. *DW* articles appeared Feb. 24, 25, 27, 28, 1936. Hathaway's role is discussed in John Earl Haynes, "Liberals, Communists, and the Popular Front in Minnesota," thesis, University of Minnesota, 1978. The series may have been prompted, in part, by a critique of the *Daily Worker,* "Review of the *Daily Worker* (U.S.) for October 1935" in *Communist International,* Jan. 1936; this critique exhorted the *Daily Worker* to denounce leftists who did not follow the party line, urging the paper to explain "why on every issue the position of the united front and the Communist party is correct."

6. VFC-NYPL, EFL letter dated Feb. 27, 1936.

7. *SPD,* Feb. 25, 1936; UP dispatch in *Washington Post,* Mar. 2, 1936.

8. MPL clipping file; Johnston's letter is in Teigan, dated Mar. 9, 1936.

9. BCA, case 5226, report dated Feb. 18, 1936.

10. Harvey's background is in *E&P,* Feb. 22, 1936; his correspondence with Roy Frank is in MAG file 695; his expense list was attached to a letter from Chicago dated Feb. 14, 1936.

11. MAG file 695.

12. MAG file 695.

13. Undated *New York Post* clipping in FBI; other items in FBI (Liggett) file 62-3978-34, 35, 36, and 37 (dated Feb. 20, 1936, from Chicago; Feb. 20, 1936, from New York; Feb. 25, 1936, from Washington, D.C.; and a memorandum for the director dated Feb. 20, 1936) all appear to concern Harvey.

14. MAG file 695, Harvey telegram from Washington, Feb. 24, 1936, and collect reply from Frank same day.

15. MAG file 695, Harvey letter from New York, dated Feb. 26, 1936.

16. MAG file 695, Frank reply dated Feb. 29, 1936.

17. MPD, FBI, BCA.

18. Wendt references in MPL include clippings dated June 28, 1936; also *E&P,* July 4, 1936. Early denial of "mystery wire" is in *SPD,* Feb. 13, 1936.

19. MPL; *MS,* Oct. 10, 13, 1936; *St. Paul News,* Oct. 10, 14, 15, 16, 1936.

20. Gilbert quote was in undated (Mar.?, 1958) *SPPP* clipping discarded from Gilbert papers at MHS.

21. MPL clipping file. Although I queried at seven likely libraries, I was unable to locate any extant copies of this senatorial probe. It has not, so far as I know, been cited, except in this clipping.

19. Home to Brooklyn

1. MPL, undated; *St. Paul News,* Mar. 2, 1936; *Washington Star,* Mar. 2, 1936. Other recollections are mine.

2. *St. Paul News,* Mar. 2, 1936, notes that EFL kept title to *MWA;* Day.

3. Memories of Brooklyn are mine.

4. My recollections and NYDA.

5. EFL, "Murder in Minneapolis," *Crime Detective,* Oct. 1938; MPL and *New York News,* Aug. 28, 1936, reported the censorship.

6. Irene Kuhn, interview, *New York World-Telegram,* Mar. 5, 1936.

7. Erskine Gosling, *New York Mirror,* Aug. 23, 1936.

8. WF; *E&P,* Dec. 5, 1936.

9. *E&P,* June 13, 1936; ACLU, Apr.–July 1936, letters between Pew and board members and to EFL.

10. Both *E&P* and *NYT* covered the American Newspaper Publishers Association convention; copies of the resolutions are in *NYT,* Apr. 23, 24, 1936; full text of ANPA's Freedom of the Press Committee is in *E&P,* Apr. 25, 1936.

11. *New York Post,* Mar. 27, 1936. Libelous articles on WWL and EFL were in *DW,* Feb. 24, 25, 27, 28, 1936, and are quoted in chapter 18. I started the chronology with newspaper clippings from the Brooklyn Public Library file of the old *Brooklyn Eagle*'s clipping file; these clippings were mostly from the *Brooklyn Eagle,* the *New York World-Telegram,* and the *New York Sun,* not all identifiable by source or even date. I supplemented these BPL clippings with *NYT* and *DW* articles, plus miscellaneous clippings from FBI file 61-7554-9 and various other numbers. Additional clippings, dated but not identified by source, come from MPL.

12. *NYT,* Feb. 9, 23, 1936; *DW,* Mar. 28, 1936.

13. Interviews with Morris Forkosch, 1987 and 1988. Records of the civil case (Case 212, New York Supreme Court, *Edith Liggett against Comprodaily Publishing Company, Inc., Clarence H. Hathaway, Hyman Colodney, and John Doe*) are filed in the basement of Brooklyn's Supreme Court Building (BSC).

14. Several thousand background pages on the *DW* criminal case (the district attorney's office files) are available as NYDA Indictments 211288-90 at Room 103, 31 Chambers Street, New York City. BSC contains a deposition by Edward Kuntz, the *DW*'s lawyer, that the *DW* kept him on retainer to handle libel suits.

15. Forkosch interviews; BSC; *DW,* Apr. 25, 1940.

16. BSC; *DW,* Apr. 26, 1940; *E&P,* Dec. 5, 1936.

17. BSC; *Brooklyn Eagle* files in BPL.

18. Forkosch interviews; *DW,* Apr. 26, 1936; *NYT,* Apr. 26, 1936.

19. NYDA, memos from O'Connell to Grafenecker, Aug. 16, 1938, to Stichman, Feb. 28, 1942; memo to O'Connell, Sept. 22, 1938 (signature not clear).

20. NYDA, letter from Stichman to O'Connell, Aug. 31, 1938.

21. NYDA, memo to O'Connell, May 27, 1939, from JK.

22. BSC; *DW,* May 1, 1938; *NYT,* May 4, 10, 14, 1938; *Brooklyn Eagle,* May 10, 14, 1938.

23. BSC; *E&P,* May 27, 1939.

24. *Brooklyn Eagle,* Aug. 2, 1939; *New York Journal American,* Aug. 2, 1939; *New York Herald Tribune,* Aug. 3, 1939; *NYT,* Aug. 3, 9, 1939, Mar. 29, 30, 1940; FBI memo dated Aug. 10, 1939.

25. BPL clippings, possibly *Brooklyn Eagle,* Aug. 2, 6, 1939; *New York Journal American,* Aug. 2, 1939; *New York Herald Tribune,* Aug. 3, 1939; *NYT,* Aug. 3, 6, 1939.

26. My memory; EFL note in NYDA.

27. BSC contains a note on the first investigation; NYDA has EFL's notes on corruption in Minnesota, and Schuldberg's deposition.

28. Edith's testimony is detailed in *New York Sun,* Apr. 2, 16, 17, 18, 19, 1940; *New York Journal-American,* Apr. 16, 17, 18, 19, 23, 1940; *SPPP,* Apr. 18, 1940; *NYT,* Apr. 18, 19, 1940; *DW,* Apr. 19, 1940. A comprehensive article on the prospective case appeared in *New York Sun,* Apr. 6, 1940.

29. *DW,* Apr. 19, 1940.

30. BSC; NYDA; *DW,* May 23, 1940; MPL clipping dated Apr. 25, 1940.

31. *DW,* Apr. 25, May 23, June 15, 1940.

32. *NYT,* Apr. 23, 1940; BPL clipping, Apr. 22, 1940.

33. ACLU; *DW,* May 5, 6, 7, 1940; *DW,* June 15, 1940; EFL to me.

34. *DW* (scanned 1938 through 1940) and general knowledge; *New York Sun,* Jan. 21, 1941 (in FBI file on Hathaway 100-9138-x); *NYT,* June 4, 1940, Feb. 4, 1942.

35. BSC.

36. *New York Journal American,* May 4, 5 (with picture), 1940; *NYT,* May 5, 1940.

37. The criminal case (*People of the State of New York vs. Comprodaily Pub. Co, Inc. & Clarence A. Hathaway*) was appealed and unanimously affirmed on Oct. 24, 1941; it is cited as 262 *App. Dev.* 1008; other sources include *New York Journal American,* Oct. 24, 1941; *NYT,* Oct. 24, 1941; and *New York Mirror,* Oct. 25, 1941. NYDA contains correspondence on transfer of the documents. Papers on Walter's murder at NYPL are cited in its *Dictionary Catalog* as "Liggett, Walter William (1886–1935), *A Collection of Material in Connection with the Murder of Walter Liggett* 4 vols., v.p., 1934–1936."

Appendix

1. These speculations provide my personal, not necessarily accurate, understanding of my father's murder.

2. *MJ,* Dec. 12, 1935.

3. MPL clipping file.

4. Letter to me from George E. MacKinnon, June 27, 1988.

5. FBI file on Olson 31-43913, Serial 16, p. 10, dated June 13, 1936.

6. MAG; Nitti's presence in Minneapolis is discussed in chapter 15.

7. Marion K. Sanders, *The Professional Radical: Conversations with Saul Alinsky* (Harper & Row, 1970), p. 21.

8. MPD.

9. FBI, file 63-30930-315, p. 82.

10. FBI, Bremer kidnapping file, Serial 1526?

11. Letter to me from Paul Maccabee, Jan. 23, 1993.

12. MAG file 695.

13. Ibid.

14. Williams.

15. MPD.

16. Henry Ehlrich, "The World's Most Generous Man," *Look,* Sept. 1947.

17. SPPL clipping file under Siegel and Murder, Inc., dates not legible, except Nov. 23? and Dec. ??, 1940. Siegel visited St. Paul at least once in 1935 and at least four times in 1936. Relevant FBI pages include 6-302-43-23 (letter from FBI, Minneapolis, Apr. 15, 1947) and file no. 404580, pp. 1, 4.

18. *MT,* Feb. 14, 1939.

19. BCA.

20. *Collier's,* Apr. 20, 1940.

21. MPL, "Looping the Loop," Feb. 22, 1936.

22. Cann's lengthy but lackluster FBI file 62-69850 provides some addresses, newspaper citations, annotated lists of arrests and indictments, a list of his Minneapolis bars, and other tidbits.

23. FBI file 62-69850.

24. Kasherman's murder is discussed in *EWC* and in *NYT,* Jan. 24, 1945; Minneapolis clippings are in MPL; MPD has two files on the investigation, including a copy of the last issue of his *Public Press.*

25. "How Mobsters Grabbed a City Transit Line," *Collier's,* Sept. 29, 1951; MPL clipping file.

26. FBI file MP 92-45, p. 18.

27. Brief accounts of the Twin Cities Rapid Transit Co. appear in *MT,* July 26, 27, 28, 29, Aug. 6, 7, 1960.

28. *MT,* May 17, 1961.

29. FBI file 62-69850; two good articles on Cann's Miami activities are "Mob Money: Silent Host in Beach Hotels," *Miami Herald,* Jan. 27, 1967, and "Who Owns Miami," *Miami Times,* Mar. 5, 1967.

30. Obituaries are in Minneapolis newspapers of June 23, 1981, and *Time,* July 5, 1981.

Index

Marda Liggett Woodbury, a retired reference librarian and library director, is a graduate of Bard College, the Columbia University School of Library Science, and the University of California at Berkeley. She has written seven reference books, including the award-winning *Childhood Information Resources* and *A Guide to Sources of Educational Information.*